The Ups and Downs
of Raising
a Bipolar Child

A SURVIVAL GUIDE FOR PARENTS

Judith Lederman

Candida Fink, M.D.

A FIRESIDE BOOK

PUBLISHED BY SIMON & SCHUSTER

NEW YORK   LONDON   TORONTO   SYDNEY

This publication contains the opinions and ideas of its author. It is intended to provide helpful and informative material on the subjects addressed in the publication. It is sold with the understanding that the author and publisher are not engaged in rendering medical, health, psychological, or any other kind of personal professional services. The reader should consult his or her medical, health, or other competent professional before adopting any of the suggestions in this book or drawing inferences from it.

The author and publisher specifically disclaim all responsibility for any liability, loss or risk, personal or otherwise, which is incurred as a consequence, directly or indirectly, of the use and application of any of the contents of this book.

FIRESIDE
Rockefeller Center
1230 Avenue of the Americas
New York, NY 10020

Copyright © 2003 by Judith S. Lederman and Candida Fink, M.D.
All rights reserved,
including the right of reproduction
in whole or in part in any form.

FIRESIDE and colophon are registered trademarks
of Simon & Schuster, Inc.

For information about special discounts for bulk purchases,
please contact Simon & Schuster Special Sales at
1-800-456-6798 or business@simonandschuster.com.

Designed by Diane Hobbing of Snap-haus Graphics
Manufactured in the United States of America
10 9 8 7 6 5 4

Library of Congress Cataloging-in-Publication Data
Lederman, Judith.
   The ups and downs of raising a bipolar child : a survival guide for
parents / Judith Lederman, Candida Fink.
      p.   cm.
   Includes bibliographical references and index.
   1. Manic depressive illness in children—Popular works.   2. Child rearing—Popular works.   I. Fink, Candida.   II. Title.
RJ506.D4L43 2003
618.92'895—dc21   2003050696
ISBN 0-7432-2940-1

I dedicate this book to my children, who always keep me on high alert, and to my loving husband, who has been with me through all the ups and downs. I also dedicate this book to Christie, a bipolar mom with a bipolar son who gave me a firsthand perspective on what a mood shift feels like, and to all the parents of children with mental illness I have met over the past few years.

—Judith Lederman

I dedicate this book to my mom, whose unconditional love informs and surrounds all that I do. Her heartfelt acceptance of others is a foundation of my work. I also dedicate this book to my children, who teach and enrich me every day, and who have supported this task with all of their hearts. And to Michael, who has been a gift to me in countless ways.

—Candida Fink, M.D.

ACKNOWLEDGMENTS

That this book finally made it to print is a minor miracle. As most parents who are reading this probably know, the constant disruption and turbulence of daily life with a bipolar child is a challenge in and of itself. Writing a book in between Committee for Special Education meetings and dashes to psychiatrists and therapists, and while being pulled away for midday crises, was definitely one of the most daunting tasks I've undertaken. Dealing with the disorder 24/7—between parenting my son and researching, interviewing, and writing—took its emotional toll. I thank my family for supporting me on this journey and for allowing me to share their lives, tell our stories, and help others.

I am grateful to the Child Adolescent Bipolar Foundation (CABF) and the National Alliance for the Mentally Ill for helping to put me in touch with so many savvy parents. The on-line listserves have been a constant source of support and a mighty shoulder for me through the years. Parents are using their knowledge to drive the mental health system forward in its quest for solutions.

Thank you to Candida Fink, M.D., my wonderful co-author, who was always there for me whenever I had a question (and there were plenty of those) and who meticulously conferred with me on each and every subject. You have been a personal and professional source of support and a true friend. And kudos to Lisa Considine, the world's most scrupulous editor, and Faith Hamlin, the agent who knew exactly where to go with my proposal.

—Judith Lederman

I would like to thank all of my patients and their parents, who have trusted me and collaborated with me through some of the most difficult and challenging times in their lives. I learn every day from my patients—they are my endless resource for knowledge and understanding.

Thank you to my coauthor, Judy Lederman. Your understanding of this disorder and your empathy for the families and children is profound. I have learned much in doing this work together. Thank you for this opportunity.

I want to thank Lisa Considine, our editor, who was always pushing us to be better. And finally, my deep appreciation goes out to Faith Hamlin, who welcomed me onto this project graciously.

—Candida Fink, M.D.

CONTENTS

INTRODUCTION   1

PART ONE:

YOUR BIPOLAR CHILD   11

1. The Diagnosis: What It Means to Be Bipolar   13

2. Mental Health Care Professionals: Picking
   Your Team   36

3. The Moods: Helping Your Child Through
   Mood Swings   71

4. The Medications: The Right Prescriptions
   for Your Child   106

5. The Structure of Daily Life: Routine Is
   Everything   125

6. Hospitalization: When and How to Get
   24/7 Care   150

PART TWO:

YOUR CHILD IN THE WORLD   173

7. Day Care, Schools, and Camps: Finding
   Safe and Appropriate Care and Education   175

8. Friends and Family: When and How to Explain Your Child's Condition   201

9. The Law: A Good Lawyer Can Help   212

PART THREE:

YOUR FAMILY   227

10. You: Caring for Yourself So You Can Care for Your Child   229

11. Relationships: Meeting the Challenge Together   239

12. Siblings: Parenting the "Normal" Ones   255

PART FOUR:

MONEY MATTERS   267

13. Career: Balancing Work and the Biggest Job You'll Ever Have   269

14. Family Finances: Paying for Special Needs Now and Later   281

RESOURCES   293

INDEX   297

INTRODUCTION

The moment I discovered that I was the mother of a child with bipolar disorder, also known as manic-depression, my life became the ultimate learning curve. I knew something was terribly wrong one summer day in Mystic, Connecticut. My son, then five years old, stood on the edge of a pier at the seaport museum and, under a sparkling summer sky, threatened to kill himself. What horrible incident triggered the outburst? An ordinary parental limit-setting moment. I'd just informed him and his brother and sister that we were headed inside the museum. He wanted to explore another ship, and when I said no, he stomped to the edge of the pier, where he teetered over the smashing waves below. His blue eyes clouded with tears as he threatened to jump into the angry sea. A crowd began to gather as my husband and I tried to talk him away from the edge. We were afraid to charge at him and grab him, afraid he might jump. I helplessly led the other children away as my husband moved closer and spoke to our sobbing child in low tones.

We waited for what seemed to be hours but was actually only about ten minutes. Finally, my husband reappeared, hand in hand with our son. I said a silent prayer and vowed to find out what was wrong. It would be three years before I got an answer.

Unlike his brother, who as a baby was always squalling and

fussing, this son was an even-tempered infant—a baby who gave me his first smile the morning after he was born (it *wasn't* gas!). He seemed exceptionally bright and would lie quietly in his crib or playpen for hours on end, amusing himself with toys and life swirling around him.

He was unusually sensitive to others' feelings. He knew instinctively how to rest his head on the shoulder of a friend who needed a cuddle, and loved sharing—toys, food, anything at all—with just about anybody.

As a toddler, he was very attached to me. When I tried to leave him with babysitters, he clung to me and refused to let me leave. I did what all the books suggest: developed a good-bye ritual, said good-bye firmly, and left without looking back. But the crying, pounding, and kicking echoed in my heart long after I left. According to the sitters, it took him a long time to get over my leaving—much longer than it took other children his age.

Before his sister was born, my son, then two and a half, kicked the Lamaze teacher as she worked with me on the floor. His angry outbursts continued after his sister was born. He adored her but got angry at her, and his aggression got worse as she grew older. The emotions were normal but the expressions of them extreme. He was genuinely bent on inflicting harm one minute, then gentle and loving the next. As he got older, these behaviors were more pronounced.

I worked from home most of the time when he was small—always nearby, but with babysitters in place to care for him and his sister. The babysitters just couldn't manage him. One reported that he charged after her and his sister with a stick. Upon tendering her resignation, another said, "In all my life, I've never heard a child curse like he does." The whirlwind of babysitters was taking a toll on my son, but we needed my income. It became harder to focus on my work as his behavior escalated.

One day I came home from a meeting to find my daughter with a deep gash down her cheek. The babysitter was devastated.

"It happened so fast—he scratched her for no reason at all," she stammered.

I blamed the sitters. I blamed my career. I blamed my horrible parenting skills. And I blamed my husband. I read every parenting book I could get my hands on and tried every system of discipline, from charts to tickets to marbles. All the blaming brought me no closer to an answer. I knew I needed help.

After the suicide attempt, I brought my son to a psychologist recommended by the school district. I was surprised when the psychologist shrugged off the incident, chalking it up to "attention-getting tactics." "He's a very manipulative child," the psychologist told me. He said I should ignore the outbursts and implement a good reward-based system. I went back to the books and looked for a method that I hadn't already tried and abandoned.

School was becoming a problem. Getting him there was half the battle. At night, he stayed up later and later, no matter how early we began his bedtime routine. In the morning, he refused to get out of bed and routinely missed the school bus. I tried to let the consequences of his decisions rest on his shoulders; when he missed the school bus, we walked to school. On really bad days when he would hide under the bed and refuse to get dressed, I'd grab my pajama-clad son in one arm, his clothes in the other, and drive him to school half dressed. One day the principal had to climb into the minivan, pry him from the backseat, throw him over his shoulder, and deposit him in his first-grade class.

When my son managed to tow the line at school, his behaviors at home got worse. The situation affected everyone in the family. My older son, going through his own teenage turmoil, didn't understand how his brother "got away" with such terrible tantrums. My daughter, who vacillated from being his best friend and caregiver to being the victim of his anger, was starting to imitate his behaviors. My husband and I argued—about parenting, about the money it would cost to bring our family to therapists, and about the budding awareness that something was seriously wrong.

Worse yet, our struggle was alienating us from our friends, our community, and even our extended family. His antics on the community baseball team—stomping off the field, refusing to go up to bat, accusing coaches of mishandling him—raised more than a few eyebrows. We felt isolated. People blamed us for our son's strange behavior.

At age eight, he slept just a few hours at night, but he had boundless energy. Then he would become sad—so sad he would cry and say he wanted to die. One morning, I woke up at 4:00 A.M. to find him marching around the house, banging on a tambourine. He said he couldn't sleep and was bored so he decided to have a parade. His aggressive behavior was worsening as well. We battled daily threats. He lay down on the railing of the deck, about eighteen feet off the ground, and threatened to roll off. He pointed a kitchen carving knife at his older brother, then later against his own wrist.

"I don't want to be here," he would cry as I tried to put him to sleep.

"Here where?" I asked.

"Here on this earth," he whispered. "I don't want to live."

In desperation, I searched our health insurance plan and called several psychologists. Few got back to me, and the earliest appointment any of them could give me was two weeks away. When one of them finally took the time to listen to the symptoms, he suggested that I bring my son to a psychiatric hospital. He gave me a few numbers, and I made an appointment for that night. My husband was opposed to the idea, but I couldn't take yet another sleepless night followed by a day of rage. I was mentally, emotionally, and physically exhausted.

Although my husband was in denial about the seriousness of the problem, I felt I had to get my son help. Leaving my husband in charge of the other two children, my son and I drove to the hospital.

The psychiatric facility, housed in an old stone mansion on the crest of a windswept hill, was eerily lit by the setting sun. We were asked to sit in a library with floor-to-ceiling shelves piled with dusty old books. A nurse brought us some markers, and we played umpteen games of tic-tac-toe. My son was relaxed, but not at all sleepy, even though it was getting quite late. As the nurse asked me detailed questions about my son's sleeping habits and rages, my son got angry that I was "telling" on him. Markers flew. He refused to listen when the nurse politely told him to stop. He kicked her when she tried to restrain him.

The nurse reached a phone, and other staff members arrived to help restrain him. They searched his pockets, inventoried his belongings, and even took away his boots, now considered dangerous since he used them to kick the nurse. I watched in horror, tears springing to my eyes, as they forced my eight-year-old child out of the room.

A psychiatrist explained to me that they would evaluate my son in the hospital. They would administer medication that would help him, and they would monitor him while he was in the hospital. I called my husband, and he was livid. The psychiatrist explained that if I didn't sign the papers, my son would be committed all the same. Based on his observations, something was terribly wrong.

"If you don't allow us to treat your son, children's protective services will be called in," he warned. "If they take over, you will be forced to forfeit your parental rights to make any decisions for your son."

I reluctantly signed papers enabling the hospital to evaluate my son for seventy-two hours.

By the time I left the hospital, it was 2:00 A.M., and it looked even creepier than before. I wiped away tears of exhaustion as I drove down the empty highway.

As I crawled into bed early that morning, one comforting thought surfaced: even as I was plagued by guilt, feeling that this was somehow my fault, I was relieved that my son was finally going to get help.

Three days later, the insurance company prevailed upon the hospital. With a diagnosis of attention deficit disorder and depression, the hospital reluctantly released my son. I was given prescriptions for three drugs: Ritalin, for hyperactivity; Seroquel, to address the rages; and Luvox, an antidepressant. I made a follow-up psychiatric appointment with a clinic recommended by the hospital. The earliest a psychiatrist could see him was in three weeks. Meanwhile, I filled the prescriptions and waited for everything to get better. To my shock and disbelief, things got worse.

On Hanukkah, my son flew into a rage, and we had to guard the candles to make sure he wouldn't deliberately burn the house down. He was like a feral animal, running outside naked and urinating on the front door. I had bruises all over my body from trying to restrain him. The rages seemed only to intensify. Those weeks on Ritalin and Luvox were three weeks of hell.

On the day he was scheduled for his follow-up, our son threatened to throw a ten-pound weight at my husband's head. Together, we managed to disarm him and carry him to the car. At the psychiatrist's office, he sat backward in a chair, playing with the light switch. He walked out of the office with one of us in tow several times.

The child psychiatrist took a family history and seemed especially interested in hearing about my husband's father, who had been diagnosed many years ago with something called "involutional melancholia." He watched quietly as our son fussed, fidgeted, and mumbled to himself. And then the psychiatrist got angry.

"I can't believe that hospital! Your son isn't ADHD. This is as clear a case of early-onset bipolar disorder as I've ever seen and they released him after only three days? I'm going to call the insurance company right now. We've got to get him treatment."

My husband and I shrugged. The diagnosis meant nothing to us at the time, but anything that would explain our son's behavior was welcome. A few minutes later, the doctor was on the phone with the insurance company, demanding in no uncertain terms that they approve another hospitalization for our son.

We were thrilled to finally have an advocate, as well as a name for our son's illness. Doctors at the new hospital, a teaching hospital, confirmed the diagnosis of early-onset bipolar disorder and explained that this mental illness causes extreme highs and lows. We were told that although the disorder sometimes goes along with hyperactivity, Ritalin can worsen the symptoms of bipolar disorder, sending patients into uncontrollable rages.

But the most amazing thing that the psychiatrist told us was that our son's behavior was not our fault. He assured us that bipolar disorder and its attendant mood swings are very, very real and that time and treatment would help. The treatment *is* helping. Although my son still gets angry and irritable, his rages seem to have ended and his depression has lifted. With our help, he manages to do most things an ordinary adolescent does. His schedule is modified. He needs special programming in school. We stay in close contact with his teachers, doctors, and other adults who work with him. We make sure they understand that although our son is a highly intelligent child, his behaviors and reactions can sometimes be unpredictable and are not to be taken lightly.

We now know that managing bipolar disorder is a lifetime effort. Mental health professionals say that bipolar disorder is one of the most treatable mental illnesses and that new medication and other breakthroughs are just around the corner. We take it one day at a time and pray that they are right. Days, even weeks and months, pass when we are challenged, but we no longer feel the helplessness that we experienced that day watching our son on the edge of a pier in Mystic.

This journey has been a learning experience; we've come a long way now that we know what we are facing. When I began this book, my son, then ten years old, routinely wore army camouflage togs. He felt safe in his camo—a soldier no one could hurt. But the real threat came from within, from inside his tousled, curly head, where his moods festered like brew in a bubbling cauldron. One minute, he smiled a beatific smile that reminded me of his sweet, calm, newborn face. Moments later he was agitated. He will always have his moods, but things have improved with time and treatment. He and my entire family are so much better and stronger now than when I started my research and writing.

I am writing this book from a unique point of view: one of a mother who suffers as she watches her child suffer from a condition that is his alone but affects just about everyone in the circle of family and friends. Over the years, as a mother and primary caregiver for my son, I have seen pieces of myself being stripped away. My career, the work that sustains me, must be set aside when his moods so dictate. His behavior can trigger copycat behavior in our other children. Leisure and entertainment are meted out in contained doses to keep him stable, as are family trips and vacations. What is normal for other families—scouting, sports practice, food shopping, a visit to the museum, the occasional movie—can, on a bad day, send my son into a tailspin, and so we curtail these activities, closely examining his moods and responses.

In each chapter, "Notes from the Couch" offers the psychiatrist's perspective on the issues being discussed. Candida Fink, M.D., my coauthor and noted child psychiatrist, has been treating children with bipolar disorder for many years. Her notes offer guidance and support.

My hope is that this book will find its way into the hands of people who shake their heads, glare, and "tsk-tsk," as they stand in line at the supermarket watching an eight-year-old bipolar child beating, cursing, and berating his helpless mom. This book is for the teachers who eschew psychologists' endless labels and claim that if given the chance, they could "do a better job" parenting a child who rants, cries, or rages each day in the classroom. This book is for the doctors who, in spite of clinical training, cannot believe bipolar disorder can manifest itself in a small child and wonder if parents are overmedicating their children to make life easy on themselves. If you recognize these people, as so many parents of bipolar children do, urge them to take the time to read this.

Most important, this book is for you, the parent of a bipolar child, who, like myself, has been trying to understand why your child seems so different from other children. Whether you suspect something is wrong or have already received a diagnosis, you'll find both practical guidance and emotional reassurance here. In these pages are information, heartfelt support, and unique coping methods to help you deal with everything from difficult spouses to legal conundrums to blood tests, road trips, camps, and schools—everyday situations inspired by the ups and downs of your child's life.

An on-line questionnaire was made available to parents of bipolar children at www.parentingbipolars.com from 2001 through 2002. To date, there have been several hundred responses. For this book, responses were tabulated and sifted through; the information is shared in quotations, through statistics, and with anecdotes. The same site is live now with information and links for anyone parenting a child with bipolar disorder.

Part One

Your Bipolar Child

CHAPTER 1

THE DIAGNOSIS

What It Means to Be Bipolar

I knew her violent behavior was beyond her control. Trying to deal with her was tearing our family apart. School had become a disaster. I was finally at the end of my rope, was powerless to help her myself. I felt like a failure having to admit I couldn't successfully parent my own child.
Candace, mom of a bipolar daughter diagnosed at age eight

Something is wrong. You feel it in your gut. Your child just doesn't behave like other children. She is prone to uncontrollable fits of rage. The terrible twos seem to have followed her through life. She impulsively opens car doors while you're driving, threatening to jump out. Sometimes she is weepy or down on everyone—friends, school, teachers, the toys she once treasured—for no apparent reason. Getting her to school is a nearly impossible task. She spends most school days talking or squabbling with other children or, more perplexing, behaving completely "normal," reserving her bad behavior for home.

A child may seem exceptionally moody or may misbehave in dramatic, unpredictable, or unusual ways for many reasons. Some moods are influenced by situations. Some misbehavior is a cry for guidance or structure. Yet when moods and behaviors regularly interfere with your child's day-to-day routines or when the moods seem explosive and dangerous, it's time to consult a mental health expert.

What Is Bipolar Disorder?

Bipolar disorder is a very real, very treatable physical brain disorder. This energetic disturbance with its fluctuating mood states frequently coexists with other mental illnesses, such as attention-deficit hyperactivity disorder (ADHD), anxiety disorder, eating disorder, obsessive-compulsive disorder, substance abuse, and Tourette's syndrome. Professional sources estimate that the condition affects at least 1 million children in the United States alone, and since it is estimated that 1 to 2 percent of the adult population suffers from bipolar disorder, many psychiatrists believe that a similarly large number of children are afflicted as well. The illness manifests itself emotionally and behaviorally, but its roots are physical in nature, and doctors are finding that it can manifest itself earlier in life than they once believed. Over the years, the condition has been called many things, including manic-depression, circular insanity, and involutional melancholia. No matter what they call it, health professionals have always classified it as a psychiatric mood disorder.

The word *bipolar* refers to the two poles of energetic extremes. Symptoms of mania include elation and grandiosity, racing speech, impulsive behavior, and boundless energy. The manic state is one that some children find pleasurable. As enjoyable, addictive, and exciting as the manic state can be, sometimes irritability, fury, suspicion, brooding, disgust, and dissatisfaction accompany the high energy. Symptoms of the depressive phase include low energy, profound sadness, apathy, hopelessness, self-loathing, morose negativity, thoughts of suicide, and in some cases actual suicide attempts.

Adults and children naturally express these symptoms differently. In adults, for example, manic or depressive moods can last months, while in children, the moods can be more frequent and fleeting. As Barbara Geller, M.D., professor of psychiatry at Washington University in St. Louis and a researcher who has been studying early-onset bipolar disorder since 1990, points out, an eight-year-old in a manic state doesn't go on a spending spree or have a reckless sexual fling. The equivalent may be an enterprising eight-year-old who opens a lemonade stand in her classroom and becomes enraged when the teacher tells her to close up shop and do schoolwork, or a child who, in the absence of sexual abuse or overstimulation, tries to grab his teacher's breasts. According to eminent psychiatrists like Joseph Biederman, M.D., mania in children frequently looks like hyperactivity and irritability.

To compound issues, the manic and depressive states in prepubescent children aren't always well defined. Children can bounce back and forth between mania and depression many times a day and often endure "mixed states," where their mania combines with depression, leaving them in a rather loud state of depression. Children who have their first episodes as adolescents tend to have more classic manic-depressive mood swings.

Bipolar disorder in children is not a new diagnosis. Worldwide case reports from the *Archive of General Psychiatry* record children on lithium for bipolar disorder as early as 1978. But the generally accepted diagnostic criteria for bipolar disorder have never been broadened to encompass the manifestation of the condition in children. Research has been lacking, but fortunately, that's changing. Thanks to psychiatrists like Demitri Papolos and other determined researchers, new studies are being done even as I write. The indications are that bipolar disorder is identifiable in children. While scientists are working to identify bipolar disorder in children as young as preschool, psychiatrists are generally wary of making a diagnosis at that age.

The Brain Science Behind the Label

Mental illnesses and their biological origins have traditionally been back-burnered in the research world, in spite of the fact that many have biochemical roots. At the heart of any discussion of moods is an area called the limbic system. It controls our emotions, our flight-or-fight response, as well as our desire to "feed and breed," in other words, our appetite for sex and food. Within the limbic system is a kind of thermostat called the hypothalamus. In its role as the gatekeeper for the pituitary gland, the hypothalamus helps control everything from our temperature to our sexual desire.

Our 100 billion or so brain cells are called neurons, which together compose an immensely sophisticated electrochemical messaging system. Messages travel through the system, jumping schisms between neurons (also called the synaptic clefts) with the help of neurotransmitter chemicals. Individually and in combination, these chemicals communicate different messages. For example, serotonin influences mood and controls sleep patterns and appetite. Dopamine controls thought patterns and helps regulate muscles and movement. Norepinephrine plays a part in focus and attention, as well as in the production of adrenaline and endorphins that modulate experiences such as fear, excitement, pain, and pleasure.

According to researchers, the absence or overabundance of neurotransmitter chemicals in the synaptic cleft, particularly serotonin and norepinephrine, appears to influence depressive and manic symptoms. Also under scrutiny is the sensitivity of the neural receptor mechanisms in bipolar patients. Armed with this information, researchers are learning how to measure the flow of chemicals and address through medication the structures that may be defective.

The neurotransmitter chemicals in the limbic region also control the endocrine system, bringing hormones into the mix. Before you latch on to a bipolar diagnosis for your child, she needs a physical workup to rule out physical diseases like thyroid conditions. Such endocrine imbalances can create symptoms of mental illness like depression.

Some research suggests that by mapping out active areas of the brain, a bipolar brain can be distinguished from its non-bipolar counterpart. Researchers are exploring several tests to map brain function and pinpoint brain disorders, including early-onset bipolar disorder. That said, there are dissenting voices. Many doctors, like Peter Jensen, M.D., director of the Center for the Advancement of Children's Mental Health, say that these are research tools, which should not and cannot be used as diagnostic tests.

The Tests

The most accurate diagnostics are an expert psychiatrist's careful examination of your child and review of symptoms as reported by you. As neuroimaging techniques are researched, tested, and perfected, they will likely prove a valuable tool in both diagnosis and treatment of bipolar disorder.

Psychiatric Evaluation
Owen had always been high maintenance even in the womb!!! It seemed as though the entire time I was carrying him, he was in motion. His psychiatrist had always suspected a mood disorder, as I myself am bipolar.
Jerri, mom of a bipolar son diagnosed at age nine

Everybody has moods, so when should a parent worry that a

child's moods are anything but normal? When high or low energy levels become debilitating, interfering with the child's ability to function normally in school or interact with peers or family, there is cause for concern. Substance use, hypersexual behaviors, conduct disorders, eating and body distortions, and talk of self-harm or actual self-harm are serious red flags that indicate that a child is in a critical phase of a mental illness.

Psychiatric diagnoses are made by assessing patients' symptoms using a set of accepted criteria found in a professional reference, the *Diagnostic and Statistical Manual of the American Psychiatric Association* (DSM), now in its fourth revision. How closely your child's symptoms match the symptoms in the DSM depends in part on the diagnosing psychiatrist's interpretation. Originally compiled in 1952, the DSM is revised periodically as new information surfaces. The latest DSM, the DSM-IV, includes few diagnoses that are specific for children. Bipolar disorder is only described for adults. The DSMs break bipolar disorder down into categories: bipolar type 1, bipolar type 2, and bipolar NOS (Not Otherwise Specified). In bipolar type 1, a person experiences at least one week of mania and may or may not experience depressive episodes. In bipolar type 2, a person experiences at least four days of hypomania (a condition of less severe mania). The bipolar NOS classification is the one that many children fall under because its myriad symptoms don't cleanly fit into the strict DSM criteria for bipolar 1 or bipolar 2. Another frequent diagnosis is cyclothymic disorder, which is a combination of hypomania and dysthymia (mild depression) for more than a year. According to the National Alliance for the Mentally Ill (NAMI), current genomic research may be leading to the discovery of even more types of bipolar disorder than we know about today.

While the next DSM revision is due around 2011, it remains to be seen whether the new checklists and descriptions will include better criteria for diagnosing bipolar disorder in children. Some doctors still lean heavily on the DSM criteria; others are developing their own criteria and even exploring other possible diagnoses.

Child psychiatrists continue to debate the question of whether adult bipolar criteria are adequate for diagnosing bipolar disorder in children since, they say, childhood-onset appears to present differently from adult-onset illness. For example, children cycle through manic and depressive episodes much more rapidly than adults do. It is also possible that what doctors have identified as early-onset bipolar disorder might be an entirely different phenomenon.

Child psychiatrists are divided on the question of bipolar diagnosis in children. Most agree that the disorder exists in childhood, but differ in their views of how and when to diagnose. A psychiatric evaluation takes into account family history, school history, parental input, and the psychiatrist's own observations of the child. She then tailors the psychopharmacologic treatment—medical prescriptions—to the individual child's symptoms.

Since there are no definitive data on how many children with bipolar symptoms will grow into adults with bipolar disorder, some doctors believe it's better to treat the symptoms and avoid the label. These doctors may employ a more generic label for a child's condition, such as "mood disorder."

What Are the Symptoms?

The first inkling of the disorder often starts with a depressive episode, which in children can be expressed by irritability or anxiety. A manic episode, often described as energetic irritability, can follow immediately or much later. Because "irritability" is a vague symptom, it is a parent's job to play detective in collecting a thorough family history and helping their child's psychiatrist understand all the potential biological and event-triggered incidents in their child's life.

Barbara Geller, M.D., professor of psychiatry at Washington University in St. Louis, Missouri, has developed an adaptation of the adult DSM criteria that is used by most National Institute of Mental Health–funded studies for establishing a bipolar diagnosis. As more psychiatrists become aware of the Geller model and the new research on early-onset bipolar disorder becomes available, these diagnostics are likely to become the norm.

Here are some things most psychiatrists take into account when considering bipolar diagnosis for a particular patient:

Attention/Organizational Levels

- Does he have attention problems?
- Does he have trouble getting or staying organized?
- Is he restless or fidgety?
- Does he have trouble starting tasks? Completing tasks?
- What is his activity level? Does he seem sluggish or going at top speed, physically and mentally?

Moods

- Does she exhibit unusual sadness?
- Does she seem irritable a good part of the time?
- Does she express a grandiose sense of herself and her abilities? Is everything too good?
- Does everything seem terrible to her most of the time?
- Do her moods and behaviors seem to cycle, that is, erupt and then calm down again, for reasons you frequently cannot see?

- Does she show significant changes in sleep, appetite, energy, or interest in friends and activities?
- Does she ever talk about or exhibit self-mutilation thoughts or behaviors?
- Has she ever expressed wishes to be dead or to kill herself?

Behavior
- Does he have unexplained rages?
- How are his judgment and impulse control?
- Does he have frequent tantrums?
- Is he prone to explosive behavior?
- How well does he tolerate frustration and transitions?
- Is he compliant when it comes to rules and regulations?

Anxiety
- Does she have seemingly unfounded fears or worries?
- Is she prone to panic attacks?
- How does she handle separation?
- Does she have regular somatic complaints (aches, pains, trips to the school nurse, refusal to go to school)?
- How are her sleep-wake cycles?
- Does she frequently wake with nightmares or night terrors?
- Is there a history of trauma or loss?

Social Skills
- Does he exhibit appropriate responses to social interactions?
- How does he handle new situations or new people and groups of people?
- Is he indiscriminately friendly?

- Does he fight with other children?
- How does he interact with adults? Other children?
- Does he exhibit stilted or awkward demeanor?
- Does he seem socially isolated?

Thought Problems
- Does she have hallucinations, delusions, or bizarre thoughts?
- Does she exhibit mistrust and suspicion of others?
- Are her thoughts slow or halting?
- Does she exhibit a rambling or disorganized thinking process?
- Does she have obsessions or compulsions? Rituals? Unreasonable superstitions?

An experienced child psychiatrist will analyze the mix of symptoms your child demonstrates to come up with an appropriate diagnosis. Your child should be evaluated very carefully by a psychiatrist before a diagnosis or treatment regime can be established. Be patient with this process, and remember that what you observe and report can be a great help to the health care professional on the case. Depending on the severity of the symptoms, hospitalization or frequent, extended appointments may be required to determine the correct diagnosis.

Neuroimaging Tests
The meds were not working, and the psychiatrist we were working with refused to change doses or drugs. I took him to the Amen Clinic in Fairfield, California, where they SPECT scanned him and changed all his meds.
Elizabeth, mom of a bipolar son diagnosed at age eight

If only we could peer into our children's bipolar brains to find out exactly how they work. It sounds like science fiction, but as we discover new imaging techniques, we may one day be able to do just that. Here are a few of the imaging tests that your child may experience.

PET Scans

Positron emission tomography detects regions in the brain where nerve cells are working and glucose is being metabolized during a mental task. PET scans are said to be sensitive to biological brain alterations during episodes of schizophrenia, depression, and other disorders.

Brain activity levels are indicated with colors that range from red, yellow, and green (most activity) to blue, violet, and black (least activity). A brain in the midst of an untreated depressive episode shows less activity than a nondepressed brain.

SPECT Scans

Single photon emission tomography can accurately identify areas of activity in the brain, according to Daniel Amen, M.D., author of *Change Your Brain, Change Your Life* and one of the pioneers of SPECT scan technology. This test measures blood flow in particular areas of the brain. According to Dr. Amen, the bipolar brain is markedly different from the typical brain. During a manic phase, patchy increased blood flow is visible across the whole surface of the brain and particularly in the thalamus. Dr. Amen calls this a hot brain overall—one that exhibits what he calls a visible "ring of fire." The depressed state shows an overactive thalamus, but usually not the patchy increased uptake.

Most doctors do not consider SPECT scans appropriate diagnostic tools, and some question the use of radioactive isotopes, a part of the scanning procedure.

EEG with Strobe Lights or with Nasal Probes

This test is used to assess seizure disorders. A relatively safe and inexpensive test, an electroencephalogram (EEG) measures the electrical activity in the brain. According to Jean Frazier, director of child outpatient services and director of the pediatric psychotic disorders program at McLean and Massachusetts General Hospital, this test is critical in determining whether a medical condition or neurological condition is causing symptoms such as explosivity, hyperactivity, irritability, periods of confusion with bizarre repetitive behavior, losing urine or feces, or psychosis. While these can be symptoms of bipolar disorder, they can also indicate an organic condition like a seizure disorder. In a sleep-deprived EEG, the child must stay up all night before the test. A sleep-deprived brain is in a stressed state and will bring out any unusual electrical activity.

If your child is sent for an EEG, she will go into a room with dim lights and sit in a reclining chair. A technician will apply leads to the child's head with a gel. It doesn't hurt at all, and your child might even fall asleep during the test, which will provide valuable data, since the sleeping brain looks different from the wakened one. Sometimes strobe lights are used as stressors to try to induce seizures. Your child may be asked to breathe heavily because this can also bring on seizure activity. The test usually takes about half an hour.

MRI and MRS

Magnetic resonance imaging (MRI) is a general imaging technique that uses magnets to produce a "picture" of the brain. MRI is not used to identify mental illnesses, but is often employed to rule out other neurological problems and abnormalities in the brain anatomy, such as small tumors, small strokes, or multiple sclerosis, that could resemble a mood disorder. If a lesion, stroke, tumor, or multiple sclerosis is present, if a particular brain structure is smaller than the normal, or if there has been severe head injury, the MRI will pick it up.

Several times Dr. Frazier has used MRI to rule out bipolar disorder in cases in which a child presented with atypical bipolar symptoms but an MRI revealed tiny brain lesions, actually caused by Lyme disease. Such children are taken off psychotropic medications, prescribed antibiotics, and generally experience full recovery.

Magnetic resonance spectroscopy (MRS), not yet available to clinicians as of this writing, is said to show promise as a diagnostic tool. It measures the concentration of the neurochemicals in the brain. For instance, it can tell how much of a medication such as lithium is actually getting into the brain and how it is changing the levels of other brain chemicals.

The Diagnosis

Misdiagnoses and Comorbidity
She was first diagnosed with ADHD and depression and was put on antidepressants. Meds just made it worse. She was hyper, not sleeping well, and had Dr. Jekyll/Mr. Hyde–style mood swings.
Rona, mom of a bipolar daughter diagnosed at age seven

Because they cause learning problems, and because they are common, attention deficit disorder (ADD) and attention deficit disorder with hyperactivity (ADHD) have taken center stage for many years, leading even the most seasoned health professionals and education experts to make swift, and often incorrect, diagnoses. Numerous symptoms, such as hyperactivity, racing thoughts, irritability, and impulsivity, are common in both ADHD and bipolar disorder, as well as obsessive-compulsive disorder, anxiety disorder, and schizophrenia.

The ADHD diagnosis often is comorbid with bipolar disorder, meaning the two coexist. According to one study, eight of ten children with bipolar disorder are actually suffering from bipolar disorder and ADHD together. Bipolar children who are misdiagnosed as ADHD are often medicated with stimulants like Ritalin or antidepressants, which can send bipolar children into a state of mania far worse than anything the child has experienced before. Even nonbipolar children can have agitated reactions to stimulants or antidepressants, which is why parents need to monitor their children closely for mood changes, especially when they start on medications (more about this in Chapter 3).

Coping with the Diagnosis

When she finally got the BP diagnosis, it was almost a relief in the sense that we could work on getting her the right treatment. Sometimes there is anger and fear too, but I believe that kind of goes with the territory for this illness.
Danielle, mom of a bipolar daughter diagnosed at age seven

Obtaining the bipolar disorder diagnosis can be an arduous process and may bring on various feelings, ranging from relief to outrage. Some parents go to psychiatrists demanding the bipolar diagnosis and find themselves in a face-off with their children's health care providers, trying to prove to them that the bipolar diagnosis makes perfect sense given their family history and their child's behavior. Other parents are devastated by the thought of their child's having a serious mental illness. For some, the diagnosis for their child is the first step in coming to grips with an illness that they might have been battling for years, perhaps without knowing it.

According to David Fassler, M.D., psychiatrist and author of *Help Me, I'm Sad,* "Bipolar disorder in young children is both under and over diagnosed." If you go to a doctor who is a specialist in early-onset bipolar disorder, you may end up with a child who is immediately labeled bipolar with few or no questions asked. After all, he notes, "A person holding a hammer sees everything as a nail."

If you go to a psychiatrist who is unfamiliar with or skeptical about the bipolar diagnosis in children (and many are), you may end up with a misdiagnosis and the wrong treatment. In some cases, this can be worse than no treatment at all. Many children who are misdiagnosed as ADHD are given stimulant medication, which can send the child into a feral state.

Dr. Fassler says that it is critical to go to a doctor who is familiar with many childhood diagnoses as well as the latest research on early-onset bipolar disorder. Don't be afraid to ask questions to ensure the psychiatrist does a thorough evaluation. A doctor may still decide that he isn't quite sure, and may want to see how your child responds to different medications to treat the symptoms.

Don't be surprised to find yourself grappling with your own feelings as you learn more about your child's diagnosis. Acceptance takes time, but it does happen eventually. Anger, denial, and a dose of healthy skepticism are normal reactions for a parent confronted with a diagnosis of early-onset bipolar disorder—or any other mental illness, for that matter. By all means, question the diagnosis; talk to doctors, health professionals, and other parents of diagnosed children. Get second and third opinions. Do everything you need to in order to educate yourself and understand your child's diagnosis. Then go on to guide your child to the best treatment you can find.

Nature or Nurture?

My husband feels his family history is the problem. I'm not big on blame.
Lenore, mom of a bipolar son diagnosed at age ten

The nature versus nurture question is one that plagues many parents. Would their child have been bipolar if circumstances were different? Current thinking indicates that there are biological and environmental components to bipolar disorder. Potentially, a child may have a genetic tendency to develop the condition, but sometimes circumstances don't awaken it.

Psychiatrists interviewed for this book confirmed that at least 50 percent, and frequently a much higher percentage, of their bipolar patients had a parent who was either suspected or confirmed bipolar. Parents who responded to my on-line questionnaire reported that 70 percent of children had someone in their family with bipolar disorder. In fact, most of the doctors I spoke with said that in 50 percent of the cases, at least one parent of their bipolar patients displayed some symptoms of the disorder.

History gets blurry when it comes to third-generation mental health histories, but you may uncover some clues. If your great-aunt Sally had a reputation of being impossible to get along with, raged on a fairly regular basis, moped for weeks at a time, or had so much energy she never slept, she may have been suffering from bipolar disorder. Aunt Sally may never have bothered to go to a psychiatrist, a tremendous stigma back in her day. She also may have managed to live a somewhat healthy, albeit chaotic and sometimes miserable, life without diagnosis and treatment. There's no reason now for our children to go through life at the mercy of their tumultuous moods.

Despite environmental factors, it appears that bipolar disorder is driven more by biology than circumstance. A child with a neurological vulnerability to bipolar illness can be triggered into an episode by a wide range of stressors. The triggering event may be simple, but in a child with bipolar wiring, it can result in a manic or depressive episode. The brain, being the wonderfully adaptive and responsive organ that it is, reacts to the episode by formulating a response. Without specific treatment, that response becomes ingrained. Over time, the brain becomes more and more sensitive, and it takes less and less to trigger an episode. Eventually a bipolar brain will cycle almost independently of environmental cues. It's on autopilot.

Moving Beyond the Stigma

He was mortified when I mentioned the words bipolar, psychiatrist, *or* therapist. *It was a part of himself that he just didn't want to confront.*
Ellen, mom of a bipolar son diagnosed at age eight

Many people are uneducated about depression and the devastating effects it can have on a child. Clinical depression is a medical condition, and children are as prone to this state as anyone else. Those who ask what children have to be depressed about don't understand the physical nature of depression. Your job as your child's parent is to educate those who interact on any level with your child. Of course, not everyone needs to know about your child's condition. (See Chapter 8 for a complete discussion of when and how to share this information.)

Untreated, people who suffer from bipolar disorder can, and all too often do, turn to suicide to end their pain, and this includes children and adolescents. The mortality rate for this disease is very high. According to the surgeon general's December 1999 report *Mental Health: A Report of the Surgeon General,* the incidence of suicide attempts reaches a peak during the midadolescent years; mortality from suicide, which increases steadily through the teens, is the third leading cause of death at that age.

The stigma of mental illness makes it difficult for many parents to accept a bipolar diagnosis. For one thing, acknowledging mental illness requires admitting that a child or teen could genuinely be out of control, a notion that is inconceivable for some people. Parents always want their children to be responsible for their actions. But when you understand the brain imbalances behind a mental illness, it becomes easier to accept. According to Dr. Gianni Faedda, psychiatrist and director of the Lucio Bini Mood Disorders Center (www.mood-center.org), bipolar disorder is perceived as a character flaw more often than other mental illnesses are. "Because during periods of remission people with bipolar disorder can lead functional lives, it appears that they can control the illness," explains Dr. Faedda. "In the midst of a bipolar episode, though, that is just not the case."

Some parents find it easier to label their children as lazy, stupid, or ADHD—anything rather than bipolar disorder. In their minds, acknowledging mental illness places stigma not only on the child but on the entire family. According to Dr. Faedda, once one family member is diagnosed, two or three more within the family can end up with the diagnosis as well—not because it's contagious but because this brain disorder is congenital, and probably it's hanging elsewhere on the family tree.

Adopted Children: Hidden Histories

Responses to my on-line questionnaire revealed a surprising fact: 14 percent of parents indicated that their bipolar child was adopted. Researchers I spoke with indicated that they too have noticed a high number of adopted children presenting with early-onset bipolar disorder, although no formal research was conducted. Some surmised that birth mothers who became pregnant out of wedlock may have been bipolar, since hypersexuality and impulsive behavior can lead to an unwanted pregnancy. Others pointed out that posttraumatic stress may trigger genetic bipolar tendencies.

Although it may difficult, try to get a thorough understanding of the mental health history (along with the physical medical history) of a child's birth parents, grandparents, and uncles and aunts when you are planning to adopt a child.

Explaining the Diagnosis to Your Child

We tell Daisy that she takes her meds so that she can be happy when she wants to be happy, sad when she wants to be sad, and angry when she wants to be angry. But when she is sad or mad all day, then she needs help from her doctor.
Glenda, mom of a bipolar daughter diagnosed at age three

Your child is undoubtedly as bewildered as you are by the diagnosis of bipolar disorder. To date, he has probably been held accountable for his turbulent moods and troubled behavior. Every child wants to belong, yet your child may feel very different—never good enough at home, at school, or with peers. Although his behavior may look awful and seem to be the source of the problem, he has most likely tried and tried again to improve, with little success.

While a parent may feel the stigma of the diagnosis, the child must deal with that as well as with the illness itself. Medication and treatment will begin to repair some of the self-control issues, but your child will need a lot of support and encouragement in the months and years to come. He will need to catch up with his peers. On top of all that, he will need to learn to cope with his illness. Dealing with the grief, accepting that he has a chronic condition that needs medication, learning to cope with the illness, and unlearning the old maladaptive coping are hard for even the most resilient child.

The American Academy of Child and Adolescent Psychiatry suggests that parents explain the diagnosis and discuss the illness with their child. Giving a child the basics of brain chemistry (with some library or on-line help), explaining that he is not alone in experiencing mental illness, and tracing the family history, if you have one, can be helpful to a child.

Use the Internet to find and print out photos of the brain. Try to make the science as visual as you can. Older children may appreciate the nuances of neurons; younger children may require a simpler approach. Children of all ages will benefit from learning that this is an illness like any other illness, and that others in their family have it and cope with it.

Keep in mind that even when a child seems out of control and seems unreceptive to the scrutiny and exams by strange new health care providers, deep down he is longing to be in control again. It is important to reassure him that talking to doctors and therapists and taking the medications prescribed will ultimately help him feel better and take away the mood swings.

Welcome to the World of Advocacy!

Throughout this most difficult and frightening process, I felt repeatedly that if I did not know how to advocate effectively for my child and know many mental health professionals, the entire thing would have been even worse than it was.
Sally, mom of a bipolar son diagnosed at age seven

You may not have realized it when you began your quest to solve your child's problem, but when your child is diagnosed with bipolar disorder, you are no longer just a parent. Even if you failed high school biology, you will learn about the intricacies of the brain. If you don't know a congressman from a senator, you will quickly learn who to petition about changing laws that affect your child's health and education. Yesterday you were "just a parent." Today you are an advocate. Even if you never took psychology and don't know the first thing about social work, you have become your child's caseworker.

Whether it is on a small scale (negotiating with your child's teacher) or a large scale (fighting with your state legislature on behalf of insurance parity), you are fighting for your child. And you need to arm yourself with knowledge and support, because the road will not always be smooth.

Making the world a better place for his or her children is every parent's job, regardless of the child's physical or psychological challenges. The bipolar parent's mission is much more. It requires making the world a place where a mentally ill child gets the health care treatment he needs, education he deserves, medicine that stabilizes him, legal assistance he occasionally may require, financial assistance he is entitled to, and the ability to stand up tall in spite of those who may stigmatize him. So welcome to the world of advocacy! May you find the strength and tenacity to wage a winning battle.

Now that you know all about bipolar disorder, here is the good news. According to the National Alliance for the Mentally Ill, the treatment success rate for bipolar disorder is 80 percent. In other words, the vast majority of people with bipolar disorder respond to treatment and are able to live comparatively stable lives. That makes bipolar disorder one of the most treatable forms of mental illness. In the next chapter, you'll learn how to take steps toward finding the help your child needs.

Notes from the Couch: A Psychiatrist's Point of View

Early-onset bipolar disorder is one of the most complex and challenging diagnoses that I make in my practice. It is just as important to avoid the diagnosis if the disorder is not present as it is to make the correct call when it is.

I often feel like a pioneer doctor from the 1800s: trying to make diagnoses without modern tools. The best tools I have are a good history and examination of the child. Without scans and blood tests available yet, much of my job comes down to convincing people that bipolar disorder and mood disorders are both real and important to treat.

The question of why their child has bipolar disorder often haunts parents, and researchers are working on the answer to that question as you read this. At the moment, all we have are educated hunches. Mood disorders appear to be hardwired into our systems, and they present themselves at certain developmental times, when they are programmed to do so. We all want to know why it happens at that time or at all, but ultimately that question is more distracting than helpful. The emotional environment of the child becomes critical in managing and ameliorating the disorder, but rest assured that parenting style alone is not likely to have caused your child's mood disorder.

Oppositional defiant disorder is an often overlapping diagnosis in children with bipolar disorder. In my practice, I tell families that until proven otherwise, oppositional defiant behavior is secondary to a neurodevelopmental issue. I would rather presume that there is something we can work on medically rather than conclude that a child simply doesn't want to behave. If the latter is true, I have few options; I just have to accept this "negative" personality. I think many kids get caught up in oppositional behavioral cycles because their moods are driving them. They try but can't achieve more successful behavior. For bipolar children, the right meds and patient, understanding parents can and do make a difference.

CHAPTER 2

MENTAL HEALTH CARE PROFESSIONALS

Picking Your Team

Ideally, parents who suspect that their child may have a problem should be able to get a swift and thorough referral to a child psychiatrist, competent evaluation, correct diagnosis, and prompt treatment that includes effective medication combined with responsive therapy. Unfortunately, it seldom plays out so perfectly. When confronted with a mental health crisis, families are often unwittingly sucked into the health care system without adequate opportunity to evaluate and choose their health care practitioners. If a crisis fuels your child's bipolar diagnosis, the system takes over, and it becomes doubly hard for you to think clearly and take the time necessary to carefully choose the practitioners who are suddenly managing your child's mental health. As difficult as it might seem at the time, it is important for parents to try to take control of the situation to the best of their ability by seeking education, support, and local resources.

The Players

It's helpful to bring as much information as you can to the professional you're turning to for help, so before you do, talk to other adults who work with or know your child. Ask if and when the behaviors you've observed occur outside the home. Have they noticed other behaviors that concern them? Sometimes a teacher might be the one to alert a parent to unusual moods or behaviors. Conversely, a teacher may be oblivious to problems that seem quite obvious to a parent. Coaches, day care providers, and other parents who are close to your child will help you to get a fuller picture of your child's day-to-day life. Keep this information at hand, and use it when you are asked to describe your child's daily interactions.

Pediatrician

After one particularly upsetting episode when he expressed how much he hated his life and wished he were dead, we consulted with the pediatrician, who referred our son for a psychiatric consult.
Phyllis, mom of a bipolar son diagnosed at age eight

How clueless can a doctor be? For years, we went to the same pediatrician, and for years he observed my son exhibiting out-of-control behavior without saying a word. On some visits, the pediatrician shrugged and told me that he couldn't complete the annual physical examination because my son was not cooperating. He never suggested that I look into these behaviors or referred me to appropriate care. Yet for many families, the pediatrician's office is the first stop on their way to finding the help their child needs.

If you suspect that your child's behavior may indicate a greater problem, you may well turn to your child's pediatrician or family doctor who, if you're lucky, will refer you to a superb child psychiatrist. I say *lucky* because, as strange as it may sound, until about five years ago, behavioral development was not part of the curriculum taught to pediatricians. As a result, some pediatricians remain unfamiliar with the signs and symptoms of early-onset bipolar disorder and other mood disorders. Some attribute behavioral concerns to bad parenting. Although parents are routinely questioned about their child's physical development (When did he start to walk? Talk? Sit up by himself?), until recently they were rarely questioned about behavioral issues (How long does a typical temper tantrum last?). A family history form may have queried about cancer and heart disease but in all likelihood did not ask about mental disorders.

According to Martin Stein, M.D., a pediatrician practicing in California and cochair of the ADHD committee for the American Academy of Pediatrics, a formal curriculum for developmental and behavioral pediatrics—an umbrella term that incorporates child psychiatry, psychology, and psychosocial issues—was recently added to the training program for pediatricians and is expected to effect a major change in the attitudes of pediatricians toward early-onset bipolar disorder. Interviewing techniques now include questions about psychosocial development and symptoms of hyperactivity, grandiosity, depression, and failure to thrive due to lack of interaction. In the future, these questions will be posed alongside those about height, weight, and head circumference.

Still, many pediatricians remain untrained and may either miss or dismiss signs that a child is mentally ill. If you are convinced that moods or behaviors are problematic, be insistent about getting a good referral from the pediatrician for a consultation with a child psychiatrist or psychologist. Dr. Stein suggests that a parent educate a pediatrician who seems to be unclear about early-onset bipolar disorder by lending or referring books (like this one) that explain the condition. Since your child's pediatrician will continue to monitor physical aspects of your child's health, it is important that she understand as much as possible about the brain science behind your child's condition, as well as the medications your child may be taking and the side effects they may have.

Psychiatrists

A psychiatrist is a medical doctor with an M.D. or D.O. degree plus at least four additional years of training in the field of psychiatry. Psychiatrists have nine to ten years of special training and can become board certified by passing a national test given by the American Board of Psychiatry and Neurology. A child and adolescent psychiatrist has two additional years of advanced training that concentrates on children, adolescents, and their families. In addition to providing evaluations, a psychiatrist can prescribe medications and schedule regular therapy sessions. Some psychiatrists prefer not to participate in active therapy and instead get feedback during the medication check visits. Often the best approach is a team approach: a psychiatrist to prescribe and maintain the medication treatment and a psychologist or social worker to administer therapy.

Because of the nature of early-onset bipolar disorder, the ideal is to find a compassionate child and adolescent psychiatrist with experience in diagnosing and treating this disorder who is likely to understand the nuances of this condition. Unfortunately, that ideal is out of reach for many. According to a 1999 American Medical Association survey, only about 6,300 fully trained child and adolescent psychiatrists currently practice in the United States. If you balance that number against the number released by the surgeon general in 1999—15 million children and adolescents with diagnosable psychiatric disorders—it's easy to imagine that finding a local specialist could be a problem. If a child and adolescent psychiatrist is not locally available, you might choose to travel to see one and delegate the therapy aspects of your child's treatment to a local child psychologist or social worker, or you may have to find a psychiatrist with a general practice who is familiar with early-onset bipolar disorder.

How Often?

In order to monitor medication, a psychiatrist usually needs to see the patient once a month. A parent might want to coordinate blood tests, if they are needed, just prior to the psychiatrist visit. In times of crisis, visits may increase to several times a month. When a child is stable and the meds are working, you may need to see your child's psychiatrist just once every three months. Parent and child need to see a psychiatrist at least quarterly since children's bodies grow and change rapidly.

At the initial evaluation, which should be at least an hour and a half long, the psychiatrist will often present parents with a questionnaire and interview them thoroughly to get a full perspective on the child's condition. Subsequent visits of between thirty minutes and an hour will usually consist of an interview with parents to find out what they have observed about their child and the child's response to medications. Usually an observation period with the child follows, during which the psychiatrist can assess neurological functions and directly observe the child's moods and behaviors.

Psychologists, Social Workers, and Therapists

Psychologists, social workers, and therapists often work as part of the treatment team when managing a bipolar child.

A psychologist, a mental health care professional with either a doctoral degree (Ph.D.) or a master's degree (M.A.) in psychology, is licensed to provide testing, evaluations, and treatment for emotional disorders and behavioral problems. Many schools have school psychologists who work with children, parents, teachers, and other school personnel when a child is identified with an emotional disability. They provide limited testing and evaluation, but primarily focus on the child's special education needs.

A clinical social worker has either a bachelor's or master's degree in social work. Social workers are often familiar with special programs and organizations and are usually experienced with managing the paperwork required by programs and insurance companies. Social workers sometimes specialize in administering therapy. Most hospitals and some schools hire social workers to help them communicate with patients and their families and serve as an interface with after-care providers and outside agencies.

A therapist may have a master's degree in counseling or some related area, but doesn't necessarily need to be a psychologist or social worker. A therapist may provide an informal evaluation, but chiefly provides treatment.

These professionals offer different types of therapy. As a parent, you are going to want to know exactly what mode of therapies (usually a mix and match of several types) is suggested for your child. Therapy may be with the child alone or include the parent for at least part of the session. Joint sessions are frequently used for addressing oppositional behavior in a child and mediating between parent and child. There are many forms of therapy, some more tested than others. Alternative therapies are also available and are discussed at the end of this chapter. The most common therapies used in treating children with bipolar disorder are:

- **Supportive therapy**—The therapist helps the child learn to identify and resolve her stress levels, cope appropriately with her moods, improve her confidence, and deal with issues that trouble many bipolar children, like feeling different, having scary nightmares, and general anxiety.
- **Play therapy**—The therapist plays a game with your child or watches him play with toys. The goal is to resolve distress by understanding and processing underlying psychic conflict. This form of therapy is helpful with children too young to articulate their feelings.
- **Cognitive therapy**—The therapist, together with the child and parents, works on derailing the thought processes that create and sustain negative emotional and behavior patterns. It is very helpful in dealing with the common obsessive behavior in bipolar children and is the recommended form of therapy for a comorbid diagnosis of obsessive-compulsive disorder (OCD).
- **Behavioral modification therapy (BMT)**—The therapist comes up with methods to identify and address particular behaviors. BMT is especially effective in dealing with impulse and attention problems and is often used when a child with bipolar disorder is also diagnosed with ADHD.

A good therapist will approach the treatment with an understanding of its biological basis, explains Nancy Austin, Psy.D., a New York–based psychologist who treats many children diagnosed with bipolar disorder. Dr. Austin begins treatment by helping the child identify the mood states, the severity, and the length of any recent mood-triggered "events."

After the child can identify this recurring process, Dr. Austin works together with child and parents to identify what might be helpful to make the mood event manageable.

Therapy is as much an intervention as is medication. As you search for a therapist, ask what modalities or therapeutic techniques each prefers and request a treatment plan. Just as medication may be adjusted during the course of treatment to address particular symptoms, therapy may also be changed to address changing target symptoms. You're looking for a therapist who is flexible and experienced with a wide repertoire of therapy styles.

How Often?

Sessions with a psychologist or social worker are usually scheduled once every week, lasting from forty-five minutes to one hour, and may consist of spending a short time with a parent to review the child's behavior and go over management techniques and time spent talking or playing with the child.

Alternatively, the therapy session may involve both the parent and the child for the entire session, with the focus on the communication between them. The therapist may want to spend sessions alone with the parents to help them learn new ways to cope with their child's behavior. Effective child therapy must always include parents as part of the treatment team.

Picking Your Team

Our insurance is horrible, *and it was difficult to get the name of anyone who even saw children. We had to make big waves to get any kind of help at all.*
Cindy, mom of a bipolar son diagnosed at age ten

The arduous task of finding the right health care professional to treat a child with behavior and mood disorders is compounded by managed care and insurance companies, which have traditionally reimbursed less for mental health issues than they have for other medical problems. The National Alliance for the Mentally Ill (NAMI) is fighting for insurance parity. As this book is written, thirty-four states have passed parity laws, putting mental illness in the same category as physical illness for insurance coverage and Medicaid. The late Senator Paul Wellstone (D, Minnesota), along with Senator Pete Domenici (R, New Mexico), introduced what is now called the Paul Wellstone Mental Health Equitable Treatment Act of 2003, a bill calling for parity on a federal level, which is expected to pass, hopefully sometime around the publication of this book.

The neurobiological basis of bipolar disorder makes it as much a physical ailment as it is a mental one. According to the Employment Discrimination Report of February 2002, a Washington, D.C., court ruled to allow a bipolar insurance plan participant to receive benefits beyond the twenty-four-month limitation for mental illnesses. The decision in this case, *Fitts* v. *Federal National Mortgage Association,* determined that bipolar disorder is a physical, not a mental, illness under the long-term disability benefit plan covering employees of the association. While this was only a local ruling, the definition of bipolar disorder as a physical illness—a neurobiological disorder that affects the physical and chemical structure of the brain—is one that may be used as illustrative case law as similar cases emerge in other jurisdictions.

Many parents are forced by financial circumstances and lack of insurance to limit mental health care for their bipolar children or, worse, to provide care by relinquishing rights to their child. That way the state assumes custody and pays the bills for long-term treatment and residential care.

If you are insured and anticipate needing mental health services, pick up the telephone. Many insurance companies have a gatekeeper system—an 800 number that must be called in order to activate mental health services. Other companies require a written referral from a primary care health provider. Be sure you know your insurance company's policy *before* visiting a hospital, psychiatrist, psychologist, or social worker, lest you find out after the fact that you are not entitled to reimbursement because you did not follow their rules.

If you are insured, working with someone in the network of providers paid for by your health plan is preferable. Unfortunately, a great many psychiatrists and psychologists do not work with insurance plans. It is not cost beneficial for them to do so. This is not to say that they won't give you a receipt so you can get the minuscule reimbursement from your insurance plan. These doctors don't want to be bothered with the day-in and day-out justifications and eternal qualifiers that they have to present to insurance companies so that we can get coverage. The bottom line is they want to get paid more than the insurance companies want to pay them.

Finding a mental health practitioner takes some basic legwork:

1. Obtain an up-to-date directory of your insurance plan's in-network providers. Check their hospital affiliations and their backgrounds through the NAMI or the Child and Adolescent Bipolar Foundation (CABF) referral service, and do an Internet search to find out more about them—for instance, whether they have published any articles on childhood disorders.
2. Find out if universities with medical schools are in

your vicinity, and call local inpatient child psychiatric hospitals for additional referrals.

3. See which practitioners are closest to you geographically. Keep in mind that psychiatrist visits occur at least once a month and psychologist or therapist visits can be as often as twice a week. Schlepping a child (and possibly siblings) to faraway doctors is doubly stressful for a bipolar child (and everyone else).

4. Cut your list down to the practitioners who are convenient or well recommended. Leave an introductory message on his or her answering machine, and see who calls back. Don't bother with anyone who doesn't call back. The last thing you need is an unresponsive health care provider.

5. Note how much time the practitioner takes to listen to you on the telephone. A practitioner who takes the time to get to know you before you have him on your payroll will likely show similar care and compassion after you commit to paying for his help and time.

Interviewing Potential Health Care Practitioners

I interviewed several doctors, looking for strong knowledge of complex children and a person who would listen to my concerns, observations, and questions. After all, I live with the child. I wanted someone open to ideas and willing to read articles that he may not have been aware of and one who was proactive and conservative, all at the same time. Insurance coverage came into play too.
Cindy, mom of a bipolar son diagnosed at age ten

Once you have made your initial appointment, you are ready

to evaluate whether this practitioner is right for you. Of course, with managed care, your choices may be limited, but the hope is that you can get comfortable enough with the practitioner so that a relationship can be established. Here is a checklist to help you interview, assess, and select appropriate mental health care for your child:

The Office
- Is the waiting room the kind of place where you and your child will feel comfortable waiting?
- Is the office stocked with toys or magazines to keep your child occupied?

The Practitioner
- Are you comfortable with the practitioner? Your child's initial reactions may not be a reliable barometer because he may be resisting or too young to understand how therapy works, so your feelings about the practitioner must come into play.
- What is her overall style? Warm and engaging? Quiet and retiring? Strict and unyielding?
- Does she fire questions at you rapidly or let you do all the talking?
- Do you feel comfortable talking to her?
- Does she answer questions clearly?
- Does she seem judgmental about your parenting skills?

The Practitioner and Your Child
- Observe the communication between the practitioner and your child. Do they seem to connect?
- Does your child seem comfortable expressing herself in his office?

- Does the practitioner make an effort to engage the child, or does he spend all his time addressing you?

Here is a list of questions that you might want to ask the practitioner you are interviewing. The questions are broken down into two groups: one for psychiatrists and the second for therapists.

Evaluation Questions for Psychiatrists
- What kind of mental illnesses do you treat most often in your practice?
- How do you diagnose and treat children with bipolar disorder?
- What are your treatment goals?
- How do you determine which medications to give to which child?
- Based on what you know about our child, what do you think is the best course of treatment?
- How would you treat comorbid conditions, if there are any?
- Would you ever consider taking my child off medications? At what point?
- What are some of the alternative approaches you might consider if you feel my child is not responding completely enough?
- How often do you expect to see my child? Are you prepared to see her more often if treatment is not working?
- Are you willing to make medication changes over the phone?
- How involved do you want me to be in the sessions? If you plan to see my child privately, do you also intend to bring me in for the end of the session?

- How long will each session last?
- What do you look for in your sessions?
- What happens if I have a question and need to contact you?
- What is the best time to contact you with questions?
- What do I do in case of an emergency?
- What happens if we cannot make it to a session? Will you charge us?
- How do you want me to keep you informed on changes from session to session? With mood charting? What do you want me to note? Do you want this information by phone? By e-mail?
- Are you planning to exchange information directly with my child's therapist?
- Do you charge for time spent on the phone between sessions?
- Do you charge for additional services (reports, representation at educational program meetings)?

Evaluation Questions for Therapists
- What kind of childhood disorders do you deal with in your practice?
- Have you treated children with bipolar disorder?
- How often do you expect to see my child?
- How long will each session last?
- How involved do you want me to be in the sessions? Do you plan to hold separate sessions with me?
- Do you plan to see the whole family at times, including siblings?
- What are your priorities in helping a bipolar child the age of my child? How will you help keep my child safe?
- What sort of therapy do you do?

- Will you be available to help us with parenting issues?
- Will you adjust the format of my child's session during unstable periods? How?
- What happens if I have a question and need to contact you?
- What happens if we have an emergency?
- If we cannot make it to a session, will you charge us anyway?
- Can you connect us with other community resources for our child?
- Will you tell us if you learn that our child is doing something potentially dangerous?
- What are your overall philosophies on discipline and child rearing? Do you have a single approach, or do you recommend different approaches depending on mood stability?
- Do you charge for time spent on the phone between sessions?
- How do you want me to keep you informed on progress? Mood charting? Behavior charts? What do you want me to note? Do you want this information by phone? By e-mail?
- Are you planning to exchange information directly with my child's psychiatrist?
- Do you charge for additional services (reports, representation at educational program meetings)?

At the end of the interviews, discuss with your partner or ask yourself these questions:

Psychiatrists

- Do you agree with the criteria the psychiatrist uses for diagnosing bipolar disorder in children?
- Does the psychiatrist's medication philosophy seem sound and safe, starting with the older well-tested mood stabilizers (see Chapter 5 on medications) and progressing as needed to treat remaining symptoms?
- Does the psychiatrist's treatment plan start with stabilizing the bipolar child and revisiting comorbid diagnoses only after the bipolar disorder is under control?

Therapists

- Does she seem to respect us as parents?
- Do his values and attitudes toward child rearing appear to resemble ours?

For Psychiatrists and Therapists

- Does this mental health practitioner seem to be someone we can trust?
- Does she have experience diagnosing and treating bipolar disorder in children?
- Did she build a rapport with our child?
- Will she be readily available if I need to reach her with a question or problem?
- Can we live with his terms, conditions, and business practices?

If the answers to the above questions are a resounding yes, book your next appointments.

Therapy Goals

When you have a child in therapy, you might find it helpful to work with the therapist in setting goals—benchmarks that, when achieved, show your child's therapeutic progress.

Examples of goals you might want to work on with your child in therapy include:

- Getting your child to acknowledge his or her condition
- Getting your child to recognize the various moods
- Dealing with specific moods and behavioral responses
- Dealing with oppositional behavior
- Making your child more independent
- Helping your child hone her social or organizational skills
- Breaking patterns of negative thoughts or behaviors
- Curbing impulsivity

After you have discussed the issues that you would like your child to resolve through therapy, use the Treatment Goal Worksheet. (Some examples are filled in.) Revisit the form every few months to assess improvements and redirect goals. The form will serve as a communications tool as well as a way to help your child.

Treatment Goal Worksheet

Date_____

Child's Name:_____

Medications:_____

Target Symptom *(e.g., explosive behavior)*

		Mon	Tues	Wed	Thurs	Fri	Sat	Sun
Time/Place	*bedtime*							
Situation	*refused lights out*							
What happened	*exploded, cursing, throwing things*							
How resolved	*fell asleep after 2 hours*							

Interventions to Practice/Homework

Parent: *deep breathing, disengaging, not listening to the provocative words, offering a drink or a snack*

Child: *noticing first signs of anger, deep breathing, getting a glass of water, taking a walk*

Other changes: *medication adjustment, changes in school program or personnel, vacations*

Other notes or thoughts:

Do Too Many Shrinks Spoil the Family?

In a word, no. At times, one psychiatrist or therapist may not be enough for one family. The number of mental health practitioners can even begin to outnumber family members. However, if siblings or a parent begins developing problems of their own, the psychiatrist or therapist may advise separate treatment. Sometimes one family member develops trust in and becomes attached to a particular psychiatrist or therapist, leaving that person resentful of sharing the professional with other family members. Or the psychiatrist or therapist may feel that treating more than one member of a family interferes with her objectivity. Still other therapists might feel that it is helpful to treat several family members at once and that this will actually give them better insight into the overall family dynamics.

Time for a Therapeutic Change

We went through a few therapists, and I thought I'd found a good one, but she ran at his first sign of rage. The therapist I have now is indescribably wonderful. She is our angel! Her help has allowed my son to go back to a mainstream public school. His rages have stopped. Now we finally have the right meds in place. I've never seen my child so happy. He's a joy to have around. I don't think it's possible to love him more or be more proud than I am these days.
Chrissie, mom of a bipolar son diagnosed at age six

Therapy for a bipolar child may be a long-term necessity, so you should periodically reevaluate the situation. Keep in mind that therapy often involves hearing things you may not want to hear. All kinds of feelings are bound to surface. It is sometimes hard to differentiate between discomfort due to a serious disagreement with the therapist and discomfort due to a deeper and perhaps more painful insight.

That said, there are also times when enough is enough: you and your child can no longer work with this person.

Here are some pointers for knowing when to stay and when to look elsewhere:

When to Stick with It
- Your child exhibits basic trust in the therapist (e.g., he uses her as a sounding board on which to base his opinion before speaking with you about an issue) but

is having trouble expressing himself because the issues are getting touchy.

- Things seem to be dragging, and you don't see immediate results or breakthroughs. Therapy, particularly with a bipolar child, takes time, and extra doses of patience are required to recover from a crisis. Changing therapists because *you* feel the therapy isn't proceeding as fast as you'd like is ill advised.
- You are having disagreements with the therapist regarding money or time.
- Something the therapist told your child is really bothering you (e.g., your child comes home and reports that Dr. P. thinks you're fat and that's why she has problems).

When to Call It Quits

- The therapist seems inflexible and unwilling to incorporate your parenting techniques into his dictates on handling particular situations or does not support your attempts to adopt alternative parenting techniques.
- The values and priorities discussed during your interview are not being upheld.
- Your therapist's approach strikes you as too odd, counterproductive, or dangerous to benefit your child. One mother who responded to my on-line survey reported that her son's therapist encouraged him to light candles as a way to calm himself—and this was a boy who had been arrested for setting off illegal fireworks in a public park! The mother fired the therapist after finding a candle that the therapist had given her son burning on the paper-strewn desk in his room.

- Your child is completely oppositional with both you and the therapist, and although it's been months, you see no real progress.
- The therapist resists seeing you and your child together, particularly on issues regarding oppositional behavior. You feel left out of the loop.
- The practitioner has no backup or support system in place when he is not available.
- The practitioner refuses to communicate with you by telephone or e-mail.
- Your clinician balks when you request a second opinion.
- You have had basic disagreements with the therapist involving money or time, and he can't accommodate you in any way.

If you decide to change therapists, do your best to ease the transition for your child. Do not communicate disrespect for the therapist to your child. She has likely established some kind of connection with this person, even if it wasn't the best relationship in the world. Ask for your therapist's help in smoothing what could otherwise be a difficult shift.

Your Role in Helping Your Child

There is much you can do to help your child and the rest of your family deal with the issues that come up when one child is bipolar. Therapy sessions can go by in a blur, and changing ingrained parenting responses takes time and patience.

Dr. James MacIntyre, a child and adolescent psychiatrist and associate professor of psychiatry at Albany Medical College in Albany, New York, encourages parents to bring a notebook or even a tape recorder to record their sessions with him. He gives parents time to ask questions and stresses that the best indicator of a good mental health provider is whether he takes time to thoroughly answer questions.

Don't be embarrassed to take out a prepared list of questions to refer to during your meetings. Questions are bound to come up between sessions, and if you don't write them down, they're easy to forget.

Whom Do You Call?

Due to managed care, our choice of psychiatrists was limited. We stayed with the same psychiatrist for about a year. My daughter got toxic on lithium, and he refused to take my calls when she was vomiting around the clock. Her med side effects have been managed by the pediatrician ever since.
Cindy, mom of a bipolar daughter diagnosed at age nine

With so many doctors on the payroll, sometimes it's hard to know whom to call and when. Here are some basic rules of thumb:

- **Behavioral meltdown.** When your child acts out, be sure to record the date and time and the details of the event when it happens so you can accurately inform the therapist at the next meeting.
- **Extreme behavioral meltdown.** If your child acts out or cycles for several hours with no sign of abating, contact your therapist and psychiatrist *immediately.* If the child is harming herself or others or is threatening to do so, call your psychiatrist and therapist's emergency numbers, and drive her to the nearest hospital emergency

room. If there is a mobile crisis unit available, call it for an at-home evaluation. If the child is too agitated and out of control to transport, dial 911 and explain that you have a mentally ill child in crisis. Many police departments have officers on staff trained to deal with mentally ill people in crisis. Don't be afraid to trust your instincts. If you think it's an emergency, it probably is.

- **Physical illness (e.g., vomiting, nausea, dizziness, headache) with or without psychiatric symptoms.** Inform the psychiatrist and pediatrician immediately. If they don't respond and you believe the symptoms are worsening, use your judgment and go to the nearest hospital emergency room. Be sure to inform the doctors there of any and all medications your child is taking. If the symptoms are mild and abate within a day or so, leave a message for the psychiatrist or tell him at the next visit. If the symptoms persist for two days or more, call the pediatrician and psychiatrist and get immediate feedback.

Sometimes psychiatric symptoms can present as physical symptoms, and sometimes a child can be exhibiting toxicity or a side effect to a psychotropic medication. Many pediatricians are unfamiliar with the side effects and toxicity of psychotropic medications. Make sure that your pediatrician or family doctor is well aware of the medications and dosage of each medication that has been prescribed for your child. Consult with your child's psychologist about any non-psychotropic medications being prescribed by your pediatrician.

Confidentiality

Confidentiality is an important topic to discuss with your therapist before it becomes a problem. Although different states have different statutes in terms of a parent's right to know precisely what goes on in therapy, individual therapists often determine precisely what can be told, to whom, and when, in the best interests of building an alliance with the child. This is the case if the therapist is an independent practitioner. School psychologists in public schools, on the other hand, are employees of their state, and therefore can breach confidentiality.

When is a child's health situation confidential, and when should a parent be privy to the details of the child's treatment? Lawyer and psychologist Donald Bersoff, professor emeritus at Villanova Law School and an adjunct professor of psychology at MCP Hahnemann Medical School at Drexel University in Philadelphia, explains that parents are generally given the right to make health care decisions for their children, so they must be informed of the course of treatment. The U.S. Supreme Court has ruled on this. However, there are exceptions to the rule. Emancipated minors—children who have moved out on their own and are self-supporting, married, or enlisted in the armed services—are treated independently and entitled to complete confidentiality.

Parents should ask about their therapist's view of confidentiality. Is he willing to discuss the therapeutic process and give you updates on your child's condition? When and how will she inform you if your child says something that she feels you should know about?

"It is the ethical obligation of a therapist to inform both the parent and the child so both know what the limits of confidentiality are," explains Dr. Bersoff. "A three-way agreement between therapist, parent, and child is a good approach. If people feel that they have a voice in the outcome, they are more likely to comply with the decision than if they're left out."

Whatever the decision is, everybody needs to know the rules of the game up front. The most crucial confidentiality issues surface when a child threatens to harm herself or others. Another serious disclosure issue occurs when a child alleges parental abuse. The therapist must assess the validity of the allegation. If he feels there is reasonable cause, he is mandated to disclose it to the proper authorities.

Record Keeping

As a parent, you are entitled to all charts and records pertaining to your child. Because care is often shifted from provider to provider and because acquiring written records can be an arduous process, request copies of your child's records periodically from every health care provider who sees your child for any length of time. Keep the information on file, and include with it any hospitalization intake and discharge summaries. You never know how or when you (or someone treating your child) will need this information. Keep your records together and file them carefully. Also keep your own charts of medication and mood changes.

Every home with a bipolar child should have the following:

- Crisis list—an easy-to-access list of crisis services and phone numbers for parents, siblings, and babysitters, in the event of an emergency
- Medication records—a file containing a history of medications your child is taking and which meds your

child has taken in the past, including dosing and frequency information

- Documents from your health care provider—any documents provided by your health care provider, including appointment slips, receipts, and any assessments or test results they share with you
- Hospitalization records—a listing of exactly when and where your child was hospitalized for both physical and mental illnesses

Research Studies

Breakthroughs often are made during exacting research performed by top scientists at well-known universities. These studies can be funded by federal grants, the nonprofit sector, or pharmaceutical and other private company funding. Some are industry-initiated studies, meaning they're initiated and paid for by the pharmaceutical industry, while others are investigator initiated, which means a particular university researcher developed the idea to do the research, obtained the funding, and created the study.

According to NAMI, many people participate in research studies because they are interested in furthering the cause of science—in other words, to help bring new information, in this case about bipolar disorder in children, to the fore. Beyond the altruistic reasons, getting into a research study allows you to learn more about your child's disorders, to get a valuable second opinion from an expert, and perhaps to try a cutting-edge treatment. The researchers often provide free clinical care, evaluations, medications, referrals, and lab tests, and sometimes they reimburse subjects' travel expenses.

A number of universities and federally funded health organizations are studying the genetics and heredity patterns in childhood-onset bipolar disorder. Your psychiatrist may mention these studies to you and suggest participation. Common goals are to establish better ways of predicting the illness and its course in children. These kinds of studies may involve psychological testing, extensive interviews, and even evaluation of other family members. Most have some kind of criteria for participation, such as a family history of a bipolar illness, repeated occurrences of the illness in more than one child in a family, or specific issues often related to severe mania.

Christie, the bipolar mom of a bipolar son diagnosed at age ten and a participant in research studies at Stanford and the University of Washington, says that her participation yielded important research information. "I learned more from these studies than from years of therapy and clinical care," recounts Christie. "We cooperated, and I milked their years of experience. Researchers love to share their ideas."

There are different types of research studies. *Retrospective studies* look at medical records of patients with certain illnesses and/or who were treated with certain medications. *Meta-analysis studies* scrutinize results from a compendium of different studies, consolidating data from a large population of subjects and examining the trends within those papers. *Epidemiological studies* look at big populations of people defined by certain nonmedical characteristics, such as age or community. Epidemiological researchers look for information about the prevalence of disease in defined populations.

The most common type of drug study that you might enroll your child in would likely be some form of a prospective, controlled, randomized project. *Prospective* or *longitudinal* means that the researcher follows the study participants forward in time, after specific medications have been introduced. *Controlled* means that there are two study groups: one getting the study medication (the study group) and one getting a placebo (the control group). *Randomized* means that the study participants are randomly placed into either the study or control group so that the researcher can't influence who gets what treatment. The last defining characteristic of a study is whether it is double-blind. In a *double-blind study,* neither the patients nor the researchers know who is getting medication and who is getting placebo. This ensures that the treatment responses and evaluations are not influenced by expectations.

In *open-label studies,* a selected group of patients is given a medication, with or without a control group to measure them against. These studies are prospective in nature but they are not blind and usually not randomized. The researcher selects which patients get a trial of the medications. These are often an informal first step to see if there is reason to mount a full-scale randomized, controlled, double-blind study.

Before entering any type of study, patients are screened, and researchers may exclude certain types of patients from their studies. In psychiatric medication studies, many people remain on their regular medications while trying either the placebo or study medicine. Although researchers strive to control the conditions of the study as much as possible, it is often unreasonable and unethical to ask a subject to abandon much-needed medication for the duration of the study. In some cases, though, there will need to be a washout period from at least one or more of the child's regular medications before she can participate in the study.

If your child is involved in a drug trial and the medication seems to work well but is not yet approved by the Food and

Drug Administration, sometimes the pharmaceutical companies will make it available for compassionate plea use—a privilege reserved for the participants of drug trials.

Not all studies are drug trials. Sometimes psychologists gathering research use patients as survey subjects. In such cases, the psychologist should explain to the parents of the child exactly what is being done and obtain written parental consent as well as the patient's assent before including him in a study. When faced with such requests, you'll want assurance that your child's privacy will be protected. Parents need to know all the material pieces of information before granting consent, such as:

- What are the material risks and benefits, and what are the alternative treatments that might be offered to your child?
- If the study is a drug study, will your child's medications be changed?
- Might your child be given a placebo?
- If something goes wrong and your child is injured, will you be compensated?
- What is the probability of the risk? How common are negative side effects? Are there potentially serious negative outcomes, such as chronic health problems or even death?
- What is the length of the treatment?
- Exactly what will the procedure be?
- How will dosages of meds be increased and adjusted?
- Who will be treating your child?
- How will the treatment be administered?
- Who will be looking at the records?
- Is there leeway within the research design if the med-

ications being tested are ineffectual or your child is in a placebo situation?

- If after a set period of time your child does not respond well, can she be switched over to the more effective treatment group within the course of the testing?

You retain the right to withdraw your child from a study if you have serious concerns.

According to Dr. David Axelson, a child and adolescent psychiatrist currently doing research at the University of Pittsburgh, the rewards of participating in a research study include the child's knowledge that he is doing something to help combat his disease. The findings may yield information on treatment that will be directly applicable to his own condition sometime in the future. He adds that research scientists may spend more time studying their subjects, which could translate into additional therapy time for the child.

If you are interested in enrolling your child in a study, a good place to start researching possibilities is on-line. Visit:

- The Child and Adolescent Bipolar Foundation (CABF) Web site, www.bpkids.org
- The National Institute of Mental Health (NIMH) Web site, www.nimh.nih.gov or www.clinicaltrials.gov
- The Stanley Foundation research site, www.bipolar-network.org
- The Juvenile Bipolar Research Foundation, www.bpchildresearch.org

If you are interested in learning more about federally funded research studies in progress, the Computer Retrieval Information on Specific Projects (CRISP) database is available on the NIMH Web site. Click on the "For Researchers" button on the right side of the menu. A new menu will come up on the left side of your screen and include a link to CRISP.

Alternative Therapies

Alternative therapies are those that are less tried-and-true than conventional ones and often rely on environmental stimuli to trigger a brain response. They are usually used in combination with conventional medicinal and therapeutic treatments to trigger responses and to encourage children with bipolar disorder to cope with their condition and express their feelings.

Creative Therapies

Some parents seek therapies that, while somewhat less conventional than traditional ones, help children express their creativity, which can be shooting out in all directions when they are manic. Creative therapies can calm and soothe the mania or inspire the dysphoric soul. They include (but aren't confined to) art, dance/movement, drama, music, and poetry and are usually administered by therapists who are trained in their respective discipline as well as in psychology.

Animal-Assisted Therapy

Animal-assisted therapies can involve a wide variety of animals, from horses to guinea pigs to dolphins. Children meet with an animal handler or trained therapist and they learn to care for and communicate with the animal. A child's needs must be matched with what the animals have to offer.

"The animal in and of itself is not a magic potion," explains Stephanie LaFarge, a psychologist and director of counseling at the ASPCA. "Animal-assisted therapy by definition includes a mental health professional who has developed a treatment plan and an animal that assists in the therapy."

Animal-assisted therapy doesn't have to be done with a therapist who has animals. An animal handler can be contracted to bring a trained animal to a child's regular therapy sessions.

One type of animal-assisted therapy is equine therapy, currently offered in over six hundred centers nationally. It began as a treatment for children with physical disabilities, but eventually came to be used as a therapy for children with emotional disabilities as well. It allows a child with emotional disabilities, who is otherwise dissuaded from risk taking, to participate in a structured "risky" behavior. A child quickly realizes that she can't misbehave around these specially trained horses; she must respect the animal to ensure her own and the horse's safety.

In equine therapy, as in other animal-assisted therapies, the therapist maps out goals for the child and works with a therapeutic riding instructor who puts together the treatment program.

"Most children are humbled around a horse," states Dr. LaFarge. "Learning to pick up the horse's hoof and use the different grooming brushes builds the child's confidence, and he's rewarded for doing it. For a child who has trouble following directions or who is known to act impulsively, learning to make a plan and then communicate his actions to a horse is a skill that teaches planning, self-control, and management of frustration."

Animals have been shown to be immensely intuitive around people. Studies have shown that dogs can predict epileptic seizures in humans. While similar research has not been done to date regarding dogs and humans suffering from bipolar episodes, many professionals offer dogs as a therapy option for emotionally disturbed children. A trained therapy animal can sense depression and other mood states that human beings don't recognize. Some animals can be trained to react to a signal by bringing a comfort item or favorite toy to a child in a particular mood.

Unstructured contact with an animal can lead to an animal or child getting hurt, so Dr. LaFarge urges parents to think carefully before bringing a pet into the home for therapeutic reasons. If you do decide to take the pet plunge, monitor the contact between the child and the animal. Time spent with the animal should be a reward for good behavior. If your child is in an "unsafe" mode, the animal must be put off-limits.

To learn more about animal-assisted therapy, contact your local Humane Society, the Delta Society (www.deltasociety.org), or the Good Dog Foundation (www.thegooddogfoundation.org), which can provide recommendations to pet therapists. Or ask your own therapist to look into incorporating animals into your child's therapy program.

Sensory Integration Therapy

He couldn't get ready for school because his shoes felt funny, his shirt was scratchy, and the breakfast he always ate and loved was undercooked, soggy, or too burned. That's my boy!
Peggy, mom of a bipolar son diagnosed at age nine

Some children with bipolar disorder have sensory problems as well. The senses—touch, hearing, sight, smell, and taste—send information to the brain, which processes and analyzes it. According to some theories, especially those pioneered by occupational therapist Dr. A. Jean Ayres, the vestibular system (the system that helps maintain balance) is affected when even one of the senses is not operating correctly. This forces some children into a state of hyperactivity as they attempt to stimulate the vestibule and regain their balance.

Children who have sensory issues tend to be overly sensitive to touch, sound, smells, and taste. In most children, information from all five senses is integrated into an accurate picture of their environs, but a child in a bipolar state may enter a state of sensory dysfunction.

Sensory integration therapies are usually administered by occupational or physical therapists and involve activities that challenge the child's ability to respond to sensory input. Movement education and gymnastics are often incorporated into the therapies to enhance motor skills training.

Auditory Integration Therapy

Ear, nose, and throat specialist Dr. Guy Berard, M.D., developed auditory integration therapy (AIT) to address disorders of the auditory system, which he found contributed to many behavior and learning disorders. Auditory integration identifies a child's hearing range and addresses hypersensitivity and other abnormalities that can lead to processing problems. Administered by an AIT-trained therapist, AIT exposes children to carefully selected music using headphones. The inner ear and brain are "exercised" to increase the auditory processing range and modulate any sensitivities. The treatment is administered in twenty thirty-minute sessions and can increase social skills and decrease irritability and distractibility.

Notes from the Couch: A Psychiatrist's Point of View

Your child's treatment team will be an intimate part of your life for many years to come. Picking the team is a delicate decision-making process on many levels—financial, logistical, and personal to name a few. Remember that this is a fluid and organic process. As your child grows, the illness changes, so you'll need to make adjustments to the treatment team. Always keep your eyes and ears open to information about quality professionals in your area. It never hurts to have a backup list and plan in place.

I remind families to speak up at every visit. Parents often dig out their written list of questions somewhat sheepishly, as if they are being silly or forgetful. Forget about it! Lists are an essential part of organizing your life. You may well forget a question you had three weeks ago if you don't write it down. And don't shy away from the hard questions. Even if I don't have an answer, we will work together to find one if we can. We can process the emotions that come up. Stay connected with your treater, and share your worries. That's how things get done.

Confidentiality is a cornerstone of my work with kids, especially teenagers. Make sure everyone knows the boundaries before setting off onto treatment. An open loop of communication is necessary in working with children and families, but confidentiality is precious as well. Balancing these needs is an ongoing challenge. When in doubt, I don't divulge confidences. Instead, I find other ways to raise the issue in question. I routinely tell parents to stay out of children's journals and diaries. I don't really want the information obtained surreptitiously. There are situations where we need to break this rule—times when parents have serious concern about a child's hurting herself or others. But discuss it with the doctor or therapist before snooping.

CHAPTER 3

THE MOODS

Helping Your Child Through Mood Swings

THE WORLD INSIDE MY HEAD

With the world inside my head I might as well be dead
Sparks flying but never dying turning into anger
Stronger and stronger my anger burns longer
Going, going never slowing running, feeding off my mind
The evil fire raging now I don't know why I don't know
*   how*
Long lasting anger longer, longer ever growing stronger,
*   stronger*
The power of hate burning in my soul sizzling and siz-
*   zling as the bell tolls*
The evil in my head is all turning red at the same time I
*   am wishing it is dead*
Eric Lederman, age eleven

Jason is laughing on the floor one minute and crying the
next, saying he wants to die. He just got out of the hospital
and seemed okay for a few days, so I sent him to school. I
feel like a bad mom. I should have kept him at home, but
I felt like I couldn't take it anymore.
Jane, mom of a bipolar twelve-year-old son

Oh, those moods. They are enough to drive even the most even-keeled mom into a state of confusion.

Most parenting books are written for parents of children who temporarily lose control but regain it after brief tantrums—children who respond to commands, rules, and positive reinforcement. Unfortunately, those books offer little for the mom whose son has decided that the cleaning lady is out to steal his baseball cards (an offense he considers punishable by death) or whose daughter reacts to a firm "no" with a fist through the nearest wall or a well-aimed punch to mom's solar plexus. If the problem were simply rage, perhaps there would be a singular way of dealing with it, but bipolar children have rapidly shifting mood swings. Whether they are raging or sad, elated or anxious, these moods are extreme. Children diagnosed with bipolar disorder can be amazingly sensitive and fine-tuned. For example, roadkill might elicit "eeuuww, yuck" from nonbipolar children, but for the bipolar child, the sight may precipitate a slide into a funk. First, he thinks about the dead raccoon, then its father, mother, children, and how it must have felt when the truck smashed him. He may have recurrent thoughts of how the animal died, picturing blood and guts spewing all over the road. It's a picture that may stay with him for days—or even years. A brief event can trigger an immediate mood reaction or a retroactive reaction later.

Ten-year-old bipolar Elizabeth is standing in line with her mom in a busy supermarket and wants one of those wonderfully tempting candy bars displayed right next to the cashier. Mom says it's too close to dinnertime. Another child might react with disappointment or whining, but to Elizabeth, that "no" triggers a tantrum. She screams at the top of her lungs. She tosses produce around. She sticks her fingers into the checkout conveyor belt to try to cause herself harm.

Elizabeth's brain is reacting in a maladaptive, disinhibited way to an environmental trigger. Her autonomic nervous system, which in a nonbipolar child is set to react only in the most extreme "flight-or-fight" circumstances, has hair-trigger settings. Elizabeth can be described as "overaroused" or "overreactive" emotionally. Now her mother, who is simultaneously struggling with her own embarrassment and with her unusually distraught child, becomes emotionally charged herself. She raises her voice, letting Elizabeth know she's angry. This escalation further arouses her daughter. Her mom has just thrown oil onto a fire. Response fuels response, and the situation escalates.

There has to be a better way! There is, and this chapter will guide you to it by explaining the moods that are the hallmarks of bipolar disorder and how to recognize their early warning signs so that you can take preemptive action to defuse them. The first step is to carefully observe and record your child's moods.

Observing and Recording the Moods

Because parents act as eyes and ears for psychiatrists and therapists who can't be there to observe their bipolar child day in and day out, it is important that you track her. Even if your child is highly verbal, she probably can't report her behaviors and moods accurately. It's up to you to do that.

In tracking your child's moods, try to stay neutral. The more neutral you can be when your child begins to erupt, the better your chances are of defusing the situation.

Being an objective observer when your child is acting out is one of the hardest things for you to do. There will be days when you watch her doing things that are so so far outside the range of normal that it's tough to keep your thoughts to yourself. Letting loose may relieve your own anger and tension, but is counterproductive and damaging to your child. Staying calm and positive takes practice. We all have bad days when we get overly involved with our child's mood swings, but putting yourself in the position of neutral observer is best for both you and your child.

Charting Moods

Mood charts can help you, and later your professional team, establish how often moods occur, their intensity, and if they have any particular pattern or frequency. Perhaps your child is prone to specific moods at particular times of the day, week, month, or year. You'll also want to note the triggers, minor and major, and your child's energy level. Notice which of your child's moods are more manageable than others. The Mood Chart shown here provides space for you to record the date and time of the mood event, the mood observed, the trigger, and your child's energy level. Describe the mood to the best of your ability. If your child is in a mixed mood state or is vacillating between moods, make a note of that too (e.g., "giddy/angry").

Mood Chart

Date	Mood Observed	Trigger (or not)	Energy Level (1 = low, 10 = high)	Time Began	Time Ended	Recent Med Change? (Y or N) note when

Sometimes when things are going well, we forget to appreciate it. Don't forget to note positive patterns too. This will prevent both you and your child from becoming too focused on the negative behaviors.

Mood Charting and Medication

Since many children, and bipolar children in general, have difficulty reflecting on their feelings, it's critical that you monitor their moods, especially during medication changes. Before starting a new medication, review all details of side effects and interactions between medications with the child's doctor and with your pharmacist:

- Familiarize yourself with your child's mood pattern before the change.
- As you record more information about moods, look for improvements or deterioration or new patterns. Is your child quieter? More hyper? Grumpier? Sillier?
- Record nonmedication changes, such as changing therapists or school programs, too.
- Bring the mood chart with you to visits with the doctor, and allow her to analyze the changes.

Keep a file of these mood charts even if your child stops taking a particular medication. Your doctor may want to try a similar drug later, in which case the mood charts you've kept on file could provide a good indicator of your child's potential reaction to the new medication. Your records can be a big help to a new doctor too.

Throughout treatment, you'll want to keep a close eye on other things that affect your child's moods, such as stress levels, activity levels, and sleep and eating patterns.

You may hear these words in relation to your bipolar child and her moods:

Labile, which means "unregulated" and refers to moods that are fluctuating rapidly with no apparent reason.

Florid, which refers to an extreme emotional condition, as in "florid psychosis," which often requires hospitalization.

Mood response, which indicates an immediate response to a stimulus, or feelings without thought intervention.

Mood regulation, the ability to tolerate and manage one's emotional responses without losing control and without swinging wildly from minute to minute; the smoothing out of one's emotional responses to stimuli.

Moods are conceptual and therefore difficult to discuss with children, who tend to think concretely. To help your child understand her mood, create, if you can, a tangible barometer to explain the different levels of emotional intensity that each mood creates. Here are some Mood Barometer ideas:

• **Color.** Assign the moods colors, and let your child help you identify her moods with markers or crayons. Have her fill out the Mood Observed column of the Mood Chart with the color that corresponds to her mood:

Red = Raging

Black = Irritable

Blue = Sad

Green = Happy
Yellow = Giddy/Giggly
Purple = Anxious

- **A punching bag.** Have your child show you, using the punching bag, how he is feeling. The harder the punch, the more intense the mood is.
- **A noisemaker or musical instrument or drum.** The rhythm, cadence, and intensity of the sound can let you know if a child is feeling mellow or ready to blow.
- **Pictures.** Ask your child to draw, or cut out of magazines, pictures that reflect her moods. Use magnets to affix the picture that corresponds to her mood on the refrigerator.
- **A calendar.** Buy your child his own calendar and a variety of stickers. Have him store the stickers in different envelopes labeled with various "moods." Each day (or several times a day), have your child put a sticker on the calendar to show how he is feeling.
- **The Mood Box.** This is a three-dimensional "mood box" created specifically to help children chart their own moods. A child selects one color and face on a die with five faces to choose from. The face is placed in a day/time slot. Visit www.parentingbipolars.com for more information.

A child can use any of these visual, auditory, and hands-on ways of expressing a mood. Because each child communicates differently, it is up to you as a parent to help him find the means of expression most comfortable to him.

Here's another way to help your child describe what she's feeling. Make a copy of the Mood Intensity chart below or have her design a similar one herself. Add in mood descriptors as needed.

Mood Intensity Chart

12	11	10	9	8	7	6	5	4	3	2	1	
Sluggish						|						Energetic
Bad						|						Good
Sad						|						Happy
Angry						|						Peaceful
Anxious						|						Calm
Irritable						|						Tranquil
Nervous						|						Confident

1. Ask your child which of the words best describe her current mood. Read the above mood descriptors to her if necessary.
2. Assuming the line in the middle is the midpoint between the two opposing moods/energy levels (12 is extreme, 6 is the midpoint, and 1 is the other end), ask her where her mood falls on the graph. Is it closer to 12 or to 1? Is it right in the middle?
3. After identifying your child's mood and defining its severity, discuss ways to deal with the mood. Keep a record of this chart to show to your therapist and psychiatrist.

Triggers

What sets him off? Once it was a balloon popping. Another time he missed the stupid purple dinosaur show. His LEGO did not do what he wanted it to do. I would not get him french fries.

Leah, mom of a bipolar son diagnosed at age eight

In nonbipolar children, a bad day at school, a fight with a friend, or being the "loser" at Candyland might trigger a bad mood. When it comes to children with bipolar disorder, parents often wonder which comes first: the mood or the trigger. The question is as elusive as the old chicken and egg conundrum. And the answer is . . . it doesn't really matter. Sometimes the mood is triggered by brain chemicals, and other times an external event will trigger a mood and move the chemicals into action. Even the most stable bipolar child will have mood swings, although they will be considerably less pronounced when she is stable and medicated. These intense moods get in the way of their ability to function. Bipolar children are, as a rule, harder to distract from a mood and more impulsive than their nonbipolar counterparts. Although you may not be able to help your child avoid a mood altogether, it is important to decelerate a situation that has severe mood warning potential before it turns into a full-blown flare-up.

Hyperarousal becomes ingrained and more automatic over time. Over time, due to what is called a kindling effect, even a mild stimulus may trigger a severe reaction. Similarly, a parent's anticipation of the child's overreaction creates automatic arousal in the adult—before anything has even happened. The nature and nurture interaction becomes a vicious cycle. Learned behaviors intertwine with automatic, maladaptive responses.

The more cycles a child goes through, the more severe and long lasting the episodes become. That is why early treatment, through medication and behavior modification, is an important factor in stopping the cycle and reducing or eliminating the kindling effect.

Moods can be influenced by the stress of school, or the transition from school to home, or a child's exposure to sunlight on a given day. Many bipolar children have been found to be particularly sensitive to seasonal affective disorder (SAD). As the winter holidays approach and the days get shorter, the child may get depressed; with springtime and longer days come mania.

Identifying the moods and their triggers is not easy. Many children deny their mood swings, and others are so caught up that they may not be able to process or communicate their feelings.

When a mood is in the process of taking over your child, there is no time for major interventions or long speeches. Your child becomes less communicative, and often all we can do as parents is help them through the storm, keeping them as safe as we possibly can while it blusters and blows. While it is impossible to predict every nuance of a mood, and not all management techniques will work with every bipolar child, here are some suggestions from psychologists, psychiatrists, other professionals, and parents on handling some of the more common bipolar moods:

- Let the child define his own mood. What a parent perceives as sadness in a child might be expressed as "indecisiveness" or just plain "feeling bad."
- Learn your child's code words and actions. This will help you interpret and communicate the mood cycles to therapists and psychiatrists.
- Anticipate triggers when you can, and plan to deal with them before they happen. If you know that something is likely to trigger your child (e.g., time of day, candy at the checkout counter of the supermarket), schedule the shopping trip for another time or find a way to bypass the counter with the candy.
- Don't let your child's mood trigger an automatic reac-

tion in yourself. Wait until you know what you are dealing with before you act.

Learn Your "BP Kidspeak" Secret Codes

Some children are expressive and will tell you exactly what they are feeling. Others are more cryptic. It's not what they say; it's body language and how they say what they say that let's you know they're in an irritable mood. Unfortunately for parents interested in keeping their child on an even keel, the latter is much more common.

A sullen look is worth a thousand words if you have deciphered your child's secret code. A brief comment that alludes to kids who make fun of her or a teacher who hates her could really be a larger statement that her meds are a little off, the days are getting shorter, and she is feeling depressed or paranoid. Tears that suddenly spring to his eyes during what ought to be ordinary sibling fisticuffs are a signal that something is happening beyond the routine teasing.

Who is better equipped than a parent to learn the unspoken language of an emotionally challenged child? We've been there from the very beginning, when they cried nonstop (as so many bipolar babies do) and when they held their hands over their ears before we so much as plugged in the vacuum cleaner.

Learn to recognize moods by observing body language, choice of words, rapidity of speech, shuffling, mumbling, facial expressions, and the various nuances that indicate that a mood is shifting. By learning how to recognize their "secret code," you can help them recognize and articulate their feelings. A "What's up, Buddy? Are you sad or just thinking about something?" or a "My, you do seem to have a lot of energy today; tell me more about what's going on . . ." invites a child to talk about her feelings.

Try to teach your child to articulate feelings. It is a key factor in helping her respond to therapy and in assuring her that you will do whatever you can to keep her safe.

Averting and Defusing Moods: Coping Techniques

Mania

He'd be awake for a few days at a time, and he would be so loud! Lenny's a rapid cycler, so it's a bit of everything all at once all the time. Like a strobe light!
Kelly, mom to a bipolar son, age seven

Mania comes in two flavors: intensely irritable and hostile (dysphoric) or elated and grandiose (euphoric). Mania also ranges in the degree of severity. Mild mania, often the start of a stronger mania or even the bipolar illness itself, is called hypomania. When a child is hypomanic, she is on the edge, supercharged. She won't sit still. Words seem to pour out in an endless stream, and her thoughts shift quickly from one topic to the next. Her voice may drown out every other voice in the room, but she doesn't even realize she's shouting. She may be giddy or giggly.

Severe mania can sometimes cross over into psychosis, causing hallucinations and delusions, a very serious state that often requires immediate hospitalization. If your child is hearing voices or seeing people who aren't there, get her to a safe, quiet place and stay with her. Contact your doctor immediately, and ask for guidance.

When in a state of mania or hypomania, your child may express the desire to be something amazing—a great actress, an FBI agent, a superhero. Her energy is boundless, and you may wonder if she will ever sleep again. She may suddenly decide to put everything in order and dash around her room rearranging her furniture or organizing her books by size and color.

Adults with bipolar disorder have described the hypomanic state as an extremely pleasurable and productive state of mind. Children too enjoy the intense highs of manic euphoria. Although it feels good, hypomania often becomes mania, and in children, the manic state can easily shift into irritability. When it is over, it often leaves in its wake depression. Here's what you can do to help:

- **Listen and learn.** The silver lining of her hypomanic state is the chance to listen and learn about your child's innermost desires. Does she want to be the funniest comedian, the best dancer, the Nobel Peace Prize winner when she grows up? Acknowledging her desires shows your child that you respect her.
- **Encourage productive expression.** A manic child is often at his most productive and most creative. Encourage your child to write a story or draw a picture. The vibrancy of the images and the sheer volume of what he produces may amaze you.
- **Put off outrageous demands.** She's consumed by an insatiable desire to fly to France! She wants to go to the airport this minute. Try not to laugh, and acknowledge that you too would someday like to go to France. Then point out some of your more immediate responsibilities: "I have to pick up Kevin from school and then put supper on the table." It may not make her want to go to France any less, but it may help anchor her.

- **Detox.** Diffuse the intensity of the mood with a bubble bath and a dab of French cologne to your aspiring Francophile. Put on a CD with songs in French, and let her dance to the music. Dig out your old college art book and show her some Renoir paintings. Find a way to use the theme of her mania to slow her down and bring her back to a more stable mood.

Sexual Inappropriateness

The babysitter came to me very distraught and said that she caught my seven-year-old son sticking toys into my four-year-old daughter's vagina. At the time, I thought it was normal kids' play—"doctor stuff"—but his constant questioning about private parts and sexual matters seemed unusual. He was picking sexual language up from the news, television, videotapes, and thin air, it seemed.
Marcy, parent of a bipolar child diagnosed at age nine

Just as bipolar children tend to be more sensitized to noise, lights, and other external stimuli, they tend to be more aware of their sexuality, and often at younger ages than their non-bipolar counterparts.

It's perfectly natural for all kinds of children to "play doctor." The bipolar child does it in a less inhibited and more impulse-driven way. He may become the instigator where "doctor" play is involved—to the point where other children may feel frightened and uncomfortable. Here's what to do:

- **Be matter-of-fact.** If you stumble on a bipolar child exhibiting sexually inappropriate behavior with a sibling or friend of approximately the same age, your first response should be a matter-of-fact one: "Aren't bodies interesting? But the rules of play are that we keep our clothes on, and we keep our hands to ourselves" will hopefully get you past the incident with minimal embarrassment to everyone.

- **No locked doors.** You value privacy, and so does your child, but for everyone's sake, locked doors should be forbidden when someone else is in the room. Closely monitor your bipolar child at play, whether he's with peers or siblings.

- **Turn off TV.** Sometimes it seems that even the network news is rated "adult content." Limit your bipolar child's viewing to videos and television shows without sexually explicit scenes. But when prime-time television programming, daytime talk shows, and news stations are full of spicy content, what is a parent to do? Just as you might turn down the lights at bedtime to help calm a child, turning off the television and carefully screening videos is a sure way to reduce your child's exposure to inappropriate stimuli.

Bipolar children may be less modest and more flamboyant than their nonbipolar counterparts. Therefore, they need more concrete and specific rules about clothing and behavior. Families differ in their tolerance of flamboyant behavior—one mom's "exhibitionist" is another mom's "individualist." If you're floundering, it's a good idea to err on the conservative side.

Rage!

Sometimes silly things trigger an episode. Once Amanda

blew up in a rage over the color of my T-shirt. Usually her rages were triggered by frustrations at school. Generally she kept them under control at school, but when she got home, she would have a total meltdown.

Leanne, mom of a bipolar daughter diagnosed at age seven

Rage is one of the toughest emotions to work through with bipolar children. The most important thing is to make your child understand that he is safe, he is loved, and you will guide him to appropriate help. Work out a safety plan—a person you will call, a place he or other members of the family can go when he is raging—so that if he can't regain control, the next steps are clear. Talk to your child about this plan, letting him know that you will use it if you feel that he might hurt someone else or himself. Everyone in the family, including siblings and babysitters, should be familiar with the safety plan and should be briefed on when and how to use it. Similar to the plan you might draw up in case of a fire, this plan should include the particulars of what should happen in the worst-case scenario. It's scary for everyone involved, but it's an unfortunate fact of life when raising a child with this illness. Here are the particulars:

- **Safety first.** First, ensure everyone's safety. Separate her immediately. As the parent of a bipolar child, you are the bomb squad. If you clip the wrong wires, *kaboom!* Assess your child's immediate environment. Make sure there are no heavy or sharp objects anywhere near your child. Train your other children to isolate themselves when your bipolar child begins to erupt. If you're in the car when your child starts raging, pull over immediately, and turn on your hazard lights.

- **The written plan.** Put your safety plan in writing and make sure everyone—family members and others who care for your child—knows where it is. The plan should include what other family members should do in the event of a crisis. A sibling might be instructed to lock herself in her parents' bedroom or run to a neighbor's home. Emergency phone numbers—a mobile crisis team if available, mental health hot lines, local police—should all be programmed into your telephone. If you've tried other measures and you believe that you, your child, or others are in danger, don't hesitate to call for help.
- **Disengage.** When your child is raging, even a look can be provocative. Keep your child within your peripheral vision. Don't stare at him. Don't talk to him when he yells at you. If you have something you must communicate to him (keep in mind that not much is likely to get through), keep your tone even and your voice low. Resist all temptation to defend yourself, cajole him, or answer him back.
- **Check *your* mood.** When your child's mood is volcanic, ask yourself if he's reflecting your own mood. If you are not composed and collected, you will not be able to handle your child's lack of composure. The last thing you want is to fuel his fire.
- **Know your comfort zone.** Keeping your bipolar child safe means keeping him within your "comfort zone," an imaginary circle of a ten-foot radius. When he is raging, he may stray as far as ten feet in any direction from you. If you move, the edge of the circle will move along with you. You want to avoid edging toward an unsafe situation—traffic, for instance, or the kitchen,

where you've left something sharp in easy reach. Your best bet is to stay in one place. Let him explore the edges of the comfort zone while he stomps, screams, cries, or whatever else. Chances are he will come closer to you when the mood has passed.

- **Detox.** If you are on the road or in a public place when the rage begins, try to eliminate or reduce all stimuli, both auditory and visual, as well as smells and motion. If you are in a car, switch off the radio and pull over. If you are inside, go outside. If you are in a crowded public place such as a supermarket, leave your shopping cart in the store, and take your child to a quiet spot either outside the market or near the rest rooms, where she can "detox" from the mood. Sit with her quietly, and take deep breaths. Hopefully she will follow your lead.

- **Rechannel.** A raging child has a lot of energy bouncing around with no place to go. See if you can rechannel the energy. If you have a basketball hoop, hand your child a basketball, and let him work out that energy on the court. If he has a drum set or personal video game player, gently guide him to it and see if he can rechannel himself. Often a child is attuned to what he needs and will respond to the diversion by becoming immersed in it. By the time he looks up, the rage is long forgotten.

- **Hydrotherapy.** There is something to be said for the healing powers of water, whether it is a warm spa bath with herbal chamomile aromas or a pounding shower to wash the angst out of the system. If your child can be reasoned with, or as she is "cooling down" after an exhausting rage, draw her a bath or shower. The water will refresh, rejuvenate, and help your child refocus.

Rage is largely unpredictable, and many siblings won't understand it or be able to ignore it as they most likely should. Explain to them why your bipolar child needs space when he's raging. If you are at home, let the child use his room as a haven during a rage. Allow him to do whatever he wants as long as he stays within the confines of those walls. It may be easier to isolate the sibling. This might take some planning, because siblings who see one child "refuse" to be isolated may dig in and refuse as well. Later, in a quiet moment, explain that when Johnny is in one of his bad moods, you need their help. Establish a secret word or signal. For example, if you point up, that means that the sibling should go up to her room right now.

Paranoia

If they misplace a book, then their brother is hiding it on purpose because he wants to get even. If they can't find a certain action figure, well then, everyone who happens to be in the room must know where it is. We of course are just keeping it a secret because . . . well, I have never really figured out why it is we are supposedly not telling them where the action figure is. Of course, there is the old "everyone at school hates me, everyone at school does it better, everyone at school [fill in the blank with whatever negative thought can be imagined about oneself].
Alison, mom of bipolar twins

Beware the evil cleaning lady, lawn mower boy, babysitter, kid who sits behind your child in school, next-door neighbor, the teacher, the therapist with an agenda, or the neighbor who drives the SUV and whose only real sin is happening to be at the wrong place at the wrong time—driving by when your child is feeling paranoid. Any of these innocent people can take on the characteristics of Osama bin Laden and his band of terrorists to a bipolar child suffering from paranoia.

Though to you it may seem ludicrous that the sweet seventy-year-old lady who bakes muffins and knits scarves for your family whenever she comes to babysit looks like evil incarnate to your bipolar child, try hard not to laugh, and do take any threats your child makes against his "enemies" very seriously. To him, the feelings are real, and his mistrust of the babysitter can have dangerous consequences.

When showing our house to a prospective buyer, I pointed to the neighboring house and began describing the terrific people who lived next door. They had been nice neighbors, but somewhere along the line, my son, who had suffered from paranoid episodes, had had a fight with one of the neighbor's boys and had since labeled him archenemy number one. Imagine the prospective buyer's shock when my son interrupted our conversation to let her know that the kid next door was a murderer who delighted in using his head for target practice. "Ah, children and their imaginations," I laughed as I quickly steered the buyer away from the kitchen. "Shall we look at the bedrooms?"

Here are some ways to deal with paranoia:

- **Wait it out.** Sometimes arguing gets you nowhere. Wait until your child seems more rational before you explain to him that you have to let the mailman (whom he has decided is engaging in germ warfare because he once saw him picking his nose before coming to your house) deliver the mail because without mail delivery, he won't get his *Ranger Rick* magazine.
- **Reality check.** Slowly ease into a rational discussion. Debbie, the mom of a bipolar teen, addresses her

son's paranoiac moods with all the empirical evidence she can collect. She uses logic and examples to explain to her child that sometimes things just aren't the way they appear. Ultimately, the convincing will have to come from within the child, and this may not come right away. Time and therapy are enormously helpful in addressing paranoia and the issues surrounding it.

- **Concrete solutions.** Lynn's bipolar eleven-year-old son was convinced that someone was following him. Her solution was to buy him a cyclist's rearview mirror, which he used while walking around and sitting at his desk in school. This allayed his concerns to the point where he was able to stay in a mainstream class in school and participate in activities without the stress and fear brought on by his paranoia.

- **Stay on guard.** While most paranoia is pretty harmless, keep in mind that if your child is truly convinced that someone is out to hurt him, the situation has the potential to end in disaster. Keep close watch on the games he plays, and make sure they don't resemble war maneuvers (digging and concealing traps, stringing wires over stairwells, plans on paper to kill someone). If the schemes to get the "bad guys" get too dangerous and he insists that he will continue to formulate them because he has to "protect himself," consult with his psychiatrist immediately.

Depression

Winter seems to bring depression on. We have a lot of darkness here in winter, and I think this has a lot to do with it.

She was severely depressed—crying every day for months and saying suicidal things daily.
Helen, resident of Alaska and mother of a seven-year-old bipolar daughter

A depressive episode is usually the first sign of bipolar disorder, preceding manic episodes, sometimes by years. Unfortunately, we often don't recognize depression because it's often masked by other moods, especially irritability.

According to Dr. David Fassler, author of *Help Me, I'm Sad,* 9 percent of all youth have attempted suicide by the time they finish high school. Ironically, of all the moods of a bipolar child, sadness is the one that is most likely to go unnoticed because a sad child is usually imploding, not exploding—and in this mood, she isn't necessarily causing her parents (or anyone else) any trouble.

Contrary to popular belief, depression is not equivalent to sadness. In fact, in my survey of parents, the word *sad* rarely appeared, although children were often described as "depressed." The depressed child may:

- Appear withdrawn
- Have weight loss or gain
- Exhibit cravings for carbohydrates and sugars
- Experience appetite changes
- Express feelings of helplessness
- Experience insomnia—middle-of-the-night waking or early-morning waking
- Nap lethargically in the middle of the day
- Exhibit decreased interest in activities
- Have decreased concentration

- Express wishes that he had never been born or talk about how he wants to die

According to Dr. Paramjit Joshi, professor of psychiatry and pediatrics and chair for the Department of Psychiatry and Behavioral Sciences at Children's National Medical Center, if a child displays five of the above symptoms for ten days to two weeks, it is very important that a parent seek help. Dr. Joshi explains that the symptoms are weighted—some are much more serious than others. Expression of suicidal thoughts is a particularly serious symptom. If your child is talking about killing himself, it is vital that you get help immediately. Expressing hopeless and helpless feelings is another "get help now" symptom. Children who express hopelessness are letting us know that they are devoid of coping skills.

SAD can produce depression in a child diagnosed with bipolar illness. According to psychiatrists, SAD is quite common when the days get shorter or longer, and especially affects people living in the polar regions—in Alaska or Australia. Less sun can produce melancholia, while more daylight can drive a child into mania, giving new meaning to the concept of spring fever.

So what can a parent do when sadness creeps its way into our child's routine whirlwind of moods? First, validate the feelings. Resist the temptation to say, "You shouldn't be feeling this way," or "Snap out of it!" If a child feels sad, telling her *not* to feel that way won't help her. Instead, let her know that you recognize her feelings. A simple "I hear what you're saying. I love you so much" and a squeeze of her hand let her know that you are listening and that you are there for her. Then adjust expectations. Recognize that a child's capabilities will change if he is depressed or sad. What he can do with his eyes closed when feeling good may seem like scaling Mount Everest in a blizzard when he is depressed. If a child seems overwhelmed by schoolwork, chores, or duties, help him scale back on the work until the sadness passes. This may require work with the school to accommodate the depression.

Fear and Anxiety

At thirteen and a half, he's afraid of the dark, abandonment, being ignored, "bad guys," not being popular or accepted. I feel that he is more fearful than a normal child. When he has a nightmare, he still crawls into my bed for comfort. He wants to be cuddled on my lap all the time. I don't really mind, except that he is bigger than I am, and heavy.

Suzy, mom of a bipolar son diagnosed at age eight

Every child has fears. Fear of strangers and separation anxiety are common childhood fears that most children struggle with at one time or another. But the bipolar child is often far more anxious and fearful than her nonbipolar counterparts.

The acid test of a mood disorder is whether the moods interfere with a child's normal functioning. Some bipolar children cannot be left with babysitters because their separation anxiety is so intense. They cry nonstop and refuse to be distracted by play or food from the time their parents leave until they return. The bipolar child wakes in the middle of the night, sees strange faces staring at her from the mirror or window, and doesn't sleep for the rest of the night. Her nightmares are often full of blood and gore and more violent than the worst horror films imaginable. She wakens exhausted the next day.

One study found that people with bipolar disorder were nineteen times more likely to develop panic disorder than people without a mood disorder. Other studies show that family members of people with bipolar disorder tend to have a higher rate of anxiety disorders.

A bipolar child is not only confronting external fears, but must face the frightening fact that he cannot control his own impulses. Imagine how alarming it must be for a child who really wants to be in control to find himself raging or fighting or hopelessly depressed with no real capacity to pull back. As his emotions take over, he loses sight of the cues that will guide him to more adaptive ways to behave. Part of him hears his mom coaxing, yelling, and begging, and he knows that he is being impossible, but he just can't stop himself from hurtling down the wrong path. That may be where fear begins.

Teach your child the following time-honored relaxation techniques when she is in a calm mood so that she can prepare for those inevitable times when she is anxious. Encourage her to practice these techniques regularly so when an episode occurs, the method will be as natural as breathing!

- **Breathing.** This is one of the oldest stress-control techniques. Teach your child to take slow, deep breaths from the pit of her belly. Have her lie down, place her hands (or, for younger children, a stuffed animal) on her belly, and watch the hands (or animal) move up and down as she breathes in through her nose and slowly exhales through her mouth. Explain that oxygen cleanses the blood and nourishes every cell in her body. Challenge her to exhale as slowly as possible, in one long, steady *whoosh*.
- **Visualization.** Ask her for her favorite illustration or photograph. The subject should be a place that makes her feel good. Hang the picture or photo in a special

place in her room. Ask her to study the picture whenever she feels scared or anxious. Where does the picture take her? Instruct her to see that picture—that place—in her mind whenever she feels anxious or scared.

- **Muscle relaxation.** Have your child sit in a chair in a relaxed position. Have him close his eyes. Tell him he is going to learn to control his muscles. Starting with his face (have him make scrunchy faces) and working down to his toes, have him tighten and release his muscles, one by one, letting each muscle go completely slack. Slowly progress down through his neck, shoulders, chest, abdomen, arms, fingers, pelvis, thighs, calves, ankles, feet, and toes. This process should take about ten minutes from start to finish and can be repeated.

- **Counting.** Some people count ceiling tiles; others count sheep or even their own breathing cycles. Each is a marvelous way of slowing down. Teach your child to count slowly when he feels tense, until he lulls himself into a rhythm and has assuaged the mood.

Mixed States: Mania + Depression

How can a child be manic yet depressed at the same time? It seems like an enigma, but if you keep in mind that bipolar disorder is an energy disturbance first and foremost, you will understand that a child could be in a high-energy, low-mood state or a low-energy, high-mood state. While it is unusual for adults to present with mixed states, it is fairly common in children.

Irritability
When she is in her more irritable states, she will yell at her

sister for little things that wouldn't even mildly annoy some-
one else.
Deirdre, mom of a bipolar daughter diagnosed at age seven

Irritability is one of the hallmarks of both manic and depressive phases. Your child is clearly disgruntled, yet you may have
a really difficult time pinning down the cause or moving her
beyond it. Irritability often strings together other moods. It
can be the harbinger of a mood change or appear concurrently
with other moods.

Irritability can be expressed through body language. A child
may hunch over or shift from foot to foot, avoiding your eyes
or mumbling incoherently about things that are bothering
her. When she is in an irritable state, anything you say can
trigger an obnoxious reaction. "The sky is so blue today," may
get a comeback like "Blue sucks," or "Yeah, so who cares?"

In an irritable state, a child may be hypersensitive to
sounds, light, smells, and other sensory stimuli. As he gets
"overloaded," the mood can accelerate into anger and even
rage.

A parent facing an irritable child may feel like a cheerleader
in front of a mob of angry fans armed with rotten tomatoes.
Your goal is to help the child through the mood so it won't accelerate into something worse. Like anger, irritability has to be
handled gently and calmly:

- **Take a break.** Give yourself a time-out. Sometimes too
  much cheerleading, too many attempts to show your
  child why today is *not* a bad day, will serve only to
  make her more irritable. Can she pull herself out of
  the mood without excessive talking on your part? If

not, just accept it. As tough as it is for a parent to let go, sometimes that's just what's called for. In the end, we have to accept aspects of our child's personality that we may not be able to change.

- **Distractions.** When irritable thoughts start piling up in his head, your child may find it hard to focus. Unlike rages, which require that a child "detox" from a situation by going to a quiet room, time alone in a quiet setting can sometimes make a child even more irritable. Thoughts begin to pile up in his head, and there's nothing to distract him. Try to get him to focus on the world—the glint of the sun on the snow, a bird winging into the sky, or the way the willow tree bends. Baking cookies is a wonderful way to distract your child. Stirring cookie dough, forming the cookies, and smelling the baking cookies take over his senses and occupy his mind. Baking cookies, playing with clay, or otherwise teaching your child to redirect his thoughts and channel his feelings into a meditative or sensory mode falls under the mindfulness-based stress reduction techniques, a core principle in the work of Dr. Marsha Linehan, Ph.D., who developed a line of therapy called dialectical behavioral therapy, designed to help those with borderline personality disorder. It also works well with mood disorders like bipolar disease. And all this time you thought you were just baking cookies!

- **Exercise.** Exercise is a great way to distract your child, but it is also a way to physically work out the neurotransmitters in your child's brain. Just about any exercise causes the brain to release serotonin and endorphins, the feel-good hormones that affect moods. If you whip out a jump rope or a punching bag, or keep a mini-trampoline in your living room, you may be making your child less irritable in several different ways.

After the Mood

Your child has finished a two-hour rage, and now the mood is over and gone. Miraculously, he is happy—perfectly happy. But you are still gritting your teeth and trying to come to grips with the rampage that you have been subjected to. How are we, the parents of bipolar children, supposed to shift gears as instantaneously as our rapid-cycling children seem to?

The only way to combat the fatigue that comes with dealing with this kind of mood intensity is to take time after the mood for yourself. It is easy to fall into destructive patterns—M&M's look particularly seductive after you've battled a mood episode with your child. Instead, try focusing on examining your own feelings, which may otherwise be lost in the madness of the mood moment. Here's what to do:

- **Detoxify.** Acknowledge the event, and give expression to your own feelings. Examine your mood, and release any tension with deep-breathing techniques, or take a walk around the block. Do a few jumping jacks. Are you depressed, puzzled, angry, relieved? Are you satisfied with the way you handled the episode?
- **Regenerate.** Just like parents with a colicky baby have to use spare moments to do something for themselves, parents with a bipolar child must learn to de-escalate

their own arousal and find respite in the periods between moods. Try taking a nap, a bath, a manicure, a shopping trip. Call a friend or spend an hour reading. Regenerating enables you to center yourself, reward yourself for a job well done, and recover your energy for the next battle.

- **Record.** As chief record keeper for your child, it is important for you to write down all the details about the mood incident shortly afterward. It's easy for one episode to blur into the next if you don't take time to do this as soon as possible. Pay special attention to potential triggers and to your child's state of mind prior to the event and just afterward. Call or e-mail your doctor and therapist, and review the incident to see if medication or some other aspect of the treatment plan needs to be changed.

- **Convene.** After a mood has passed is often a good time to revisit the episode with your child. If the topic seems to agitate him, drop it, but if he seems amenable, ask him what he thinks caused the mood. Ask him if he thinks some of the techniques discussed earlier in this chapter might have helped.

Work with your child to design an early warning system— a code word, a gesture, or even a lunge for one particular toy that he might use in the future to indicate that he is losing control. While he might not be able to say, "Mom, I'm about to blow," the lunge for the computer game, or the act of plastering on headphones and turning up the volume extra loud, may be the signal to help both you and your child identify a mood that's about to erupt. Eventually, it may even help your child keep the rage in check.

A Contract to Avoid Conflict

Only after the mood is over can you revisit some of the issues that may have precipitated it. Perhaps your bipolar child was raging because he lost computer-time privileges for bad behavior. After the rage is over, revisit the topic with him. Keep in mind that when in a bipolar state, the child may not be able to process the logic that goes along with a verbal contract, so put it in writing. On one side, print the specific conditions that must be satisfied in order to retain the goal—for example, "Every day you must take your medicines, do your homework, and go to your room when you are feeling angry." On the reverse side of the paper, write what the child will earn as a result of satisfying the conditions: "In return, you will earn two books from the school book club each month." When a contract has been agreed on in writing, it is there as a reference tool and will hopefully help your child deal with the triggers and avoid revisiting the conflict.

Here are some guidelines for writing a contract:

- Keep it simple and be specific. Make sure that the goals and terms of your contract are stated in language your child can understand.
- Make the requirements just challenging enough for your child to find interesting, keeping in mind that her ability to address these challenges may fluctuate with her moods.
- Make sure there's a "buy-in." For the child to succeed, he must buy in to the deal. Set goals together, and agree on the terms of your contract.
- Use feedback techniques to give the child pointers on

his performance. This can be done on a daily, weekly, or monthly basis.

- Remember to update and change the contract regularly.

Some of the tried-and-true feedback techniques include these:

- Use marbles or gumballs to fill a jar each time your child stays on task or fulfills her obligation. When the jar is filled, a reward is given. Empty the jar and start again.
- Have the child draw a picture of an item or prize he wants. Cut the picture into pieces. As the child achieves goals each week, give the child a piece of the picture to tape onto the refrigerator. When the picture is complete, the child has earned the prize.
- As your child meets behavioral and other goals, place tokens to a sports entertainment center in a jar. When the jar is full, the child has earned a trip to the entertainment center. For a variation on a theme, fill the jar with popcorn kernels; when the jar is full, pop the corn, and take the child to the movies.
- The behavior chart is the most basic tool. Use stars or checks to keep your child on track.

It's Puberty Time! Dealing with Bipolar Adolescents

Dennis had his first really noticeable depression last fall and winter, as the days started to get shorter. It happened again this year, but it was much worse—he is twelve and entering puberty.

Gayle, mom of a bipolar son diagnosed at age eleven

Just when your child seems stable and adjusted to his medications, he grows a few inches and becomes oppositional and impossible to deal with. The hormones that spearhead puberty and normal adolescence in a child can wreak havoc with a bipolar child.

While the biochemistry of these interactions is still under scientific study, the increase in testosterone and other sex hormones appears to affect neurotransmitters, creating a whole new set of impulses. And just as her hormones increase and change, her brain makes some massive changes as well. During the first years of life, the brain has created millions of extra synapses to be used for different learning functions. Some are used repeatedly and become etched into brain function. During adolescence, the brain does a spring cleaning. It begins a process called pruning, shedding the excess synapses and leaving room for more efficient neural circuitry. By late adolescence, parents will see an improvement in a child's judgment, and as bipolar teens approach adulthood, they may begin to fall into a more classic bipolar model, cycling more slowly and predictably.

The teen years are seldom joyrides for parents. Even "normal" teens may exhibit impulsive behavior like shoplifting and driving dangerously. By their very nature, teens are impulsive. That said, how can you differentiate between normal teen experimentation and bipolar behavior, especially when your child has yet to be diagnosed? Once again, the frequency, duration, and severity of the mood swings will be an important clue. Is her behavior interfering with day-to-day functioning? Is he able to meet developmental tasks in spite of the moods?

If an adolescent with bipolar disorder has developed oppositional behaviors that therapy can't correct, they can become ingrained, leading to oppositional defiant disorder (ODD), which is defined by patterns of hostility, lack of cooperation, and defiant behaviors. A sometimes comorbid condition, conduct disorder, is a combination of behavioral and emotional problems that lead to rule breaking and often aggressive noncompliance. Treatment involves behavioral therapy to change existing thought and behavior patterns. Because these behaviors are more difficult to control as children get older, it is important for parents to seek treatment as soon as they have identified them.

Notes from the Couch: A Psychiatrist's Point of View

Moodiness doesn't equal bipolar disorder, but dramatic moods are a characteristic feature of bipolar disorder. Parents often come to me with the chief complaint that their child has mood swings and someone suggested the problem was "clearly bipolar disorder." Bipolar disorder is a complex diagnosis based on many features other than moodiness. The moods that are seen in bipolar disorder are bigger than life—louder, longer, and more disabling than typical mood patterns. And the moods of bipolar disorder are persistent—they always come back.

Rage and anger can be part of bipolar disorder, but like moodiness, they are not enough to make the diagnosis. Anger and outbursts are some of the most common symptoms that I see in my practice. They can arise from many sources: depression, anxiety, premenstrual syndromes, medical disorders, seizures, and grief, to name a few. Handling rage, regardless of the source, is a priority in treatment because safety becomes an issue. However, these symptoms can be stubborn and unyielding to treatment. Learning how to reduce the rages by reducing environmental arousal, and how to ride out the rages safely, without making things worse, is a critical component of treating pediatric bipolar disorder.

Mania is often a confusing term. Manic symptoms include

excessive energy, poor judgment, sleep disturbance, increased activity, euphoria, irritability, and grandiosity. To be considered manic, a person must have at least some period of euphoria and excitement and some grandiose ideas. Irritable mood can be part of mania, but it doesn't make the diagnosis. Actually, having manic symptoms alone does not imply a diagnosis of bipolar disorder. One can get these symptoms from other things, such as medical illness, personality disorders, or medications. Just as sadness doesn't equal depression, mania doesn't equal bipolar disorder. Bipolar symptoms are cyclical and persistent and not explained by other things.

I have seen many youngsters with anxiety disorders who have been misdiagnosed with bipolar disorder—and vice versa. Anxiety can mimic a lot of the mood reactivity and difficulty that children with bipolar disorder have. It's also one of the most treatable conditions of childhood. Make sure it doesn't get missed.

CHAPTER 4

THE MEDICATIONS

The Right Prescriptions for Your Child

Although we are not where we need to be with Barry's meds yet, I am so grateful that we finally know what we are dealing with. Yes, we will still have to play the pin the tail on the donkey game until we get the right combo and amount of meds, but at least this time, the blindfold is off.
Mom of a bipolar son

Treatment for bipolar disorder is usually a combination of medication, therapy, and parental retraining. There is seldom a magic pill that by itself solves the problem. Doctors can't guarantee a particular child will react to specific medications the way everyone hopes he will, and finding the right cocktail of meds is difficult. Because psychotropic medications often take several weeks to build up in the bloodstream, parents need to monitor medicated children closely. Any physical, behavioral, mood, or energy change is worth noting and discussing with your doctor. Your observations will help the psychiatrist adjust the dosage and medications from time to time. Even when the diagnosis seems crystal clear, medications aren't always 100 percent effective. But the right medication mix will take the edge off of some of the more intense moods and, combined with therapy and a low-stress environment, will help a child live a more normal childhood.

Lithium? Depakote? Luvox? Haldol? These words were gibberish to me until I had to start counting pills, cutting them in half, filling pillboxes, and sending notes about how many milligrams of each pill my son was to take and when. And the blood tests! Oh, those blood tests—a monthly, sometimes weekly, necessity. The blood tests measure the amount of medicine in the bloodstream, to make sure it is not too much or too little. Many of the classic medications used for bipolar disorder have had little testing in children, and no longitudinal data are available on the long-term side effects of those that have been tested. So what is a parent to do? Read on.

The Medications

The use of psychotropic medication is complicated and evolving. Few are actually approved for use in children under age twelve. Yet just because a medication doesn't have formal FDA approval for children doesn't mean it can't be used. In making treatment decisions, child psychiatrists do look at data obtained from studies on children, but these studies are much less common than studies with adults, so psychiatrists also rely on information reported in adult studies. This common practice is the most appropriate solution for addressing the needs of children with bipolar disorder. Your doctor will prescribe medications based on the best available scientific data and her own experience in treating this condition. Your doctor can also tap into the experiences of other clinicians. Professional meetings, Web-based discussion groups, and informal consultation with colleagues are some of the ways physicians work at developing consensus on treatment. Don't hesitate to ask, "Why this drug for my child?" Your doctor should be able to walk you through her decision-making process.

Numerous other challenges arise when prescribing medication for children with mental illness. An accurate diagnosis is the most important starting point, but even with one, predicting how a particular child will respond to a particular drug is difficult. Children's brains differ significantly from adult brains. In addition, your child's brain is growing rapidly, so his response to medication can change over time. Furthermore, monitoring for positive responses to medication is tricky. Changes in emotions and behavior are often subtle.

Monitoring for side effects is also a layered and difficult process. Some side effects appear right away and then fade; other side effects show up down the road. Dangerous side effects must be differentiated from bothersome ones, as well as from breakthrough symptoms of the underlying illness. Long-term side effects of these medications on children's brains are not well established.

General Guidelines

Before I describe the families of drugs generally prescribed for treatment of bipolar disorder, here are some rules of thumb:

- **What is the desired effect of the medication?** Be sure you and your doctor have defined specific target symptoms that should improve as a result of the medication. Understand how long it should take to achieve these improvements. Meet with the doctor at least every four to six weeks during medication changes. Ask the doctor how you can measure the positive effects, and try to involve your child in this plan. Getting your child to help report on her symptoms is the start of a learning process for her. The hope is that she'll someday be able to monitor her own symptoms and seek appropriate help when she needs it.

- **One medication is better than two or more.** The fewer medications, the lower the risk of side effects. Drug interactions are also reduced when the number of medications is kept to a minimum. However, given the multiple symptoms in children with bipolar disorder, a single medication is often inadequate. Doctors should avoid simply adding more and more meds to the mix and instead identify medications that aren't working and take them out of the regimen. Doctors also look for medications that treat more than one symptom.
- **One medication change at a time.** Without this control, it is hard to tell which benefits or side effects are the result of what medication interventions. This careful approach is preferred but not always possible, especially in the hospital or in a crisis.
- **Less or more?** If a child's symptoms get worse with a new medication, it generally means one of two things: (1) the medication is the problem or (2) the dosage is not high enough to control the symptoms effectively. Do you increase or decrease the dosage? If symptoms are suddenly worse, sustained, dramatically different from baseline, or dangerous, the typical approach is to decrease or stop the medication. If the symptoms are similar to baseline—somewhat worse but not dangerous, up and down in their occurrence or gradual in presentation—it may be better to see if a higher dose will improve things. Your doctor is more likely to stick with a medication if significant benefits outweigh the side effects.
- **Watch for interactions.** Check with your doctor before giving any other medications, including over-the-

counter medications, vitamins, supplements, and herbal preparations. Make sure your pharmacy maintains a complete list of the medications your child is currently taking.

- **Be careful of alcohol and drug use.** Alcohol and street drugs can create a dangerous mix with psychiatric medications, and this topic must be honestly and firmly discussed with adolescents.

- **Risks of medication in pregnancy.** Teenagers who are sexually active need to be counseled about the risks of taking psychiatric medicines while pregnant. Birth control should be discussed at length.

- **Consider the risk of overdose.** Some psychiatric medications can be quite dangerous in overdose. Whenever a doctor prescribes medications to someone with mood disorders, she must consider the risk that the patient may use the medications to overdose. Older antidepressants and lithium are among the most toxic. They can cause irregular heartbeats, slowing of the brain, and, in many cases, death. The serotonergic agents carry a much lower risk of overdose. Keep all medications safely out of reach of emotionally fragile and impulsive children.

- **Don't suddenly stop medications without speaking to the doctor.** If the medication changes feel endless or unproductive, talk to the doctor. Communication, persistence, and patience are the watchwords in finding the right mix of medications for children with bipolar disorder. Here is one mom's experience: "This past summer, she was taken off all her meds. Her pediatrician and former therapist wanted to see what would happen. We all knew she was not just a depressed kid, but no one wanted to label her bipolar. I had to stop going to work to take care of her. I watched her get worse and worse until I had to admit her to save her life . . . and mine."

- **How long?** Parents are naturally interested in knowing how long a child needs to stay on medications, but that's a difficult question to answer. Current research suggests that a physician shouldn't consider tapering medications until the patient has had no symptoms for at least twelve months. The specifics depend on your doctor and family. Years of medication without reevaluation are as dangerous as stopping medication too soon. Some kids require long-term medication to remain stable; some can take fewer or no medications during long periods of stability. This area is one for ongoing discussion with your doctor.

Prescription Medications

Mood Stabilizers

Mood stabilizers are used to help regulate moods in people with bipolar disorder. They act at several levels: they can reduce acute episodes of mania or hypomania, reduce the frequency of mood cycles, and sometimes help with depression. In general, mood stabilizers have not yet been shown to be as consistently effective in children as they are in adults, but these are the options available to doctors. The "gold standard" of mood stabilizers is lithium. It has been used for many years and has been typically effective in adults with bipolar disorder. The rest of the mood stabilizers are antiseizure or antipsychotic medications that have been found to have some mood stabilizing effect.

Your doctor may need to adjust the dosage of these medications over a period of weeks or even months before they produce the desired effects. Your child may require regular blood tests while on these medications. Side effects, though often numerous and irksome, usually dissipate with time. Many people with bipolar disorder resist taking their mood stabilizers because they miss the manic highs. They feel flat on these medications. Because pediatric bipolar disorder is so complex, children are often prescribed more than one mood stabilizer.

Mood Stabilizers
lithium (Lithobid, Eskalith)
valproic acid (Depakote, Depakene)
carbemazepine (Tegretol)
oxcarbazepine (Trileptal)
lamotrigine (Lamictal)
gabapentin (Neurontin)
topiramate (Topomax)
olanzapine (Zyprexa)

Antipsychotics
This family of drugs is used primarily in the treatment of psychosis: hallucinations, delusions, bizarre behavior, losing touch with reality. Bipolar disorder can include psychosis, and so these medications are frequently prescribed for children with bipolar illness. Beyond the clear-cut psychotic symptoms, antipsychotics are also effective in reducing severe agitation, rages, and dangerous impulsivity—all target symptoms in these children. These meds work by blocking the transmission of dopamine in the brain. Dopamine is related to many emotional and behavioral functions.

Precursors of today's powerful antipsychotics carried high risks of movement disorders, including a potentially irreversible side effect of abnormal involuntary movements called tardive dyskinesia. Antipsychotics prescribed today seem to have far fewer movement disorders associated with them but carry their own risks, including weight gain, cardiac rhythm changes, and abnormalities in sugar and lipid metabolism. One of the antipsychotics, Zyprexa, is also a well-documented mood stabilizer. Therefore, it is included in both categories.

Antipsychotics
olanzapine (Zyprexa)
risperdone (Risperdal)
quetiapine (Seroquel)
ziprasidone (Geodon)
clozapine (Clozaril); requires weekly blood draws—can hurt white blood cells
haloperidol (Haldol)
perphenazine (Trilafan)
thioridazine (Mellaril)
chloropromazine (Thorazine)
molindone (Moban)

Antidepressants
Since by definition bipolar disorder usually includes episodes of depression as well as mania and hypomania, psychiatrists commonly prescribe drugs to treat both. For bipolar patients, the downside to antidepressants is that they have been known to agitate and even induce mania, so don't be surprised if at some point you're warned against them. That said, clinical depression shouldn't be ignored. Balancing the mood stabilizers and antidepressants is unquestionably a delicate task, so you and your child's treatment team will have to weigh the risks of side effects carefully against the threats posed by your child's depressive episodes.

Serotonergic Agents

The most commonly used antidepressants increase serotonin, a neurotransmitter that is associated with mood, fear, and self-regulation states (the "feed and breed" system). Some of these medications also affect transmitters in addition to serotonin. These meds are popular because they are effective, and the side effects are usually pretty mild. The latter can include agitation or mania, as well as changes in sexual function. Minor weight gain is a risk in this class of drugs. Many of these medications are not particularly sedating; others are specifically prescribed because they help with sleep.

Serotonin-Enhancing Medications
fluoxetine (Prozac)
sertraline (Zoloft)
paroxetine (Paxil)
fluvoxamine (Luvox)
citalopram (Celexa)
venlafaxine (Effexor)
mirtazapine (Remeron)
nefazodone (Serzone)
trazodone (Desyrel)

Buproprion (Wellbutrin)

Wellbutrin is an antidepressant in a category of its own. As of this writing, there are no similarly structured antidepressants. Wellbutrin predominantly affects dopamine, a brain transmitter that helps to regulate mood, fear, and attentional/alerting mechanisms. Two specific benefits are the absence of any sexual or weight gain side effects.

This medication has a prominent role in treating people with bipolar disorder because it carries a lower risk of inducing mania, although it is still a possible side effect. It also may have some benefit in treating the attentional difficulties common in people with bipolar disorder. Side effects can include nervousness, insomnia, and headaches. There is increased risk of seizures with this medication as well. It should not be prescribed for those with a history of seizures or eating disorders.

Tricyclic Antidepressants

This is an older class of antidepressants, in use since the early 1960s. They are seldom prescribed today because they are associated with a greater number of side effects—including dry mouth, dizziness, constipation, and blurry vision—than the newer agents. They can induce mania and cause weight gain and sexual side effects. There is an effect on the heart as well. Children on these medications must be monitored with electrocardiograms. In the 1970s and 1980s, several children on these medications died suddenly, precipitating the drugs' fall from grace within the psychiatric community.

Tricyclic Antidepressants
nortryptyline (Pamelor)
imipramine (Tofranil)
amitriptyline (Elavil)
desipramine (Norpramin)
clomipramine (Anafranil); used primarily for obsessive-
    compulsive symptoms

Monoamine Oxidase Inhibitors

Like the tricyclics, these medications are older and less commonly prescribed. Certain foods can interact with these medications, creating dangerous acute high blood pressure states, so children prescribed MAO inhibitors must adhere strictly to dietary limitations. Other troubling side effects include dizziness and weight gain. MAOs are nevertheless effective antidepressants and still prescribed on occasion.

MAO Inhibitors
tranylcypromine (Parnate)
phenelzine (Nardil)

Stimulants

Stimulants are used primarily to treat attentional difficulties and hyperactivity. They increase brain concentrations of the transmitter dopamine and, in some cases, norepinephrine, another transmitter related to mood and attentional states. Bipolar disorder is highly correlated with attention problems and hyperactivity, both motor and mental types of hyperactivity. In theory, treating the mood disorder effectively should alleviate these symptoms, but you may well find that even when the mood disorder is under control, the attention deficit and hyperactivity remain.

Stimulants can worsen mania and increase irritability. In vulnerable kids, they can even precipitate psychotic symptoms. For these reasons, the use of stimulants in children with bipolar disorder is controversial. However, in certain cases, the stimulants may be employed, very carefully, to assist with the residual attentional problems. Stimulants can also lead to sleep problems, another trigger for mania, so children on these drugs must be monitored carefully. Decrease in appetite is also a side effect of stimulants. In a small number of children, stimulants can induce motor or vocal tics. Stimulants can be used as drugs of abuse, so this is an issue with adolescents.

Stimulants
methylphenidate (Ritalin, Concerta, Metadate)
dextroamphetamine (Dexedrine, Dextrostat, Dexedrine Spansules)
multiple amphetamine salt combinations (Adderall)

Sleep Agents
Difficulty with sleep is a common symptom of both depression and mania. Sleep deprivation can trigger mania. Sleep-deprived kids are more impulsive and crankier, and their concentration is impaired. Assisting with sleep is often essential to symptom resolution, but the benefit of a a good night's sleep must be weighed against the risks these medicines carry. Morning "hangover" from sleep aids is a common worry for parents, and rightly so. The amount of such residual sleepiness will vary from child to child and medication to medication. Sleep medicines for children include antihistamines, sedating antidepressants, "designer" sleep aids, and others.

Sleep Agents
mirtazapine (Remeron)
amytriptyline (Elavil)
clonidine (Catapres)
hydroxyzine (Atarax)
zolpidem (Ambien)

Tranquilizers
This class of medicines can be used to reduce agitation, reduce severe or acute anxiety, and sometimes reduce mania itself. They can be used as sleep aids as well. On the downside, tranquilizers can be disinhibiting in kids, meaning they can make

a child more agitated or impulsive. These medications can also become habit-forming and have the potential to be abused or sold to those who abuse them. They are sedating and may interfere with activities such as driving. They can be lethal with alcohol. Without clear and significant benefits, they're generally not worth the risks.

Tranquilizers
clonazepam (Klonopin)
diazepam (Valium)
lorazepam (Ativan)

Nonprescription Medication and Alternative Therapies

Light Therapy
The use of bright lights to reduce symptoms of seasonal depression has sound scientific backing. Not all children's depression has a seasonal component, but light therapy may be helpful in more general depression as well. Side effects of light therapy can include headache, nausea, or jitteriness, but these are not usually severe. The lights used to provide this treatment are specially designed to expose patients to high-intensity targeted bands of the light spectrum.

Herbal Preparations
Some herbal over-the-counter products are believed to offer some relief for those who suffer from mood disorders and associated symptoms. Most of the data available on these preparations are inconsistent, with the exception of melatonin as a sleep agent for children, which has been well studied and supported.

One cautionary note: Just because these products are labeled "herbal" and "natural" doesn't mean they're unquestionably safe or free of side effects. Plenty of natural compounds can be harmful to humans. Talk to your doctor before you give your child any herbal preparation. This is especially important if your child is taking prescription medications, as there may be dangerous interactions.

Herbal Preparations
St. John's wort
S-adenosyl-methionine (SAM-e)
melatonin

Essential Fatty Acids
Fatty acids are building blocks of human cells, located in the cell membrane, which help to regulate transmission of information between cells. Certain fatty acids—the "essential" fatty acids—cannot be produced by our bodies, and so must be taken in through our diet. People with depression and bipolar disorder appear to have low levels of a certain type of essential fatty acid, omega 3 fatty acids, in their cell membranes. Scientists have theorized that this affects the transmission of emotional information, so there has been growing interest in dietary supplements of these fatty acids to help treat mood disorders. There have been some positive results showing decreased symptoms of mania when high-dose supplements of these nutrients are added to the patient's regular medications. The data have not been as good for depression. One possible side effect is stomach distress or low compliance because the doses are high, and the oils may have a bad taste. Some companies are marketing blended oils in packets with flavoring to address that complaint.

Many psychiatrists are encouraging patients to add these supplements as a low-risk, possibly beneficial intervention.

Omega 3 Supplements
fish oil capsules
flaxseed oil and flaxseed oil capsules

Drug and Alcohol Experimentation and Medication

Tom was abusing drugs, stealing from the family, stealing from neighbors and family friends. His rages were destructive and traumatic.
Kaylee, mom of a bipolar teenage son diagnosed at age thirteen

The adolescent and teen years are when many children begin to experiment with drugs and alcohol. A child with psychiatric problems is more likely to try substances, sometimes as a means of self-medicating. It's a way for them to ease emotional pain, regulate the high and low moods, or deal with problems they cannot express. Bipolar children who are on medication should be made very aware that drugs and alcohol are even more detrimental to them than they are to other teens. The fact is that mixing illicit substances with mood stabilizers, antidepressants, and stimulants can be deadly. Furthermore, unregulated bipolar teens are at higher risk for alcohol toxicity. People with bipolar disorder have a higher rate of substance abuse in general.

Teens Going "Off-Meds"

Paradoxically, medicated bipolar teens face a serious risk when they are feeling most stable and subsequently decide to take themselves off medication. Drug side effects (e.g., weight gain, pimples) push them in that direction too. And because no parent can physically force a teen to do anything, they often are relegated to standing by and watching the situation play out. Parents too can be lulled into a false sense of security when a child has been stable for a while.

In between health plans, Alice, the mom of a fourteen-year-old bipolar teen, inadvertently took her daughter off her medications for five days while waiting for the new health plan to take effect. First, she noticed that her daughter's energy had increased, which she thought was a great thing, but soon an angry mood prevailed. When her daughter, a star basketball player and team captain, wound up to hit another player in the middle of a game, both Alice and her daughter were reminded of how important her meds were to everyone's well-being.

It may take your teen some time to recover from a severe mood episode even after the medications are reinstated. Be sure to let her know that no matter how great she feels or how troubled by the side effects, going off meds without a doctor's input is a really bad idea.

Frequently Asked Questions

- **How do I prepare my child for her monthly blood test?** Prepare a "blood test box" full of toys, and reserve it for blood test days. Fill it with fun pens, a small pad, a squeeze object, Silly Putty, magic slates, and other small items that can serve as a combination distraction and reward for your child's cooperation. When your child is getting ready for the "stick," have her try to find the vein for the phlebotomist. Exercising a degree of control over the process may make the blood test seem less intimidating. A routine stopover at a nearby coffee shop for a doughnut and fruit juice may be the perfect after-blood-test treat.

- **My son has been gaining weight since going on medications. Why is this happening, and what can I do about it?** Weight gain is a side effect of many medications used to treat bipolar disorder. It is due to increased appetite and changes in the metabolic system that can lead to lipid and cholesterol problems. Your doctor should carefully monitor for signs of both, as well as for diabetes. There are no easy answers to this dilemma. Weight gain is highly problematic in kids and teens. Healthy diet and exercise are helpful tools in treating kids with mood disorders and can certainly help reduce the weight gain side effects of meds. But the battles over food can be traumatic and dangerous. Some studies point to the use of various medications to reduce the weight gain associated with Zyprexa and Risperdal. Not every child gains weight on medications, but it is a serious risk that must be discussed in detail before and during the use of psychiatric medications.

- **What if we forget the medications? For a day? For a week?** In most cases, if you forget the medication for one dose or one day, simply pick up right where you left off. If you leave on vacation and forget the bottle, you may be able to get a small emergency supply from a local pharmacy if you contact your doctor. This is harder with stimulant medications, because they are heavily monitored by the government and prescriptions cannot be called in to a pharmacy in most cases. But sometimes an emergency supply can be arranged.

If you stop the medication for more than a day or two, you will need to check with your doctor about how to restart it. Your child may have to build up to the full dose again.

- **Should my child be responsible for her own medication?** New skills take time to learn. For kids with bipolar disorder, the learning curve is sometimes more gradual. Your child should participate in organizing and taking the medications, but don't rely on her to take them on her own until you have good evidence that she can do it consistently. Older teenagers may be resistant to heavy supervision, but it should be in place, at least to begin with. Even if your child is self-medicating, keep an eye on the supply—both to monitor compliance and so that you know when to call the pharmacy for a refill.

- **How about medications at school and camp?** Schools are increasingly familiar with children on medication. When medications have to be given during the day, the school nurse will often administer them. Schools have forms and policies around these procedures. In most cases, school personnel should be aware of a child's diagnosis and medications in case something goes wrong. Some families are hesitant about sharing this information about their child, and that is understandable. But in the long run, open lines of communication will be more beneficial to your child and everyone involved. Take a close look at your reasons for not sharing information with the school.

Camps are also more and more adept at giving medications. A director of a large sleep-away camp once stated that between one-fourth and one-third of her campers were on some form of psychotropic medications—and this was not a special needs camp. You will need to fill out forms and understand policies to get the medications dispensed at camp.

Notes from the Couch: A Psychiatrist's Perspective

Choosing to use psychiatric medications in the treatment of a child's mood disorder is one of the biggest decisions parents will ever make. It is important to respect the power of the medications—the power to be healing and the power to cause side effects. Power is necessary in battling this condition, but it must be handled carefully.

Information about medications for psychiatric illness in children is in constant flux. Don't get too caught up in the "drug of the day" or the "drug scare of the day." Stay as focused as possible on valid, scientific information. Get it translated into real language by a trusted ally—the pediatrician or psychiatrist, for example. Gut instincts are important in caring for a child, but be careful not to let emotions and prejudices cloud medical decision making. There is art and science to medicine, but the art will not be useful unless the science is accurate.

THE STRUCTURE OF DAILY LIFE

Routine Is Everything

Change of routine, school holidays, less structure, all make
her irritable.
Rona, mom of a bipolar daughter diagnosed at age seven

It may have been ages since you've followed a structured schedule. Most of us are fine, sometimes even invigorated, by meeting life's challenges moment by moment. Bipolar children aren't. Because they can't control their own moods, they're enormously comforted by stability in their daily routine and in their environment. Establishing and maintaining a consistent structure of their day will help your bipolar child reclaim a sense of control even when her own body refuses to cooperate. From the time she wakes in the morning until her early bedtime, there should be a plan of how each day is going to go, and it's your job to stick to the plan. Rules and rewards—lots of positive reinforcement—can help keep bipolar kids on track (well, some of the time). We can't expect bipolar children to toe the line consistently, but we can help them feel both secure and cared for.

It's All About Transitions

The purpose of structure is to help your child manage transitions, something most bipolar children tend to be very slow in processing. From natural transitions (the changing seasons) to those that would make even nonbipolar children anxious (moving to a new house or new school), these children have hair-trigger mood responses to them all.

Every command or request is in a way a transition for a bipolar child. You're asking her to shift focus from one activity to another. Oppositional stances are often a product of being unable to make this mini-transition as quickly as a nonbipolar child would.

Plan for back-to-school and end-of-school transitions well in advance. If your child attends a camp, plan for that transition too. Help your child begin to make the shift weeks before the actual event. As the end of the school year approaches, line up play dates and other activities that begin immediately after school ends. Two weeks before the fall semester starts, put your child back on a school schedule, setting her alarm earlier and enforcing school-night bedtime. Try to plan major transitions, such as moves to a new neighborhood or school, well in advance, and factor seasonal mood swings into your plans. Moving and starting a new school during the winter months, for instance, is a recipe for disaster if your child shows signs of seasonal affective disorder.

Returning to work full-time after being at home for months is a transition for everyone, not just you. A new babysitter or housekeeper is a transition. Become sensitive to the transitions in your bipolar child's life, and you may be able to anticipate and ease an impending mood cycle—or possibly even avoid one altogether. Use the Transition Form for Bipolar Kids shown here, or create your own, to prepare for an upcoming transition and to help you track your child's moods from start to finish.

Transition Form for Bipolar Kids

Expected Transition *(e.g., move, new school)*:_____
Date transition will begin:_____
Date transition will be complete:_____
PREPARATIONS:
Beginning date:_____
Tactics to include:
- Reading books about transition
- Talking about transition
- "Walk-through" of new situation
- Work with child to design schedule for transition period
- Other:_____
MOOD OBSERVATIONS
Pretransition:_____
Day before transition:_____
Day of transition:_____
Posttransition:_____
Two weeks posttransition:_____

Suggestions for Easing Transition

I have learned to appreciate the good moments, have patience and understanding through the bad, and concentrate on the wonderful qualities that make her unique.
Anna, mom of a bipolar daughter diagnosed at age eight

After all we've learned about parenting, it is hard for parents of bipolar children to let go when it comes to the basics. The problem is that for this child, normal rules don't apply. It is not so much that you should lower expectations with a bipolar child, but rather reframe them. Just as we would shift our expectations if our child were disabled in another way—blind, deaf, or mentally retarded—we must understand and accept our child's capabilities and limitations. Because bipolar children don't physically express their problem, it is easy to fool yourself into expecting more than they can reasonably give. Should we attempt to hold them to a basic standard? Absolutely. Will they consistently meet our expectations? Only if we know how and when to raise and lower the bar!

Stick to the Schedule

He gets in a lot of trouble at school. He doesn't get his work done. He's belligerent. When I try to punish him, he curses.
Mitzi, mom of a bipolar son diagnosed at age twelve

There will be days when, in spite of all of your best-laid plans, schedules, and structure, your child is unable to cooperate. There will be times when you must mete out a well-deserved punishment, but there will also be times when the punitive approach can't possibly work because your child is too distracted by her own emotional chaos to respond to the rules. The threat of punishment—grounding, taking away a favorite toy, withholding a Christmas present or allowance money, or a time-out—will generally be ignored and defied by a bipolar child in the throes of a mood swing.

It's up to you as a parent to judge whether your child is in control enough to listen and care when he is being punished. It's not easy at first, but eventually you will recognize when your bipolar child is stable and when he is not. During stable times, you can punish a bipolar child just as you would a non-bipolar child. When he is unstable, your efforts must be refocused. Your goal will be, first and foremost, to stabilize him and help him confront his feelings and reactions. You would never punish an infant for soiling a diaper because she simply can't control herself. By the same token, there's no sense in punishing a bipolar child for behavior that he cannot control.

Earn Bonus Miles

Talking, taking space, points systems, breathing, and a reinforcing behavior plan are some of our calming rituals.
Lisa, mom of a bipolar son diagnosed at age thirteen

The "earn bonus miles" concept is a simple one. Help a child to recover from an unstable episode by awarding points for everything the child does that is on task. This approach is used in inpatient psychiatric wards and seems to be the method of choice for inspiring rapid-cycling, difficult-to-manage bipolar children. Children are awarded points for waking up, getting dressed, even breathing without an untoward incident. Their behavior is monitored closely and the points add up. If a child is noncompliant or is off task, he is not awarded any points for that segment of time. At the end of the day, the child can trade in his points for privileges, such as a special dessert, a toy, or play money that he can save up and apply toward a prize. The more points, the more or better the privileges. Bedtime is also keyed to this system, which makes wonderful sense, since children with bipolar disorder really do need lots of sleep, and the less stable they are, the more sleep they need.

A note of caution: Although this system works well in a controlled hospital setting, it's easy for a points system to go from being positive to being punitive at home. When Kelly becomes bored with the system and the prizes or you become lax in tallying up the day's points, the system can unravel. Make sure you continuously accentuate the positive. Don't slip into the giveaway mode when working with your child.

Communicate Through Transitions

Use empathy and "I" sentences to help you communicate with your child, especially when he seems oppositional or distracted. Instead of, "You must go to bed right now," try, "I know you are anxious about that test tomorrow, but you still need to sleep. It's time for bed now."

Using empathy will make your child realize that you do understand her feelings. A firm and concise command lets her know that although you are listening to her complaints and objections, the directive is nonnegotiable.

Other Ways to Say "No!"

We were at the county fair, and he'd spent all the money we'd given him for the rides and games. When he asked for more and I said no, he took off his hat, threw it on the ground, and jumped on it like a three-year-old having a tantrum.

Betsy, mom of a bipolar son diagnosed at age eight

Discipline can be difficult for parents to administer. According to Nancy Austin, Psy.D., a psychologist in New York who works with bipolar children and their families, parents with bipolar children frequently suffer from posttraumatic stress disorder, a by-product of daily coping with a child's extreme moods. This manifests itself as a tendency to avoid conflicts with their child at any cost.

Many parents with children diagnosed as bipolar report that the word *no* is a trigger for their children. Some parents feel that the only way to handle their bipolar children is to avoid that word at all costs. As one mother explains, "If the kids are relatively stable, I always answer their request in positive language. 'Yes, when the toys are picked up. Yes, you can—after homework. Yes, when your shower is finished.' There's no question that some words can set them off, so I've learned how to parent without the word *no*."

It's hard to avoid saying no altogether, but if your child has a meltdown whenever he hears it, look for other ways to say what you need to say. Choose your battles: a *no* over something stupid is a wasted *no*.

"No, you cannot have a BB gun, not now and not ever. I don't think it is an appropriate plaything for you," is something you as a parent may have to say, even if you are staunchly opposed to using the word *no*. Telling the child "yes, but maybe later . . ." when you have no intention of buying a BB gun gives the child the message that you don't keep your word. Sooner or later, he'll try that technique too.

Watch Out of the Corner of Your Eye

As parents of bipolar children, we are often forced to put our children under a microscope—to examine their behaviors more closely than parents of nonbipolar children do. Is scrutiny equivalent to rewarding bad or unusual behaviors with your undivided attention, thereby reinforcing them? Dr. David Fassler often sees this in his practice: "Parents of children with bipolar disorder can become very focused on detecting signs of trouble. To an extent, this is appropriate and important. Parents are a critical part of the child's early warning system. They need to pick up on such signs. But if parents focus primarily on a child's difficulties, it will eventually affect the child's self-esteem. The child may also learn that he can get attention by getting in trouble. It's important to find ways to counterbalance the attention and to give kids lots of positive feedback for the things they're doing well."

On the most difficult days, try to point out even fleeting

glimmers of good behavior, and compliment the child for doing well. I try to employ what I call the 4:1 rule: for every negative piece of feedback you give a child, try to give her four positives. If Kathy comes home in an awful mood, throws a chair at her sister, and glares at you, compliment her on how she remembered to close the door without slamming it on her way in (1). Tell her how much you appreciate her remembering to take her medications in the afternoon (2) and the fact that she completed her homework last night without being asked (3). Finally, tell her how proud you are that she didn't leave a mess after breakfast in the morning (4). Leave out the fact that she didn't put her dirty dishes in the sink but stacked them on the counter instead. Then deal with the chair throwing. Learn to celebrate the small, albeit incomplete, victories.

A Day in the Life of a Bipolar Child

It seems that every hour is a "witching hour" for bipolar kids, but some hours seem more difficult to maneuver than others, owing to their transitional nature. Daily transitions that we take for granted include sleeping and waking up each day. It is important to establish a morning and evening routine to help ease these transitions. Spending fifteen minutes each morning to wake your child up in a consistent manner, using a gentle shake on the shoulder or three five-minute reminders to turn off the alarm, and another fifteen minutes to read a bedtime story at night can really help. Routines can and should also be developed for the home-from-school transition time. Here are some suggestions to manage a day in the life of your child.

Mornings

My wife and I just get sick to our stomachs at 7:30 each morning.

Larry, father of a thirteen-year-old bipolar daughter

According to many of the moms of bipolar children I've interviewed, mornings are an absolute horror story—"the ultimate challenge," said one mom. Getting a bipolar child out of bed and ready to face the day is a daunting task. Often, their drug cocktails make them woozy, and since their medication level is at "trough"—the lowest level in the day—they can be irritable and unhappy. One mom ended the screaming fights with her son by letting him watch TV or log on to the computer; formerly, both were before-school no-nos. She said that while he still has occasional problems on those days when the moods kick in, the electronics, plus a lot of humor, have helped.

Once they are involved in the routine of their school day, bipolar kids who are stable and have no other outstanding stressors tend to get into a groove.

Studies on depression indicate that mornings and evenings are particularly troublesome times for depressed adults. Although no research has been completed on depressed children or adolescents as of this writing, there are studies in process to try to determine exactly how the various times of day and night affect adolescents diagnosed with bipolar disorder.

School Refusal

One of the biggest morning problems is school refusal, an all-too-common issue with bipolar children. I've heard stories of parents pushing, pulling, hoisting, and physically carrying their children from house to car, from car to school. When kids get too big to lift, other tactics must be employed.

"Your child must understand that while you will do all you can to make him comfortable in school, there will always be things that you cannot change," explains Dr. Erika Karres, Ph.D., former teacher and professor in education at the University of North Carolina. "You may not be able to change the classmates, switch teachers, or change his seat in the classroom. This is a life lesson. In some situations, the only thing we have control over is our attitude."

Dr. Karres suggests that parents encourage children to keep journals of what aggravates them about school. Go over his journal entries with him, and reward him for going to school in spite of the things that drive him crazy.

Tracey Lynn Trudeau, a psychologist with the Edmonton Department of Emotional Behavioral Services in Edmonton, Canada, says school refusal among bipolar children is anxiety based. She suggests a combination of exposure and cognitive therapies. An exposure therapy approach entails controlled incrementally greater exposure. In other words, the goal for day 1 could be nothing more than walking him halfway to school, followed by all the way to school the next day, actually attending school for one hour the following day, and so on. At the same time, his therapist would use cognitive therapy to work on dismantling negative thought patterns that are likely keeping the child from school.

Many educators express surprise when parents describe harrowing pre- and postschool antics of a child who appears to them to be perfectly comported. The stress of transitions can bring out the worst in a bipolar child.

Midday

Getting him up, dressed, and off to school sucks the life out of us. By 8:00 A.M., we have barely enough energy to work.

It's such a struggle, and then we dread the afternoon.
Sharon, mom of a bipolar son diagnosed at age ten

Drop Everything!

The simple solution for easing the after-school transition is to give it your complete undivided attention for as long as it takes your child to unwind and relax. Adults often need a cocktail hour or its equivalent after a busy day at work, and so does a child who is particularly sensitive to stress. While she can't sip a martini, a glass of milk and a cookie or a crunchy apple may have the same effect, particularly if you are standing by to listen to her.

Give Them Shelter

People used to laugh when I told them that I threw away the television set. Watching the news is pretty important to me as a writer and public relations consultant. But I banished the television from my children's lives, limiting myself to a small, ancient TV that stays in my room, because I found television hyperstimulating to my bipolar child. Its effect on the other children wasn't terrific either.

Parents have asked me how I do it. The answer is quite simple. It's a big, overwhelming world out there, particularly for the bipolar child. It is full of sound, fury, and visuals that can trigger uncontrollable moods in my child. I know his limitations and feel that it is my job as a parent to shelter him from things he is not equipped to handle. You wouldn't let a child just learning to use a wheelchair navigate a busy traffic crossing alone, and I don't give my emotionally challenged child carte blanche with the remote control—or any other form of media, for that matter.

Places to Avoid When Your Child Is Symptomatic
Probably one of the worst public meltdowns was when he screamed very loudly in a restaurant and overturned the table. I left the restaurant, and my husband paid the bill.
Sally, mom of a bipolar son diagnosed at age seven

Crowded stores, bowling alleys, brightly lit arcades, and movie theaters are hard to navigate with a child who is symptomatic or in any way unstable. Sometimes it's impossible to avoid them, so it's a good idea to come up with a game plan to detoxify the situation. Here are some ideas:

- Crowded stores. Try to find a corner where you can get away from it all. Bring a handheld computer game so the child can "zone" into fantasyland in spite of the chaos and confusion around him.
- Noisy places. Earplugs, earmuffs, or a warm, fuzzy hat will block out some of the noise. A personal CD player with relaxing music can drown out vacuum cleaners and other noises that a sensitive child can find unbearable.
- Places with bright lighting or other stimulants. Carry a pillow, blanket, or stuffed animal that the child can snuggle or bury his head into for comfort. Your lap or shoulder will do in a pinch.
- Emotional places. Cemeteries, memorial exhibits, fiery rallies, and picket lines are situations where emotions run high. Bipolar children with their hypersensitive minds may find places like this overwhelming.

Places to Go When Your Child Is Symptomatic
To help your child shift into a peaceful or productive mood,

seek out places that will restore, refresh, and rejuvenate his mind. Try these:

- The playground or park. Let your child "shake her sillies out" in the sandpit, on the monkey bars, on the swings, or walking along a wooded path.
- The swimming pool. Exercise plus hydrotherapy is a wonderful way for a child to relax and elicits soothing brain chemicals.
- Gym. Punch punching bags, ride exercise bikes, use rowing machines, play basketball—anything to expend that energy in a positive manner.
- The library. You can't find a quieter place than a library. Find a book for you and your child, and sit down together to read.
- A nature center. Animals often bring out the best in a child with raging emotions. Just petting a friendly dog can be therapeutic. Watch your child closely to make sure that he handles the animals with care.
- A music store. Let him bang the drum slowly, or quickly, whatever helps him express himself, tickle the ivories, or try out a guitar. Even if your child is not musical, he will appreciate the opportunity to work out his feelings through sound.
- Home. There is no place like home. Home is the best place for a bipolar child to let her hair down.

Nighttime

Bipolar children often have a tough time winding down at night. Leaving their homework for the last minute only makes them more anxious. It is not unusual for mania, depression, or anxiety to present at night, often combined with obsessive-compulsive behavior. Some children get unusually clingy at bedtime, insisting that you stay with them until they fall asleep.

The best thing you can do for a bipolar child is to establish an early bedtime. That means limiting the number of nighttime activities or cutting them short if necessary so that you stick to your schedule. The "let them play until they drop" routine doesn't work for bipolar children. They are likely to stay wound up, not drop from exhaustion. Make sure your babysitters are well versed in your established bedtime routine. Here are some hints to help:

- Invest a half hour each night to help your child unwind. Read to her, massage her feet (if she'll let you), sing to her, or say prayers. Develop and stick to a routine.
- Use a reward system to reinforce positive behavior. For each night your child goes to sleep on time and lets you leave the room before falling asleep, she earns a privilege. Eventually, you will no longer have to reward the effort; it will become routine.
- Try visualization audiotapes and CDs that lull her to sleep. Sleep tapes are available at www.chinaberry.com.
- One psychiatrist recommends Verilux lamps to his patients. These lamps simulate natural light and have a range of dimmer options. One model even has sleep and wake sounds: babbling brooks, birds tweeting, crickets in the forest. The psychiatrist feels that the sounds are soothing and that the simulated light makes the transition of day to night and night to day more palatable for bipolar children. You can find the Verilux products online at shop.store.yahoo.com/ampr/verilux.html.

Adhering to the Daily Schedule

Clearly, transitions, even the simplest ones, can be difficult for the bipolar child. So you may be wondering how realistic it is to expect that you can get your child to conform to any kind of structured schedule. It is hard to keep going when you know that at any time or place, your child may be unable to stick with the program you've mapped out. So why bother? Here's why.

Although bipolar children may have difficulty adhering to schedules, the schedules need to stay in place, with the understanding that there will be times that the child cannot fully participate in them. Structuring gives a child a sense of what will happen next, and there is safety in that knowledge. Prescribed routines let a child know that there is order in her world, even if her moods are out of control. The knowledge that a bedtime story is followed by a foot massage and lights out is very reassuring to these children, even though there will be days when it is all but impossible for her to sit quietly and listen to a story. Eventually, the mood will pass and you'll get back on track. Patience and flexibility will help you weather the gales.

Sick Days and School Holiday

I wanted to be a stay-at-home mom, but this is taking it to the limit. When she is sick, my life comes to a dead stop. Planning is nearly impossible.
Maria, mom of a bipolar daughter diagnosed at age three

When your bipolar child is sick, your life grinds to a halt. After dealing with the practical matters—a doctor's visit, prescriptions—you will be called on to put on your detective hat. Determining how much of a child's illness is physiologically based, how much is emotionally based, and how much may be due to toxicity from medication requires more than one or two parents; it calls for a triage team. Psychosomatic (or emotionally based) symptoms can include stomachaches, headaches, sore throat, nausea, shortness of breath, hyperventilation, muscle aches—all the things you would generally associate with serious illness. These symptoms aren't faked; they are real. The body releases chemicals in response to emotions, which create genuine physiological distress. You may see your child doubled over in very real pain from a psychosomatic illness. Work with your pediatrician or family doctor as well as with your psychiatrist to determine the cause of the illness. When my son stays home sick from school, he's not allowed overstimulating television and videos. Instead, he has free access to a "sick box" filled with books, games, and puzzles.

When a Holiday Is No Picnic!

I wish I could take him to Nochristmasland between Halloween and December 24 because the lights and music and all of civilization thrumming are just too much for him.
Deborah, mom of a bipolar son diagnosed at age eleven

While the rest of the world may look forward to the falling leaves and the first snowflakes of the season, parents of bipolar children know that the shorter, crisper days of autumn often bring with them dreaded depression and shifts in their meds. Conversely, longer and brighter days of spring can trigger mania. Fifty-three percent of parents of bipolar children who responded to my on-line questionnaire noticed mood changes around the change of seasons, and 63 percent noticed mood changes around the holidays.

Combine seasonal changes with overstimulating events like Halloween parades, Christmas parties, Passover Seders that stretch late into the evening, exciting vacations, school breaks, and lack of sleep due to late-night family get-togethers, and even nonbipolar children may feel stressed. The child with bipolar disorder has more trouble than others fine-tuning her system to cope with the changes. Sometimes the problem can be addressed with a subtle medication change. Other times, more intensive care is needed to get through seasons and holiday shifts.

Stick to the Schedule

Especially during vacation time, it is important for children, especially those with bipolar disorder, to have a schedule. When children know exactly how their day (or week) will progress, it gives them a certain sense of security. Although you don't have to give them a printed agenda, it is a good idea to sit down with them at breakfast (which should be eaten at a reasonable time in the morning) and clearly explain what you will be doing each day. Even if much of what they will do will be fun, they should know what time lunch and dinner are served, from when to when they will play outside, and what time they are expected to get ready for bed. If you are traveling or going on a trip, be sure to schedule in plenty of downtime, which may just be supervised TV time in the hotel room or time spent at the hotel pool.

Your Daily Schedule chart will help you plan holiday, vacation, and other transitory times. Fill in activities and note the exact time you expect to do them. An example of this chart with activities filled in is provided.

DAILY SCHEDULE

Holiday:_____

Day of Week:_____

Activity	Time	Activity Details
Wake Up		
Breakfast		
A.M. Activity		
Lunch		
P.M. Activity		
P.M. Activity		
Dinner		
Postdinner		
Bedtime		

Our school holiday schedules typically look something like this:

DAILY SCHEDULE   Holiday: Martin Luther King, Jr., Day

Day of Week: *Monday*

Activity	Time	Activity Details
Wake Up	8:00 A.M.	*Brush teeth, get dressed, come downstairs.*
Breakfast	8:30 A.M.	*Take meds.*
A.M. Activity	9:00 A.M.	*Videos, construction toy, let Mom work (for reward!).*
Lunch	11:30 A.M.	*Make peanut butter sandwiches. Take meds.*
P.M. Activity	12:30 P.M.	*Mom will take us ice-skating!*
P.M. Activity	3:00 P.M.	*Play outside with Patty.*
Dinner	5:30 P.M.	*Set table.*
Postdinner	6:30 P.M.	*Clear table. Get books ready for school tomorrow.*
Bedtime	8:30 P.M.	*Take meds. Mom is reading* Holes *by Louis Sacher.*

Gift Giving

The holiday seasons are just too much for him. He can't handle the people and gets manic when there are too many gifts.
Midge, mom of a bipolar son diagnosed at age eight

What is it about a stack of presents that makes a child impossible to deal with? Besides the excitement of opening them all, there are almost always other emotions to negotiate: disappointment when she doesn't get exactly what she wanted, jealousy because someone else did, frustration when the toy didn't come with batteries, disappointment when somebody "forgot" a present at home. It is important to try to avoid the arousal and overstimulation that come along with gift-centered holidays. Opening gifts in a subdued environment, away from crowds of family members, lights down, soft music, and the scent of sandalwood wafting through the air certainly couldn't hurt.

A Houseful of Guests

The day after Christmas, after dinner at my dad's, I noticed some signs he was getting ready to lose it—his face was flushed and he said he was "burning up." I quickly grabbed our things to leave. As we drove off, he melted down. He started screaming how much he hates everyone. He kicked the dashboard, cracking it in several places, and kicked the radio and the window. I pulled over to try and calm him down. He tried to get out, but I had the child safety on, so he couldn't open the door from the inside. He punched me, kicked me, and then bit my finger so hard I needed stitches. Then he started beating himself up. This lasted about an hour and a half. Once he snapped out of it, he was so upset about what he'd done that he said he wanted to kill himself.

He is a very compassionate and caring, loving child, and when he loses it like that, he feels terrible about it afterward.
Debbie, mom of a bipolar son diagnosed at age seven

A houseful of people is stress enough for adults. Children feel it too, whether they are bipolar or not. Children with bipolar disorder, however, are more likely to find crowds distressing and overstimulating. While other children are hugging their grandparents and charming the grown-ups with their cute antics, your child may be off in a corner, kicking a wall in a fretful moment or giddily jumping off the landing of your split-level home. Although a modicum of decorum is to be expected (demanding gifts from Aunt Mary as she walks through the front door is a *don't*), recognize that your child has limitations. The entire scene may be taxing his very limited resources. The good news is you can do some advance planning to avoid disasters:

- Quiet zone. Make sure that when you are entertaining, your bipolar child has a special place to go to "detoxify" during stressful periods. You may want to close off his room and announce that this area is off-limits to guests, so that he will have the space he needs to be by himself and relax.
- The great outdoors. Try to schedule some outdoor time in a nearby park or in the backyard.
- Games. Rent some new video games prior to the party, so if things get out of hand, you can pull a rabbit out of your hat. If your child is in an unstable mood state, make sure the video games are of the tamer variety.

Happy Birthday AARGH!

Birthdays often mean large groups of people, gifts, and sugary treats, often a disastrous combination for children with bipolar disorder. Here are some ways to minimize the birthday chaos and still celebrate your child's big day:

- Keep it small. Let your child choose just one friend to have over for a sleepover instead of partying with an entire crew. Take them out somewhere special the next day.
- Just family. This works only for younger children who will be stimulated enough by a family party and are less likely to notice the absence of friends.
- School party. Celebrate your child's birthday in school, which gives everybody a sense of structure instead of the usual party chaos.

If you do choose to have a big birthday party, which sometimes is unavoidable, invite kids *and* their folks. A near-equal number of adults and children will ensure that everyone, including the birthday child, has a great time, providing that the adults are focused on helping supervise their children.

Holiday Travel

Just recently, Thanksgiving was approaching, and Ben knew it was his father's turn to have the kids at his house for that holiday. As it got closer, Ben's stability started to slip. I finally asked him outright what was going on. He said it was just too hard to be what they expected him to be for a whole week. I chose to let him stay here, and called his dad and told him. After that, he was fine within a day or so.

Ricky, mom of a bipolar son diagnosed at age thirteen

Any disruption to a regular schedule is particularly rough on bipolar children, so it stands to reason that holiday traveling with them has to be done with extreme caution, serious planning, and the ultimate flexibility to do things differently. For the brave and the bold who decide to travel with a bipolar child, here are some tips:

- If possible, use refundable or flexible travel sources so you can retain the option of canceling, postponing, or changing plans at the last moment if necessary.
- Obtain a letter from your psychiatrist explaining your child's diagnosis and how it might affect him in a travel situation. Present the letter to customer relations to qualify your child for special privileges.
- If your vacation involves fun in the sun, remember that children on medications for bipolar disorder can be especially sensitive to the sun and heat. Make sure they stay hydrated at all times, and keep them cool and in the shade when possible. *Always* make sure they wear a hat, and take frequent breaks out of the sun to avoid toxicity and sun exhaustion.
- If possible, bring a child care provider, adult friend, or relative along to accompany your bipolar child. That way, she can go at her own pace, without slowing down the rest of the family.
- Call your planned destination spot, and let them know that you are traveling with a child with a diagnosed mood disorder and you were wondering what sort of accommodations the place might have to make your trip a bit smoother. In order to receive special accommodations, some places will require a letter; others won't. Some will have special methods enabling

you to cut through long lines and avoid meltdowns. Others may have special "rest areas" where children can "detox." While these amenities may not help you avoid every travel-related meltdown, taking advantage of these options can remove some of the stressors that can trigger an episode in a child with bipolar disorder.

Here are some questions you might want to ask as you're planning a trip:

Hotels, Resorts, and Cruise Ships

- I am traveling with a mentally ill child. Are there any local health organizations that may be helpful to me?
- If you have day care programs, what accommodations are available for children who are mentally ill?
- What is the ratio of adults to children in your day care program?
- Can you recommend a local babysitter who may be able to shadow my child at day care and camp activities?

Theme Parks

- What special accommodations, if any, do you have for children who are diagnosed with a mental illness?
- May the rest of the family accompany the child?
- Are there designated places for the child to take a break, away from the hustle and bustle of the park?
- Are there special staff members whom families can call on in case of an emergency?
- If we have to interrupt our visit because of the child's condition, may we return without having to pay again later that day? Later that week?

Notes from the Couch: A Psychiatrist's Point of View

In my experience, parents must be strongly encouraged to take care of themselves. Learning to soothe your own emotional reactions is a prerequisite for teaching your child the same skills. A frantic reaction to a child's meltdown will trigger an entirely different cascade of events than a calm, measured reaction will.

I encourage parents and teachers not to confuse structure with rigidity. Predictability is a building block in caring for your child, but keep in mind that meeting schedules and demands is extremely hard for children with mood disorders. Leave some slack in the system, and try not to turn the predictably unpredictable into major defeats for you and your child. Expect a rough road, and prepare for it. It makes all the difference in your responses.

I have banned the words *manipulative* and *attention getting* from my office. Bipolar kids are not in control of themselves when the moods are in charge. They aren't manipulating anything; they are being manipulated by their internal storms. They aren't seeking attention; they are getting unwanted negative responses, over and over again, and they can't change the cycle. These words are negative and pejorative. They serve no purpose in problem solving and strategizing with these children.

Giving commands and directions is a central part of parenting. Each time we give such a directive, the child must shift attention and energy from what he is doing to what the environment wants him to do. Children with bipolar disorder are not good at changing direction. Their mood and feeling brain centers are more in charge than their thinking centers. So if it feels bad to stop what they are doing, they don't. Don't interpret every slow response to commands as stubbornness or troublemaking. View it as a task more challenging to your child than it is to other children. Unfortunately, these slow responses can trigger a lot of shame and anger in us; we feel disrespected and powerless. But don't turn it into a power struggle.

My most common refrain with parents, especially parents of a child with reactive moods, is, "Stop talking." You can't convince your child that your interventions are right. You can't cajole him into the appropriate response. If you have made a decision that a particular negative behavior is under his control and needs correcting, state the behavior, outline the consequence, and walk away. Don't get caught up in a verbal barrage. Ignore it. Later, you will mete out the consequence and talk to the child—but only when everyone is calm.

CHAPTER 6

HOSPITALIZATION

When and How to Get 24/7 Care

According to Antonio Blanco, M.D., a child and adolescent psychiatrist at SLS Health in Brewster, New York, (www.slshealth.com), my frightening first experience with a psychiatric facility was a common one. Parents frequently balk at the thought of hospitalization. On the other hand, children are often willing, sometimes eager, patients. "It is very common for parents to experience guilt when their child needs hospitalization," explains Dr. Blanco.

Although the whole family is in crisis when a child is brought to the hospital, too often other family members' feelings are swept aside in the urgency to get help for the child at the center of it all. Part of seeing that child through the crisis is ensuring that the whole family comes to terms with what happened. My son's subsequent hospitalizations were done with as much planning, foresight, and cooperation from him as possible. In some cases, he had time to pack his pajamas and his favorite toys. He made a list of friends he would like notified so they could visit him. He even let me know what flavor cake he wanted for his "welcome home" party. Preparation makes a huge difference.

According to Paramjit Joshi, M.D., professor of psychiatry and pediatrics and chair of the Department of Psychiatry and Behavioral Sciences at Children's National Medical Center in Washington, D.C., 70 percent of admissions to her hospital's inpatient children's psychiatric unit are emergency admissions, giving parents and their children little, if any, time to prepare.

The data gleaned from my on-line survey back Dr. Joshi's claim: most respondents admitted their children in emergency situations.

More than half of the respondents to my on-line questionnaire indicated that their children have been hospitalized at one time or another for their bipolar disorder. Forty-two percent rated experiences at the hospitals as "fair," while 37 percent felt the experience was "poor." Only 21 percent of respondents had "good" experiences with their child's hospitalization. With some preparation, parents can assuage their guilt and cope better with the hospitalizations, and their children in turn will feel better about the transition. Your child may be on a downhill mood course, or the psychiatrist or therapist specifically suggests hospitalization. That's your cue to familiarize yourself with nearby hospitals, their admission and inpatient procedures, and their staff—before you have a full-blown crisis on your hands.

When Does a Child Need Hospitalization?

After a manic mood swing day in which he threatened to burn down our house and set me on fire, we hospitalized him. I did not know what putting him in a hospital would do for him. Our hearts broke when we had to leave him.
Jerry, dad of a bipolar son diagnosed at age eleven

A child going into a hospital is usually at a point where he is no longer able to control his actions, and his behavior has deteriorated to a point that his parents cannot keep him safe or protect other members of the family. Hospitalization is usually in order when the family is faced with one of the following situations:

- Evidence of potential harm or threat to harm self and/or others. Your child's anger and frustration are escalating in spite of therapeutic efforts, and she has been making threats or taking actions that could harm herself or others.
- Psychosis. If your child is hearing voices or dealing with acute paranoia or other psychotic symptoms, your doctors should evaluate the severity of his symptoms and may admit him to a hospital.
- Diagnostic clarification and observation. When the treatment team (psychiatrist and therapist) feels that all outpatient options have been exhausted and your child's symptoms continue to escalate, hospitalization is often the solution. There the professionals can closely study her on a twenty-four-hour basis.
- Medicine changes. A child who is in need of new medication or dosage changes may be hospitalized to ensure that no adverse or toxic effects result. This is usually done when the change has to be effected quickly and the shift can have serious ramifications.

Where Will You Go?

Most hospitals with children's psychiatric units tend to be academic centers—in other words, teaching hospitals affiliated with medical schools. Upon admission, an attending physician is assigned to your child, and residents, interns, medical students, psychologists, and therapists, all with various degrees of training, will be caring for or simply observing your child. There are professors and psychiatrists who, in teaching their students, may use your child's condition as an example of bipolar illness or ask you to enroll in a study.

Many teaching hospitals are high on the list of "best hospitals" compiled in *U.S. News & World Report's Best Psychiatric Hospitals for 2001.* Top hospitals included Massachusetts General in Boston; New York Presbyterian in New York City; C. F. Menninger Memorial in Topeka, Kansas; McLean Hospital near Boston; and Johns Hopkins in Baltimore.

Some independent private hospitals have children's psychiatric units, and some of these offer admitting privileges to psychiatrists with private practices, but this is the exception rather than the rule. If you prefer to have your own psychiatrist attend your child in the event of a hospitalization, you may want to find a psychiatrist associated with a hospital that you find acceptable.

Since you never know when a crisis may occur, it is a good idea to learn as much as you can beforehand and to stay updated on the status and changes of your choices of hospitals. Hospitals add programs and cut them. As your child grows, he may become ineligible for certain hospital programs and eligible for others, so the updating process is an ongoing one. Your child's psychiatrist and therapist should be aware of changes at area hospitals, so start by asking them for information.

You will also want to stay current with your insurance company, because its contracts with hospitals may change over time. Be sure to call ahead and find out which is the preferred hospital on your insurance plan and which hospital stays, if any, will be reimbursable.

When considering a child for a particular hospital program, doctors seek the environment that will be least restrictive. Because some hospitals offer partial hospitalization or outpatient programs, there are often choices that will be made based on your child's condition and particular needs.

While hospitals aren't always the most pleasant surroundings, they do provide around-the-clock observation, proper medication, on-site testing, and a stable environment. Families are encouraged to participate in the child's care. Done right, a hospitalization is a healing experience for the child and family.

Questions to Ask About Hospitalization

Prepare to wait an inordinate amount of time—hours and hours. Prepare for the possibility of being treated as if you were looking for free babysitting for the weekend. Prepare to be looked at like you have three heads if you ask, say, to be notified before any med changes are made or stray from the docile, angry, crying, scared parent plan, which is apparently how some staff members would prefer you. Prepare for the possibility of a total lack of compassion from any person you meet. Don't act too surprised if your experience is handled with compassion, expeditiousness, and competency.
Deborah, mom of a bipolar son diagnosed at age eleven

Here are some questions you should ask when your child is being considered for inpatient hospitalization. If the situation is not yet urgent and you are considering a hospitalization, call the hospitals ahead of time and weigh the answers against one another carefully. When the time comes and you need a bed, there may not be a lot of choices, but it's nevertheless wise to do your homework beforehand so you can express your preferences.

Contacts and Communication
- Who will be my key contact, and when is the best time and place to reach him or her?
- How will the inpatient treatment team communicate

with my child's own psychiatrist, pediatrician, and therapist?
- What happens when children get agitated? How are they handled?
- Will I be contacted if my child needs seclusion or restraint?
- If there is a medical concern, how will it be handled?
- What are the limits and rules about calls, both incoming and outgoing?
- Whom do I talk to if my child or I has a complaint about something on the unit?

Treatment Plan
- Will my child be aware of the treatment plan and the goals being set for her?
- How often will the treatment team meet with my child?
- What is the anticipated course of treatment for my child? If you can't tell me now, when do you expect to decide on one?
- What sort of therapies will be used in treating my child? To whom can I talk about them?
- What is the behavioral reward system in place for children as they master new emotional and behavioral skills?
- How can we as a family work with the treatment team to facilitate my child's recovery?
- What happens in the event of a dispute between the insurance company and the treatment team?

Medications
- What medications will be tried or changed?
- Will I be provided with complete information on all medications being administered?

Schedule

- What will my child's daily schedule be like?
- Is there therapy every day or just a "check-in" with the doctor or therapist?
- When are visiting hours, and how often do you recommend family visits?

Staff

- What is the staff-to-patient ratio?
- What kind of training does the general staff have in handling an agitated child?
- How will my child be taken care of in the event that another child on the unit has a psychiatric emergency?

Types of Programs

Partial Hospitalization Programs

Outpatient hospitalization, also called partial programs, provide daytime care only. Your child will sleep at home but spend each day in a school-like setting that is more contained than an ordinary school. A treatment team will be assigned to your child, just as in inpatient care. The focus of a partial program is to transition a child, stabilize medications, or offer the child clinical services that a school would be unable to effect. As with inpatient care, you might be offered the opportunity to participate in programs designed to train both family and child in living skills.

Residential Treatment Center

If a child is deemed too fragile, aggressive, or unstable to go home but is no longer so sick that she requires a hospital, she may be referred to a residential treatment center. (Chapter 7 provides more information about these programs.)

What If I Don't Choose Hospitalization?

There may be times when, in spite of dangerous symptoms, you may want to try to keep your child out of the hospital. It's hard to do with a deteriorating child and will take a certain level of commitment on your part as a parent. Avoiding the hospital will require the following from you:

- The commitment to be physically with your child 24/7. Only a parent or very close guardian—someone who is fully versed in what to do in case of emergency—should be trusted with your child when she is in a crisis mode.
- A crisis plan. This means that you and everyone else in your household must be 100 percent clear on what to do in case of a crisis. Who calls the police? How will you restrain your child? At what point will you do this?
- Immediate access to your child's psychiatrist or a crisis intervention team that can help talk you through situations as they arise.
- The commitment to increase the frequency of psychiatrist and therapist visits (e.g., to monitor your child or inform the care team of medication reactions).
- Immediate cessation of any and all negative stimuli (e.g., with school and siblings). This may mean sending siblings away to stay with friends or relatives for a few weeks and taking the bipolar child out of school until she is able to be eased back into some kind of program.

Siblings may need special attention and therapy sessions to help them work through the situation.

- Backup! Backup! Backup! If two parents are living in the household, it is important that *both* share the responsibility of caring for the child in this fragile state. If the child lives in a single-parent household or one parent refuses to help out, the child's caregiver must find some solid form of backup, be it a neighbor, a grandparent, or a best friend. If you attempt to keep your child out of the hospital without backup, you will drive yourself into a terrible state.

If you choose to avoid the hospital and assume this level of responsibility for your child, be sure to arrange for some kind of psychological support for yourself. The intensity of this level of care is bound to affect you, and you must factor in your own recreational and therapy time so you can continue to be there for your child.

What to Expect from Hospitalization

The Cast of Characters

Even if your child has been treated before, when he is hospitalized, there is a moment when primary care shifts from his private psychiatrist and therapist to a whole new cast of characters—a multidisciplinary treatment team. This usually includes a psychiatrist, psychiatric nursing staff, a psychiatric social worker, a special education teacher, a speech and language pathologist, expressive therapists (e.g., art, music, dance, and recreation therapists), a pediatrician, and staff mental health workers with varying levels of training. Your child's private psychiatrist and therapist will be given updates, but treatment decisions are wholly in the hands of the hospital crew.

Even if your child's psychiatrist is affiliated with the admitting hospital, he or she will often opt out of treating your child during the hospitalization so as not to interrupt the structure and continuity of care on the inpatient unit.

Of course, information still needs to flow between regular providers, parents, and hospital providers. The sharing of information is often facilitated during the admission process by a series of questionnaires and consent forms that parents must fill out and sign, enabling the hospital staff to collect information from other health care providers.

There is no question that this shift to a whole new network of providers, who will only temporarily care for your child, is a challenge. Be patient, and provide this new set of professionals as much information about your child's condition as possible so they can work well with your child.

Treatment Plan

The treatment plan designed by the treatment team should clearly delineate the diagnoses, target symptoms, short- and long-term goals, and criteria for discharge. It should also clarify what interventions are being used to achieve these goals. A good hospital program should inform the child of her goals so that she can participate in meeting them.

You will be asked to sign forms authorizing the hospital to administer medications to your child. This will include authorization to administer everything from prescription medications to Maalox in case of indigestion or Benadryl as a tranquilizing agent. You are entitled to information on all medications being administered.

According to Dr. Joshi, parents are an integral part of the treatment process, but they can sometimes be intrusive or, worse, lack involvement altogether. It is important for you to tread the fine line between advocacy for your child and interference with the healing process. It is also important to take advantage of the many opportunities hospitals have to offer. They range from group therapy to sibling management to participation in art therapy, recreation therapy, and other programs with your child.

On the Unit

Your first visit to a children's psychiatric ward may be eye-opening. Most facilities are kept locked. Staff members will use keys to admit you and unlock doors to let you out. Some hospitals have combination locks, and parents are given the entry codes.

Children are assigned rooms, sometimes private, and structure on the unit is usually extremely tight, often with a strict behavioral point system designed to monitor children from the time they wake up in the morning until the moment they go to sleep. In some hospitals, everything, including visits, is a "privilege" that is earned, in which case you may be turned away from visiting your child because she didn't earn the privilege that day. Other hospitals place a high value on parental visits, and while they may withhold snacks, treats, walks, or other incentives, they will postpone, not prohibit, parental visits when a child is agitated. Parents are usually given the opportunity to visit every day, and doctors agree that it is a good idea to visit often. That said, you should prepare to follow the rules carefully because you will be held to the same tight structure and discipline that is helping your child recover. "No candy" means *no* candy, and visiting hours are set in stone—no exceptions!

In the hospital, your child will be doing quite a bit of work. A typical day on one children's unit includes an hour and a half of individual sessions, an anger management group, "school" (a teacher comes in to work on academics), pet therapy or self-esteem or community project groups, arts and crafts or leisure skills, and a parent-child group. Snacks and meals are worked into the plan, and bedtime is at a fixed time.

Seclusion and Restraint

At the age of six, my son became hysterical over losing a game to me. This escalated into two and a half hours of his running, ranting, raging, and trying to push a pencil into his heart. I was scared he'd hurt himself, so I called a center, and they told me to bring him in for assessment. He ultimately stayed for six days. He got so upset when he realized that we were leaving him at the center that he carried on, and they tied him down to a bed, like an animal!!! I will never forget this as long as I live.

Shari, mom of a bipolar son diagnosed at age six

Much has been written about seclusion and restraint. In 1998, the *Hartford Courant* launched a national investigation that revealed over 142 deaths over a ten-year period due to the improper use of restraints on psychiatric patients, many of them children. Following this investigation, NAMI continued to compile reports of abuses. In September 2000, the U.S. Congress passed legislation that established national standards restricting the use of restraints and seclusion (R/S) in psychiatric facilities receiving federal funds and in nonmedical community-based facilities for children and youth. The resulting provisions ensure that restraints and involuntary seclusion may be imposed only to ensure the physical safety of a patient. They cannot be used as punishment or for staff convenience and may be imposed only under written order of physician or licensed practitioner under state law with specifics regarding duration and circumstances.

Just the thought of your child in restraints is heart wrenching, but the system is sometimes necessary in the course of treating mentally ill patients to protect your child and others in the immediate vicinity. Each hospital has its own policies, but usually when a child becomes agitated, the ideal response from the staff is one that defuses the situation and calms (not punishes) the child. The goal is to soothe the child and avert an explosion. Usually, the initial reaction by hospital staff is to halt the escalation with verbal prompts and reminders of the rules. Sometimes it works, and everything returns to normal. Other times, the child continues to escalate, and the staff places him in a time-out situation, to reduce stimuli and help calm his nervous system. This is an open time-out; he won't be shut behind a locked door, and the emphasis is on arousal reduction.

If an open time-out doesn't work, the next step is seclusion. Most hospitals have a "quiet room" that is windowless and sometimes lined with exercise mats. The child is put behind closed doors and observed, often by camera, usually with a staff member posted just outside. Most hospitals have stringent rules for observation during seclusion. Seclusion should be used only when other interventions have failed.

Sometimes a child cannot be trusted alone in a room. He may be trying to scratch or hurt himself in some way. That is when restraints are used. Smaller children are restrained by therapeutic holds—holding techniques that enable an adult to restrain a child with their arms and legs. It is considered calming and effective when done correctly, but it is not an option for bigger and stronger children and teens. For them, leather mechanical restraints are used because they are the safest and most effective means of protecting the patient and others. Two-point restraints bind two extremities (usually arms), and four-point restraints tie down all four extremities. If a patient is spitting or biting, her mouth may be covered with some form of light cloth. If she is flailing about and turning over the gurney, a net may be used to hold her torso down.

Straitjackets and blanket holds are older methods of restraint. Although they are still employed in some hospitals, they are not considered safe or optimal. Restraint is a delicate and risky process and should be done only by trained individuals. It should be done as quietly and efficiently as possible and in a way that doesn't humiliate or punish the patient. There are very strict rules for medical observation during restraint, and these should be followed to the letter, as it is a very serious business. On a well-run unit, restraint should be rare.

Be wary of hospitals that teach parents restraint techniques. They are *not* to be tried at home. Children have died as a result of being restrained improperly. If a child is so out of control that you feel you need to restrain him, it's time to look at inpatient programs.

Sometimes medication is used to help de-escalate an episode of agitation. Early on, a patient may be offered a mild sedative, to be taken by mouth, either an antihistamine like Benadryl or Risperdal, a more serious sedative. If a child is dangerously out of control or psychotic and seems to require restraints, an intramuscular medication like Ativan (a mild tranquilizer) or Haldol or Thorazine (antipsychotics) may be used. These stronger meds require parental permission (you will be asked to fill out medication administration forms "just in case" when your child is admitted), but it can be done without a parent's permission if it is considered a true emergency and the child is at risk of hurting himself or others.

Chemical restraint is sometimes seen as more humane than mechanical restraint. In any case, it is very serious business and should be discussed *before* there is a crisis, so a parent understands the situations that might arise and the options the hospital may use to address them.

Sibling and Other Visitors

He is the youngest and has three older siblings. They each visited him at the hospital. It's been hardest on the fourteen- and eighteen-year-olds. When he was first admitted, we took time to talk about it. We also took time to enjoy dinner out together and a little bit of a breather from a very stressful home life.

Lisa, mom of a bipolar son diagnosed at age ten

The first visitors besides parents are likely to be siblings. Because a visit to the children's unit of a psychiatric hospital can be intense, Dr. Joshi recommends that sibling visits be conducted in the hospital cafeteria or in a place similarly secluded from the stark realities of life on the unit. This isn't always possible.

A psychiatric hospitalization can be difficult to explain to siblings, who might perceive the hospital as "punishment" for bad behavior. When explaining the reasons for hospitalization, be sure to stress that you are doing it to keep your bipolar child safe and to make her better. Use your judgment to determine how much about the medical situation siblings are likely to understand, and keep it age appropriate. It is important that everyone feels comfortable with—or at least not alarmed by—hospitalization. This will help your bipolar child accept the situation and expedite recovery.

Visits are important to help boost the morale of the recovering child. Ask your child for a list of adult friends of the family whom you can tell about the hospitalization. Inform those friends, and invite them to visit. Remember that if your child was in the hospital for a physical illness, visitors would likely be streaming in and out, and balloons and flowers would brighten his room. These touches help a child realize that people love and support him and take away any shame about the hospitalization he may be feeling.

Take Advantage of All the Programs

While your child is in the hospital and possibly even after she is discharged, there are likely to be programs that you can participate in as a family and on your own. They range from art programs, to recreational programs, to group therapy (a terrific way to meet other families in similar situations). If your child is in an academic facility, you may be asked to participate in comprehensive programs that study your interactions as a family. Before you agree to participate in such a study, ask how it will benefit you. What will you and your family get out of the project besides a videotape of your family playing tic-tac-toe? If the answer is that your family will provide the teaching hospital with another case study to add to its collection, you can and probably should demur. Your time and energy are better spent in helping your child get better.

If you have family issues, now is the ideal time to work them out. Use couples therapy to help you get in sync with your spouse, and get siblings into family therapy to work out issues they may have with their bipolar sibling. Deal with events and issues that led to hospitalizations, and plan for the transitions ahead.

If your child is being treated at a teaching hospital, you are perfectly within your rights to limit your interactions with interns and medical students who may stop by with lists of questions of their own. If you have just finished answering the same set of questions and have had quite enough, inform them politely that you prefer to deal with the attending psychiatrist and that he has already gotten that information from you.

Appealing the Length of Stay

If you belong to a managed care organization, it will have rigid guidelines on coverage for inpatient hospital treatment and will try to reduce the stay to as short a time as possible.

Hospitalization can last for weeks, but insurance companies are only too anxious to get children out of the hospital, so some visits are so short that they give only a rudimentary evaluation and diagnosis. This can lead to erroneous diagnosis. If you feel that your child's hospitalization is being cut short by the insurance company before she has been thoroughly examined, correctly diagnosed, and treated, you may have to fight the battle, according to attorney Darcy Gruttadaro, author of NAMI's managed care litigation guide and director of the NAMI Child and Adolescent Action Center.

Here is a step-by-step guide to keeping your child an inpatient if you feel she needs more time in the hospital:

- **Due diligence.** Every insurance plan is required to have an internal appeal process. Review your insurance documents for information about the internal appeal process or expediting reviews. Then work the phones. Call your managed care company to find out who made the clinical decision to send your child home. If a customer service representative can't or won't answer your question, ask for a manager. While you are on the telephone, see if you can get the name of the highest-ranking official who decides clinical matters.

- **Contact.** Call the persons you've identified, and ask how to expedite an immediate appeals process. Get e-mail and fax numbers so you can send backup information. Keep track of all conversations, taking copious notes when you speak with anyone involved in this process.

- **Get providers to back you up.** Ask your child's attending psychiatrist to write a letter stating that it is medically necessary for your child to continue at this level of care. If you can, get your private psychiatrist to write a letter as well. Use faxes, e-mail, and other immediate means of getting the information to the insurance company.

- **Contact your state's Department of Insurance.** Each state has one. Call yours and ask for the ombudsperson in charge. Explain your situation, and ask if he or she can help you.

- **Use an attorney.** If you can afford it, hire an attorney to write a letter and help you fight to get your child the care she needs.

Going Home

Before a hospital will release a child, it is likely to offer the family the opportunity to take him out on the grounds of the hospitals, on short trips, and eventually home for a night or weekend to reacclimatize the child and the family. A child coming home from a hospitalization, whether for physical or mental illness, is fragile, and his adjustment should be gradual. Keep in mind that transitions are tough for everyone. Make every effort to ensure that home visits are as low stress as possible. Since the child is coming out of a very structured environment, now is the perfect time to establish behavioral systems and charts to help the child stay on track. Ask the hospital for copies of its point system, and keep it going, not just for the bipolar child but for siblings as well. Use the Sample Hospital Point System provided here. Psychiatric hospitals deal with large numbers of mentally ill children, and through these programs, they manage to keep vast numbers of them in line.

Ask your hospital contact for specific directions on how to adjust its system to your life at home, and begin the program the minute your child leaves the hospital. There is nothing like starting off on the right foot.

Sample Hospital Point System

Earn 4 points each hour—42 squares = 42 points
Level 1 = 32–42 points
Level 2 = 25–32 points
Level 3 = 15–25 points

Objective: Get to Level 1 and stay there.

Time	Gave Respect	Followed Rules	Stayed on Task	Feedback TO = Time Out NFD = Not Following Directions SFD = Slow to Follow Directions D = Disrespectful GW = Good Work NJ = Nice Job
Night–8 A.M.				
8–9 A.M.				
9–10 A.M.				

10–11 A.M.				
11 A.M.–12 P.M.				
12–1 P.M.				
1–2 P.M.				
2–3 P.M.				
3–4 P.M.				
4–5 P.M.				
6–7 P.M.				
7–8 P.M.				
8–9 P.M.				
Nighttime				

Hospital Discharge

Upon the child's discharge, parents will be given a discharge summary, which often states the patient's diagnosis and follow-up care regimen, including setting up an appointment with either an outside practitioner or one connected to the hospital within about ten days. Because it takes a little time to process the paperwork, you will have to wait to put in a request for a complete copy of your child's chart, which you'll need for your personal files. Dr. Joshi notes that doctors do record whatever they happen to observe and that some parents may not like their interpretations. You're still better off with it than without it. Since your child's school will want to see the records, read them carefully and judiciously screen out particular parts of the chart that you want to keep confidential, ensuring that the school gets the information it requires. "While chart information cannot be changed, addenda can be made to 'correct' any misstatements that were made during the admission process," Dr. Joshi points out.

Reentry

The transition from hospital to home can be a jolting one. Your child is coming from a place where he was under twenty-four-hour watch, held to strict discipline methods, and monitored for everything from drug compliance and behavior to grooming habits. You, as a parent, have adapted to living a disrupted lifestyle. Keep the homecoming as mellow as possible (*don't* throw a "welcome back" party with all of your child's friends).

You must be prepared for your child to take a slow but steady recuperative course. Everyone's feelings are tender, and getting back to what was once routine may take some time. A child may harbor resentment toward whoever suggested hospitalization in the first place. Others may be harboring guilt too. Continue family therapy as a tool to help the family reconnect.

Back to School

After the hospitalization, you may need to evaluate whether your school situation will work for your child. Some hospitals have transitional programs, such as partial programs that help the children ease back to school. Tracey Lynn Trudeau, a psychologist with the Edmonton Department of Emotional Behavioral Services in Edmonton, Canada, suggests that parents observe their child on return from the hospital:

- Is he well enough to attend school?
- Can he maintain a daily schedule and negotiate a routine successfully?
- Is he able to retain information, or does his memory seem impaired?
- Is he showing interest in hobbies and outside pursuits?

Often a hospital-homebound program can be put into place in the interim period before a child transitions back to school. During this period, a teacher from the school system is dispatched for a limited amount of time each day to help the child adjust and catch up on the schoolwork that might have been missed. The availability of homebound education largely depends on your school system.

Dr. Trudeau suggests we take our cues from the child, who may seem ready to take on a little bit more each day, from talking on the phone to rollerblading. She then suggests we ease our child back to the school situation we have worked out, anticipating possible anxiety that could stem from the child's being away from school for so long. Should the child balk or use manipulation to try to stay out of school, parents should use as evidence of improvement the fact that the child is now able to go shopping at the mall or spend two hours outside rollerblading.

During the homebound period, it is especially important for you to find time for yourself and your partner. Because you may not want to leave your child alone for any length of time (depending on the age and degree of stability displayed), you may well feel especially stressed-out at this time. Find support, whether it be a grandparent or neighbor. Depending on where you live, some mental health departments offer respite workers and peer advocates. At times like these, even a five-minute run to the grocery for a container of milk can seem like a two-week tropical vacation. You deserve it!

Although hospitalization is a gut-wrenching experience, it is often the first step on the path to better mental health.

Notes from the Couch: A Psychiatrist's Point of View

I have run many inpatient units and can definitively say that the single most important factor in a positive experience is a unit based on compassion and support rather than on judgment and punishment. Too many units focus on blaming the children or the parents or both. Get a sense of the unit by talking to the nurse manager or clinical director. Try to discern their general attitude and style. Sometimes reading between the lines of conversations is as important as what the person actually says.

Ask the hospital for a summary of the restraint and seclusion data on the unit. This may not be available to you, but showing your interest will alert the staff that you are seriously concerned about these interventions and won't take them lightly. There is a lot of heated debate in the psychiatric world about seclusion and restraint. Some experts say that it should never be used. I tend to agree. Make sure the unit you admit your child to has a very specific plan for reducing "arousal" and therefore frequency of seclusion and restraints.

Make sure discharge planning starts the minute your child is admitted. Who from the hospital team is talking to the school? What will be the plan for school after discharge? What other community resources can be mobilized? Can you get help with disability or insurance concerns? These questions can take a while to answer, and given the likelihood of a short hospital stay and possibly precipitous discharge based on insurance, you need to be prepared.

Part Two

Your Child in the World

DAY CARE, SCHOOLS, AND CAMPS

Finding Safe and Appropriate Care and Education

When she was three years old, her day care insisted I take her for counseling because she was assaulting the other children.
Anna, mom of a bipolar daughter diagnosed at age eight

For many parents of bipolar children, the first indication that something is terribly wrong is the seemingly revolving door of child care situations. About half of the respondents to my on-line questionnaire indicated that they had used child care (nanny, day care center, or family day care program) at one time or another. Those who used it frequently found new situations short-lived. Nannies left abruptly, many with explanations about the difficulties of the child. Family day care providers warned them about aggressive behaviors and the use of four-letter words. Day care centers battled daily with children over chronic separation anxiety. Many children were thrown out of day care centers for behavior that threatened other children. Often moms were forced to quit jobs and end careers to stay home with their child.

Day Care

It's difficult to find qualified, trained professionals for children *without* bipolar disorder. Add to this a child who is nearly impossible to discipline, who is irritable, manic, or depressed, who attacks siblings or other children, and the search becomes nearly impossible. If you are lucky enough to find a person who understands your child's condition, keep her forever and pay her well, because child care providers like this are hard to find and even harder to keep. Burnout is a frequent by-product of the child care field, particularly when caring for a bipolar child, so don't take providers for granted. Remember that we parents sometimes find dealing with our bipolar children overwhelming. Imagine how it is for caregivers who are *not* related to the child.

If you choose to use family day care or a day care center, be very mindful of the ratio of children to caregivers. Choose the smaller situation over the larger one, and find out if the provider or day care center has any experience with special needs children.

Whatever form of child care you opt to use, interview potential providers carefully. Here are some questions you may want to ask:

> "What did you like most about your last job? What did you dislike?" Listen carefully for clues about clashes she may have had with the children or employers.
>
> "Tell me about an average day on your last job." Compare in your mind the scope of responsibilities at her last job to those of caring for your bipolar child. Do they match up?
>
> "What do you feel a children's caregiver is responsible for?" If your child is disorganized and tends to strew

toys and clothing around and the child care provider is opposed to picking them up or helping a child pick up, you may have a problem.

"When is it okay to hit an unruly child?" This is a trick question. The answer, of course, is *never,* but you'd be surprised how many folks may come up with excuses for this one.

"How do you handle a child who is acting dangerously?" Of course, if you use this child care provider, you will give her guidelines as to how to handle your child, but see if she has a clue about what to do without your prompting.

"Complete this sentence: The biggest mistake today's parents make with their children is . . ." Listen for anything that indicates that she will be impatient or refuse to handle your child in the manner in which you would like him handled.

"What TV shows should a child never miss?" This is another trick question. There is *no* TV show that a child should never miss—unless the babysitter plans on teaching the child to tell time according to what TV show is on.

"What kind of physical activity do you like? How often do you do it?" Athletics are always a plus with any children, but especially with bipolar children, for whom activity is a natural serotonin regulator.

School

She was suspended and then expelled from kindergarten. We hadn't stabilized her on medications for first grade, so we had to fight for the "emotionally disturbed" label that

would get her into a smaller, more monitored program.
Patty, mom of a bipolar daughter

I refused to let the school label him "emotionally disturbed."
He was already "learning disabled," so they labeled him
"other health impaired."
Sharon, mom of an eleven-year-old bipolar son

Children diagnosed with bipolar disorder who have issues that interfere with their functioning at school will fall under the banner of learning disabled (LD), emotionally disturbed (ED), severely emotionally disturbed (SED), or other health impaired (OHI). Many parents resist letting educators apply labels to their child. There's no question these labels can be scary and stigmatic, but they can also translate into valuable special services for your child's education. Without that label, your child can't get the help she needs.

The Evaluation

Dr. Erika Karres, Ph.D., former teacher and professor in education at the University of North Carolina, says that many parents believe that their child will outgrow problems or erroneously believe that the only way to keep their child in the mainstream is to avoid labels. The strategy can backfire, Dr. Karres points out, because these children, although they may be very bright, are often lumped together with underachievers due to their lack of social and organizational skills. "The best thing a parent can do for her child is to get the diagnosis and an appropriate label," she asserts. "Mainstream teachers may not be prepared for children like this. They simply are not trained to deal with their problems. But if more parents embraced labels, the school system would be forced to provide more services."

State education systems receive federal funding to provide services for children like yours and have a responsibility to do so. The Individuals with Disabilities Education Act (IDEA) ensures that children with disabilities receive "free and appropriate" education. Note the word *appropriate,* which rarely, if ever, amounts to the best education available. That said, if a school system truly doesn't have what your child needs in place, it must find some other way to accommodate that child. Federal IDEA laws are being challenged as this book goes to press.

According to renowned educational attorney Reed Martin, three additional federal laws—the Americans with Disabilities Act (ADA), Section 504 of the Rehabilitation Act, and the Federal and Educational Rights and Privacy Act (FERPA)—also support your child's right to a special education. Significant time may elapse between the time your child begins school and the time when you and your school become aware of the scope of services that your child needs in order to thrive. And while the system is in place and must by law be made available to you, a budget-strapped school system may well resist spending on special services for your child unless you give the administrators no choice. Some school districts will take special needs seriously, but many do not. It's vital that you address your child's educational issues promptly, familiarize yourself with the options available to you, and steel yourself for a fight to get your child his due. The first step is having your child's needs formally evaluated.

Request in writing an evaluation from your school or from your local education department if your child is enrolled in private school. The department typically has thirty days to get it done. At the same time, you can have your child tested privately. Although not all schools accept the results of private testing, some do. In addition, the trained educational advocates who administer these tests will often guide you through the entire testing process.

Your child will be called out of class to spend time with the school psychologist or one contracted by the school. They will test his intelligence, observe his behavior, and administer other tests that measure academic achievement. If there is a school psychiatrist, he or she may be called in to evaluate your child's medical records and behavior. Your child's teacher will also submit information on where your child stands in comparison to other children (known as a grade-level comparison). The report is assembled in preparation for a meeting with the Special Education Committee.

Special Education Committee Meeting

Ideally, the Special Education Committee (SEC) meeting attendees will function as a team. The team will typically include:

- Director of special education or some similarly high-ranking special education official
- Your child's teacher
- The school psychologist (if there is one)
- The school social worker (if there is one)
- Any resource room teachers with whom your child might be working
- You and your spouse, therapist, and anyone else on your team
- In some cases, a school-appointed parent advocate
- In some cases, your child. Elementary school students may be invited to portions of the meeting depending on their maturity level and desire to be involved.

When the meeting involves transition planning for high school, the child must be invited.

Because there is safety and solidarity in numbers, prepare a united approach to the SEC meetings. Your team may also include your child's therapist and a paid or unpaid parent advocate of your own. Ask your psychiatrist for her recommendations in writing, and bring them along. Anyone who knows your child well—a grandmother or clergy member—can attend and speak on behalf of your child. Much depends on whether your school district is accommodating or combative when it comes to providing services. In certain situations, you may have to hire an educational attorney. If you bring your attorney, the district will likely bring an attorney to represent the district as well.

You can prepare for the meeting in other ways too:

- **A picture is worth a thousand words.** Tracey Lynn Trudeau, a psychologist with the Edmonton Department of Emotional Behavioral Services, has used PET scan pictures to show educators exactly what bipolar brains look like. In a study that she conducted on children returning to school after hospitalization for mental illness, one participant noted that if a child came back to school with an obvious disability, such as a leg amputated, school staff would immediately understand the problem and accommodate the child. Because mental illness is invisible—your child doesn't look any different than he did before his diagnosis—the school administration may assume that there's nothing really wrong. PET scans are a tangible means of showing educators that there is a measurable problem.
- **Hire an education advocate.** Education advocates are

often special education teachers or parents of children who at one time needed special education services; all are familiar with education law. These advocates guide parents through the process of obtaining services from the school district . . . for a fee.

Linda Dannemiller, an Arizona-based professional education advocate with a degree in psychology, educates parents on the fine points of the law and negotiates directly with schools on their behalf. "Parents are too trusting, and they often do not ask for things in writing," she states. "My rule of thumb is that if it's not in writing, it didn't happen. Ask for prior written notice from the school if it plans to deny a requested service. Written refusals like these can be taken to the state and appealed or taken to a court proceeding called due process."

Although hiring an education advocate is less costly than hiring an attorney, they're still expensive and usually paid for on a retainer basis. Education advocates don't commonly file lawsuits, although they may file complaints. They often do work with attorneys when cases turn into litigation.

If you decide to use an advocate, look for someone with a real understanding of bipolar disorder. You must feel comfortable in speaking with your advocate. How familiar is he with the staff at the state department of education? How closely does her agenda follow your own? Good oral and written skills are a must. Don't hesitate to ask for references from parents and professionals (psychiatrists, lawyers, and psychologists) who have worked with the advocate before.

- **Meet my child.** Missy, a mom who shares a bipolar diagnosis with her sixteen-year-old son, put together information packets and passed them out to everyone who came to her son's SEC meeting. The packets included a photo of her son and information on what she would like for him, as well as what he would like for himself. Also included was an explanation of the bipolar condition and tips that Missy wrote about how best to deal with her bipolar child.

- **Play the role of education advocate however you can.** Collect and disseminate informational leaflets and brochures (NAMI and other mental health organizations have plenty of handouts); refer school system staff to Web sites; or offer to loan your own books and materials to teachers, special education staff, and the administration. Smaller school districts especially may have had very little experience with bipolar disorder, so it's up to you to trailblaze for your child and for others who will undoubtedly follow in your child's footsteps.

It is a good idea to go into your SEC meeting with a very clear picture of what your child needs educationally, socially, and emotionally to succeed in school. If you are unclear about the range of services you're within your rights to request, have a discussion with your child's therapist or consult with a professional advocate or attorney on educational solutions for your child. The evaluations and testing will help to determine if your child has a learning disability (as many bipolar children do), physical problems (such as speech or grapho-motor disorders), or emotional problems that interfere with learning.

The Individualized Education Program

The outcome of the SEC meeting is an Individualized Education Program (IEP) to help your child through school. This program will be amended as your child grows and her needs change. Although IEP formats vary by school and state, the following general information must be contained in the IEP document:

- The child's performance level academically, socially, and psychologically
- Goals and objectives, both long and short term
- Specific tools for measuring progress
- Program modifications, devices and supplementary aids, special education services, and other allowances that will be made for your child
- Extent of mainstreaming with nondisabled children
- Test-taking allowances for statewide exams
- Specifics regarding when the program will start, how long it will be in effect, and the extent of services to be offered
- Reporting methods to be used to communicate progress
- Transitioning services (from age fourteen on) that discuss agencies that may take over providing services after high school
- A statement that a child who is reaching adulthood (one year prior) is informed about the transition that will take place

Destination: School

As you negotiate and navigate the various options available in schooling, you may be fortunate not to have to make too many stops. Other parents may need to stay on the "school bus" a bit longer until they reach their destination.

> ### First Stop: To Mainstream or Not to Mainstream
> *They attempted to keep him in mainstream, but after he had stabbed the first-grade teacher with the tip of his pencil and was suspended from school, they put him in a self-contained class—a small class with kids with emotional problems. That was awful. They have now placed him out of district at a behavioral school.*
> **Kitty, mom of a bipolar son diagnosed at age seven**

One of the biggest questions you will face on your quest to find an optimal learning environment for your child is whether to mainstream. Being in the mainstream keeps a child in the vast social circle of school. He doesn't feel singled out or abnormal. On the other hand, when a child returns to school after an episode or hospitalization, his emotional fragility may make it difficult for him to get back into the swing of things. As children approach middle school, they are often expected to exhibit more emotional maturity and independence. For some bipolar children, this level of independence can be overwhelming. Should your child be mainstreamed or in a self-contained class? Here are some issues to consider:

- Does he have difficulties being in a mainstream-size classroom?
- Is she able to focus in a regular classroom?
- Is he able to behave in a regular classroom?
- Will her anxieties interfere with her learning?

- Will he be able to handle the social scene at recess or lunch when adult supervision is generally at its most lax?
- Does she need so much one-on-one attention from the teacher that she'll call attention to herself?
- Does the mainstream teacher truly understand his condition and know what to do in the event of a mood meltdown?
- Is she able to make and maintain social relationships in the mainstream?
- Does he feel intimidated by the crowds, noise level, or other aspects of the school?
- Is she able to get into a routine at school?
- How well can school faculty respond to his needs?
- Will the mainstream teachers be able to implement crisis plans for her?

Dr. Trudeau points out that your child's response to medication (or lack thereof) will play a large role in determining whether he should be mainstreamed. She urges parents to make decisions based on the child's needs, not their own, and strongly suggests that parents honestly examine their own feelings about the issue. Is guilt or social stigma, rather than your child's needs, driving your decision to mainstream?

For some, mainstreaming feels like setting your child adrift in the Pacific on a raft. But a smaller class chock-full of emotionally disturbed children comes with its own set of problems. Children with psychiatric problems often fall into one of two categories: those with fragile personalities and those who have developed conduct disorders such as oppositional defiant disorder (ODD) or other aggressive tendencies. Putting a fragile bipolar child with paranoid tendencies into a roomful of adolescents with ODD can be a terrible mistake. Some schools separate out the fragile children and have special classes just for them. Others do not. It is imperative that you visit the classrooms before you make a decision. Are children learning independently? What support systems are in place for those who need extra learning help and emotional support?

Mainstreaming can be more difficult as a child enters middle school. He must exhibit independence—getting from class to class unsupervised, organizing a voluminous and sometimes confusing workload, and dealing with a new level of coed socializing. Frequently bipolar children lack the maturity and social skills to negotiate these mainstream challenges without a strong support system such as social skills classes and therapy.

If you are trying to maintain your child in a public school setting, your wish list of accommodations will largely depend on the symptoms that your child exhibits. An excellent listing of bipolar symptoms and accommodations parents can ask for is available on the Child and Adolescent Bipolar Foundation (CABF) Web site at www.bpkids.org.

Second Stop: In-District Therapeutic Support Programs

If the mainstream public school is not meeting your child's educational needs, some schools offer in-district therapeutic support programs (TSP). These programs are usually small, self-contained classes, often with fewer than ten children, with two or sometimes three dedicated staff members (a teacher and one or two aides). In addition, therapeutic programs usually include individual or group therapy sessions and a self-contained gym class. Some include music, art, or drama therapy classes. The workload is often scaled back to alleviate stress, and the children are encouraged to achieve by positive reinforcement programs, such as "earning" pizza parties, prizes, and privileges that will enable them to slowly rejoin the mainstream school community. Your schools may offer a variation on this theme. You're looking for a situation where educators can adjust workloads to accommodate the student's fluctuating moods and provide therapy when meltdowns do occur.

Third Stop: Out-of-District Public Schools

Smaller districts don't always have enough students in need of special services to fill a therapeutic class. The logical solution to this problem is to send the child to a nearby school that does. If an out-of-district placement is decided on, parents are usually offered the opportunity to visit several schools to determine whether the program will accommodate their child. Use your wish list to determine whether the class offers accommodations that will work for your child. Find out how long the placement will be in effect because some classes cater only to certain grade levels, and then you will have to look around for another placement, which means yet another transition for your child.

Fourth Stop: Private School Placement

Each stop along the road to finding the right school for your child represents a greater financial commitment from your school district. Don't be surprised if the SEC balks, particularly when a private school placement is on your agenda. These schools are far more costly than the public schools. You will have to prove to the district that this is the only school that will suit your child's needs. This will take preparation and research on your part, and will likely necessitate bringing in an attorney to help you make your case.

If you have been approved for an out-of-district placement, your school district will likely inform you of some of the choices available to you, but don't rely on them alone. Do your own research into private schools and their amenities. Here are some questions to ask:

- How many children are in the class, and what is the maximum that may be enrolled?
- What are the diagnoses of the other children? Are they fragile or conduct disordered?
- What is the staff-to-student ratio?
- How does the school help children with their social skills?
- Are there social skills classes?
- Is there one-to-one counseling?
- Is there group counseling?
- What other programs are designed to help children with bipolar disorder?
- Where would my child place in the class academically?
- Are there children who live near me enrolled at the school?
- What kind of extracurricular programs does the school offer, and how are they supervised?

The Last Stop: Residential Treatment Facility (RTC)

If you've tried more than one option offered by the school district and your child is still teetering on the edge of instability (his safety and others' is still at risk), there is one more option: residential treatment. Residential treatment centers are the most restrictive settings for bipolar treatment, but many parents turn to them when they feel they can no longer cope with the daily challenge of caring for their child.

"It's hard to say what might cause an imbalance that will necessitate residential care," explains Mona Swanson, A.C.S.W., and a vice president at Children's Village, a residential treatment center based in Dobbs Ferry, New York. "Changes in the family, developmental changes in the child, difficult social situations or school situations that just aren't working, the onset of adolescence—any of those shifts could start you thinking seriously about residential treatment."

After her nine-year-old bipolar son flew into several uncontrollable rages at school, Cynthia was forced to put Josh in a residential treatment center, the option deemed least restrictive for his situation. Residential facilities range from secure locked facilities to an open campus where residents come and go as they please. A good residential treatment center will combine meticulous structure with plenty of recreational activities. The child who does best in a residential facility is one who has trouble negotiating a toxic situation at home—perhaps an unstable bipolar parent or an abusive situation. A wide range of situations make it hard for a bipolar child to function and interact normally with others in the family. The ideal residential facility will allow a child or adolescent to earn privileges of greater freedom and less structure for good behavior. Some facilities compensate residents for chores.

According to Mona Swanson, the length of stay at a residential facility can range from six months to several years.

Before putting your child in a residential program, ascertain how the facility will involve you as a parent:

• Will you have open access to your child's caseworker and to other school personnel?

- Will you be consulted about medication and treatment changes?
- Will you be informed about outstanding incidents (your child ran away, had a fight, somehow obtained a tattoo)?
- Will there be team meetings or some other form of involvement to update you on your child's condition?
- How will the school handle it if the child wants nothing to do with you?

Make sure you are on the same page as the treatment facility and that it will value your involvement. If the facility doesn't care to involve you, find another facility—one that closer matches your own philosophy. A good residential facility should aim toward eventually releasing your child to a less restrictive environment.

If the School Says No

According to education advocate Linda Dannemiller, an IEP is a contract. If a school refuses to provide services agreed on in the IEP, a parent is entitled to file a complaint with the state department of education. In most states, an investigator is sent within sixty days to ensure that all elements of the IDEA are being followed. If the law is being violated, a "Letter of Finding" will be sent out indicating that the school district has violated federal law. Corrective action will be instituted, which can range from in-house training to compensatory education, which can be tutoring or financial reimbursements for catchup or summer programs. In Arizona and Montana, parents work with a compliance officer as soon as a problem surfaces to expedite early complaint resolutions.

The Final Responsibility

If you cannot find an out-of-district placement that is appropriate or could accommodate your child, the situation has to be reevaluated. Ultimately, it is the school district's responsibility to provide a program for a child with special needs. If the program doesn't exist, the school district must create it, according to current IDEA laws. Linda Dannemiller believes that schools must exercise creativity in such circumstances. For instance, new services may be added to an existing school program that was previously deemed unsuitable. "The first letter in the acronym IDEA stands for *individual*," explains Dannemiller. "The program may have to be customized for just one child. If that's the only way the school can provide for that child, so be it!"

Document Everything

Just as you did with your child's medical records and information on her moods and medications, it is important that you document all day care (and other school-related) documents as well. Keep this information in a dedicated file on the computer or in your file cabinet. Put as much as you can in writing. Keep a log of phone calls, documenting what was said and when. Follow up every telephone promise with a written note to everyone involved. Documenting things will create a paper trail that can help you get what you need from the bureaucratic educational and legal systems that may be less than forthcoming. Sometimes a well-timed letter or documented phone call can make the difference between receiving or being denied certain services.

Homeschooling

Last year, we had to pull him out and homeschool him due to numerous suspensions and escalating behaviors.
Tim and Tricia, parents of a bipolar son diagnosed at age nine.

Over the years, homeschooling has evolved into a viable alternative for children who don't respond well to the traditional school system, as well as for parents who object to the school policies and curricula. Sometimes homeschooling is imposed on a family after an incident at school or posthospitalization.

Cindy decided to homeschool her bipolar child after getting regular calls about her child "shutting down" at school. Finally, the school asked him to leave. The school system labeled her child as a behavior problem and said it could not meet his needs. Cindy agreed, but she felt that the next step— a self-contained school that the school wanted her to try and higher doses of medication—was an unacceptable solution. The school district planned to contribute nothing in terms of professional therapy, money, or books.

Cindy says homeschooling puts a lot less pressure on her; she is not "jumping every time the phone rings." On the other hand, the barrage of chatter from the minute her son gets up until bedtime makes her yearn for a well-earned break. She hopes eventually to find a better placement for her son and views homeschooling as an interim solution.

Should you feel that homeschooling is a better option than the ones the school system is offering you, you can negotiate with the school using legal means to try to get it to pay for some or part of it. In some cases, the district will provide or pay for tutors. In other cases, you might receive no more than textbooks. Unfortunately, in the vast majority of cases, you'll have no district support.

Jennie Rakestraw, associate dean of education at Georgia Southern University, an expert in homeschooling, counsels that parents considering homeschooling their bipolar child do their homework carefully. "Parents should look within their community and state to find a homeschool support network near them," she suggests. "Almost every state has an established network through which you can reach other homeschoolers. Look for families who share your concerns, and ask a lot of questions before making the commitment to homeschooling."

If you are planning to homeschool, here are some suggestions, put together with the help of Dr. Rakestraw:

- Research, research, research. There are voluminous sources on the Internet to help you decide if homeschooling will work for you. Contact homeschooling parents, and ask lots of questions.
- Before you decide to homeschool, ask to observe your child in the classroom to get a sense of her strengths and weaknesses in various subject areas. If she is in an interim situation (hospital or home), sit in on her tutoring sessions.
- Contact your school district to find out the state and local laws about homeschooling (a great place to start is www.homeschoolcentral.com).
- Visit your local college bookstore, and look for methods books on teaching. Understand that you will have to teach subjects you are not particularly fond of and things that your child may not like either. Try to come up with creative ways to relearn the things you've for-

gotten. You may have to find someone else to teach certain subjects to your child.

- Just as a regular school program would incorporate accommodations for your child, you will have to scale your curricula and program to accommodate your child's special needs.

Summer Strategies

As your child emerges from her winter doldrums, you'll need to focus on what she's going to do for the summer. It is hard to plan too far in advance if your child isn't very stable, but you are going to have to do some advance planning and hope for the best.

Twelve-Month IEPs

It is possible to obtain a year-round IEP that will entitle your child to summer schooling, which is usually less academically rigorous and involves physical activity and programmed trips. It is ideal for those with children who are seriously challenged by the school start and summer break transitions.

Mainstream Camp

If your child is able to negotiate mainstream camp, it is terrific for both parent and child. A mainstream camp can give a child with bipolar disorder the opportunity to start anew with friends who aren't necessarily familiar with his spotty history. It is no longer unusual for mainstream camps to accept children on medication. One camp director told me that most of her campers were medicated for one thing or another.

If you are sending your child to overnight camp, make sure the camp doctor and nurse are very aware of the need to keep your child medicated (if he is) and to watch for side effects. Educate them about the bipolar diagnosis, and help them put together a crisis plan, just in case. If your child is going to day camp, you may remain in charge of his meds, but you'll definitely want to tell the camp doctor or nurse to watch for side effects. Counselors should be informed of his condition just as his teachers are.

According to Karenne Bloomgarden, camp consultant, special education teacher, and overall children's advocate, some parents actually take their children off medications rather than deal with the stigma of having the child take medications at camp. This is a *huge mistake*. Doing it during a transition period like summer vacation can cause a child to start cycling.

When a mainstream camp director says that he will accept a child, ask how he plans to prepare the staff. It is not always as cut-and-dried as a camp director might like to think, and it is up to you to ensure that the camp is adequately prepared. If a camp director says that he doesn't know if the camp can accommodate your child, Bloomgarden says not to push it. The camp director may be telling you that counselors are simply not capable of dealing with children who need special attention. Unless the camp director seems eager to accommodate your child, it's better to seek out another situation.

If you want to keep your child in a mainstream camp but are uneasy about how she will get along with the other children, you can hire a shadow to be there just for your child. A shadow is a specially hired counselor, sometimes a counselor-in-training, who stays with your child and her bunkmates and helps your child in the event of a social problem or conflict. It can be costly but worth the peace of mind if you doubt whether your child will successfully negotiate the pressures of a mainstream environment. Sometimes the camp director will guide you to someone appropriate, but more often, it will be your job to provide the shadow. Find a neighborhood teen who has a special relationship with your child, or post a bulletin board advertisement in a college with special education programs.

Special Camps

Camps for children with emotional and developmental disabilities are few and far between, according to Karenne Bloomgarden. Given the additional costs of caring for a special needs population (e.g., more staff, trained health professionals), it simply isn't very profitable.

Special needs camps exist, but they are either very expensive or run by nonprofit organizations. The latter have sliding-scale fees and generally cannot afford to provide the best facilities and counselors. The pricier camps can cost $7,500 and upward for a summer. There are also outdoors wilderness and twelve-step type camps, but these are usually reserved for troubled teens, not for younger or fragile children with emotional disorders.

The pricier camps are often staffed by special education teachers, but that does not necessarily ensure quality, says Bloomgarden. She suggests that when choosing a camp for your child with bipolar disorder, you ask the following questions:

"Will the cabin counselor be with my child twenty-four hours a day?" It is important to ensure that your child has someone available to him at all times. Find out who that person is likely to be and who will be there when that person is not.

"Who else will be with my child each day?" Find out how educated and trained the other counselors will be.

"Will the counselors be specialists?" Here is your chance to find out how many, if any, special education teachers or other professionals will be working at this camp.

"Are the counselors foreign students?" Some camps hire foreign staff for a variety of reasons. Find out how many, if any, will be working at the camp and in what capacity. You might also want to find out if they all speak English and if they have any familiarity with working with emotionally disturbed children.

"Are all kids—those with developmental, behavioral, and emotional problems—mixed together?" While it is wonderful to develop tolerance, a child with bipolar disorder may become quite frustrated if his day is spent with children who are developmentally less functional than he is. Ask about the milieu and how and when the campers spend time together.

"How team-sport-oriented is the camp?" You can assess this by taking a look at the camp schedule. If it appears that the children are hopping from one sport to another, the atmosphere may prove to be quite competitive. Does your child fare well in this type of atmosphere?

"My child is not a competitive type and the camp seems oriented to specific sports or activities. How will you incorporate him into the activities?" Again, depending on the answers, this camp may or may not be right for your child.

"Does the camp employ people with disabilities?" This could give you a hint as to how tolerant a camp would be about your child's disability.

"Will there be social skills groups, therapy, or other interventions to help children have a successful summer experience?" For a bipolar child, these can make the difference between a successful camp experience and one that is unsatisfactory.

Notes from the Couch: A Psychiatrist's Point of View

In terms of school planning, networking with other parents is invaluable. Informal and formal groups of interested parents always form around kids with special needs. One of my parents calls it the "Mommy Mafia." You can find out lots of information about rights and resources from parents who have been there. You also get emotional support. Don't be shy. Go to meetings. If your district doesn't have a "special education PTA," start one—either alone or with other districts if your district is small. Contact special education departments at local colleges for information and ideas. I often ask very involved parents if I can share their names with other families. Most are happy to help. They have been down this road and know it can be dark and lonely. They'll give what guidance they can.

In general, I prefer that families keep lines of communication open with schools. Some parents are reluctant to inform school staff when their child is diagnosed because they fear stigma and backlash. I am actually much more worried about ignorance than I am about stigma. I want the schools to know that this is an illness that can be treated. I've run into a few teachers and administrators who don't believe bipolar disorder is "real" or who respond poorly, but they are the minority. And I would rather work with those hard-core naysayers than communicate through our actions that we are ashamed of the illness and unwilling to talk about it.

I work with school districts and am also an advocate for my private patients when they go to special education meetings. I am sometimes stunned at the lack of services or lack of professional educators' awareness. Other times I'm amazed at the skill and sensitivity displayed by overworked teachers and administrators. Hang in there. You will find the right placement as long as you keep plugging and as long as you eventually find someone in the system who "gets it."

CHAPTER 8

FRIENDS AND FAMILY

When and How to Explain
Your Child's Condition

*I'm very open about it. We needed to come out of the closet
to gain acceptance and to help others who struggle silently.*
Jenna, mom of a bipolar son diagnosed at age nine

*The behaviors can be very embarrassing at times. If some-
one I don't know asks what the problem is, I sometimes say
she has rages she can't control and leave it at that.*
**Leslie, mom of a bipolar daughter diagnosed at age
thirteen**

"I was hoping the girls in the back of the van didn't notice," the
mom of one of my Girl Scouts sadly informed me. "But they
did. They asked why he was saying such terrible things to his
mother—to their scout leader. I didn't know what to tell them."

I didn't know what to tell them either, nor did I have a clue
how to explain it to this mom. My son had just had a full-
blown fit, complete with cursing and crying. He threatened to
jump out of the carful of Girl Scouts I was driving home from
a local event. What could I say? Should I tell her the truth? I've
learned that if I am going to circulate in public, there will be
incidents like this one. There are times when the situations
seem to demand a public apology. There are times when I just
don't know where to begin.

For some families, the pain of having to explain such behaviors is so overwhelming that they isolate themselves. They withdraw their child from sports activities, from extracurricular programs, from community centers, and from youth groups. They withdraw themselves, opting out of the PTA, church, and social activities. But sharing the burden can be cathartic. Withdrawing is often the *worst* thing a child and family can do. You would be surprised how many people really do want to understand or have been through something a lot like what you're struggling with. The best part about "telling" is connecting with others who have similar challenges. They can be a tremendous support.

The issue boils down to determining whom it is appropriate to inform. Most of the parents interviewed for this book felt that in spite of the stigma, it was vital to spread the word and educate people about their children's disorder. "One of the contributing factors of stigma is keeping it in the closet," says Stella March, coordinator of NAMI's Stigma Busters e-mail alert campaign and the mom of a son with severe mental illness. "If you come out and talk about it, you'll often find that the person you're chatting with knows somebody or is related to somebody with a mental disorder—which makes sense, since an estimated one in five people has a mental illness."

Whom to Tell

I talk to friends and family to maintain a cushion of support, and I pray.
Janice, mom of a bipolar son diagnosed at age fifteen

This is the crux of the problem. On the one hand, parents often desperately need to reach out. After all, it vindicates our parenting skills. We can "explain" our child's eccentricities as something (anything!) other than "bad behavior." But on the other hand, no child wants to live with the disgrace of being "mental" or "nuts"—terms that children mindlessly toss around in the schoolyard. Sadly, these labels are often reinforced by an uneducated and uncaring media.

As Told by Ginger, a show broadcast on Nickelodeon, featured an episode titled "Lunatic Lake" where a "crazy bipolar man" escaped from a mental institution. The cartoon, which is geared for adolescents, portrayed the bipolar patient barking like a dog and generally acting crazy. My son was insulted by the portrayal and fired off an angry missive to its writers and producers. Without informing them of his condition, he let them know exactly how he felt about the bipolar character: "Not many bipolar people that I know move their eyes in circles and bark like dogs—and I've known many! I wonder if in the future you will have characters that are autistic, diabetic, bald from cancer treatments or limping from polio? I think you should make an episode of *As Told by Ginger* where there's a quiet bipolar kid who keeps getting bullied and eventually becomes very popular. That way you could teach people that being bipolar doesn't mean you're crazy. If you need help thinking of ideas, feel free to contact me." He never got a response.

Because mental illness, unlike other illnesses, carries a unique stigma, particularly for its youngest victims, you need to know how to make good decisions about whom to share this sensitive information with. Everyone you and your family interact with falls into one of three categories:

- Those who absolutely must be told
- Those who should probably never be told
- Those who should be told judiciously as needed

The "Whom to Tell" Venn diagram shows who might belong in the categories.

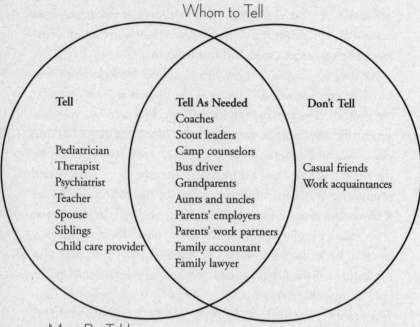

Whom to Tell

Tell

Pediatrician
Therapist
Psychiatrist
Teacher
Spouse
Siblings
Child care provider

Tell As Needed
Coaches
Scout leaders
Camp counselors
Bus driver
Grandparents
Aunts and uncles
Parents' employers
Parents' work partners
Family accountant
Family lawyer

Don't Tell

Casual friends
Work acquaintances

Must Be Told

Depending on the severity of your child's symptoms and recurrences, there will be people who must be told about her diagnosis and treatment. Using a Venn diagram like the one shown here, make a list of the people who must be told. These should include any medical staff who deal with your child and will likely include people who interact closely with your child on a daily basis, such as teachers, after-school child care providers, or regular babysitters.

Tell As Needed or Don't Tell

The people on your "as-needed" list should include anyone

who has close contact with your child and whom you or family members may call on during a crisis. You may ask them to dispense medication during a sleepover, monitor behavior and report back to you during a play date, or consult for their professional nonmedical advice on issues pertaining to your child. The list can also include anyone whom you feel comfortable enough to confide in or who may be able to provide support. It could include sports coaches, neighbors, and close relatives who may be called on to care for a sibling during your bipolar child's hospitalization. There is never a hard-and-fast rule for this category. It is largely up to you. Ask yourself:

- What is the downside of telling this person?
- How is she likely to react?
- Can I rely on her to offer emotional or tangible support to my family when my child is in crisis?
- Is she a gossip? If I tell her, will the whole community or workplace soon know?
- Is my child likely to mind that I shared our situation?

Use your answers to determine whom to put into the "as-needed" and "don't tell" categories. Review your diagram and weigh the options of telling versus keeping silent. When making this decision, balance your need for support against your child's desire for privacy. No one ever said it would be easy.

When You Decide to Share

Do not let parents of "normal" children berate you. Remember that you can educate them too.
Sue Ellen, mom of a bipolar son diagnosed at age thirteen

There are a lot of judgmental people out there, particularly when it comes to child rearing. Helen, mom of Peter, diagnosed at age nine with bipolar disorder, felt she had to let her son's baseball coach know about his illness after her son stalked off the field in the midst of an important game. He was becoming increasingly unstable, and she wanted to make sure that the coach knew what to look out for in terms of warning signs. Taking the coach aside, she explained the illness to him, and she braced for a scornful reaction. She was surprised when he sympathetically took her hand. "He said it explained a lot of the small incidents that had been happening at practices when I wasn't around," Helen said. "He said that knowing about my son's illness would help him—not just in relating to Peter but also in just-in-case backup planning for future games. He even struck a private deal with Peter, awarding him baseball cards each time he held it together at a practice or a game. It made an immense difference to Peter and to us."

Shortly after the conversation, Peter was hospitalized, and his coach visited him in the hospital. Helen was even more amazed when, during the ten-day hospitalization, the coach's wife showed up at her doorstep with a casserole. "Our whole family, not just Peter, really benefited from the disclosure," Helen recalled.

Telling about your child's bipolar condition can feel like you're "outing" yourself and your child. Here are some guidelines for talking about your child's illness:

- Explain that she has a neurobiological illness called bipolar disorder.
- Briefly describe some of the symptoms that the person may have observed in your child.
- If you are telling the person for a particular reason

(e.g., to effect changes in how your child is treated, or to see if your friend will take your bipolar child's sibling while you run with him to the therapist), be direct and explain your needs.

- If the person seems uncomfortable discussing the illness or is unable to provide you with the support you need, smile and end the discussion.

The Toughest Audience: Parent Bullies

Parents of well-behaved children can be the sternest critics. Some are afraid that your child will influence or harm other children. They nod politely as you explain your child's condition and avoid any future contact with you or your child. The key to changing their behavior is to get to know them on a one-to-one basis.

Sam, diagnosed bipolar at age seven, became fast friends with Zachary in kindergarten and soon best friends. Although their parents weren't particularly close, the boys enjoyed many play dates together over the years. Kathy, Sam's mom, didn't tell Zachary's mom, Anne, about the diagnosis right away, but when the boys were twelve years old, Sam became less stable and began refusing to go to school. When Zachary inquired about Sam's repeated absences, Kathy finally got up the nerve to tell Anne about Sam's illness. Anne seemed sympathetic at first, but when Kathy encouraged Sam to get together with Zachary, Anne balked, saying she was just too busy to get the boys together. Sam missed his friend. After umpteen turndowns, Anne told Kathy that although Zachary was pining to see Sam again outside school, she just didn't feel right about having a child who had such severe emotional problems in her house and around her son. What if the behaviors "rubbed off"? Kathy was devastated. Her "true confession" had cost Sam his best friend.

Conversely, some parent bullies may try to persuade you that a child trying to cut his wrists with shards of a plastic cup in a community center is perfectly normal. They may even use their own nonbipolar children as examples. *Their* kids occasionally need a "time-out" from a baseball game, stomping off the field. In short, they dismiss the diagnosis as nonsense and you as an alarmist. They conveniently overlook your child's engaging in behaviors that are impulsive and possibly dangerous. There are some people who will never be convinced that you are advocating for your child and doing what is best for him. That is why it is imperative to choose your friends and confidants wisely and to build a support network of people who can give you reinforcement and solid ideas to help you meet your child's challenges. If you tell someone and that person really refuses to understand, drop the subject and don't discuss your child's behavior with her again.

Kathy Noll, author of "Taking the Bully by the Horns" (http://hometown.aol.com/kthynoll), offers the following tips for dealing with parent bullies:

- **Don't let other parents intimidate you.** They are no better at parenting than you are. Usually people will invalidate others because they have low self-esteem. Don't mistake arrogance for high self-esteem. If they're so competent and confident, why the need to control others? That's what bullying is about: control.
- **Stick up for your child (and yourself).** Before responding to verbal bullying, take a deep breath and think for a moment. Be firm and polite. Let others see that you are strong and they can't take advantage of you.

- **If someone refuses to listen to you or becomes ver-bally abusive, walk away.** Ignoring a bully takes away the power this person thinks he or she has over you. When he sees he is no longer "getting to you," the control game is over.
- **Be yourself.** Bullies will try very hard to make you think there is something wrong with you (or your child). Recognize that they are simply venting all their own anger and their frustrations with life.

Remember that you are doing all you can to better understand your child's condition and advocate for him. Bullies need help too, but their problems aren't your responsibility.

When You Decide Not to Share

What do you say when you're in public and your child is acting in a bizarre manner? A wise psychiatrist once advised me simply to change the subject. And certainly in many situations, it works. You needn't provide a history of your child's illness, hospitalizations, and medications to every person who witnesses one of her meltdowns. Here are several "change the subject" questions or comments to help you move off the topic of your child's misbehaviors or eccentricities and onto less controversial and embarrassing issues:

"So how did *your* child do in school this year?"
"Are you planning to go away during spring break? We're still trying to decide."
"Did your child have Ms. Mitchell last year? What did he think of her?"
"Do you have a good recipe for pot roast?"

"Have you read your children the latest Harry Potter book?"

"I've always wondered where you buy your scarves. They are so attractive."

"How about those [name of sports team]?"

The art of changing the subject is to change it to something that will slyly shift the focus off the topic you are uncomfortable with—your child and his illness—and onto something that the other person cannot resist talking about. Usually that's himself or something that he greatly enjoys. Keep it light and complimentary when you can.

Don't Let It Get You Down

Circulating publicly can sometimes get you down, especially when you observe friends with well-adjusted children who are doing things that your child may never do. Try to remember that not every picture is as rosy as it appears; not every child is as well adjusted as she seems. Everyone has her share of burdens to bear. Instead of getting gloomy, count your blessings. Think about people who aren't as fortunate as you or your family; then make a list of all that you've got to be grateful for. Visit a soup kitchen or homeless shelter, and you will begin to appreciate how relative everything really is.

Notes from the Couch: A Psychiatrist's Point of View

You need a support network. Sharing with those you trust is essential in navigating this journey through bipolar illness with your child. Don't try to do everything yourself; it will only backfire in the end.

Develop a mantra for keeping focused when your "embarrassment meter" is off the charts: "I am doing the best I can" or "My child is in pain. He needs me to stay in control" are examples. Practice saying it over and over during your child's most outrageous moments, and hold on tight. Lots of people will think they have the right to judge you, but as Eleanor Roosevelt once said, "No one can make you feel inferior without your permission." If you don't value those people's input, it has no meaning.

I tell families all the time that a sense of humor is a powerful tool. Laughter lightens emotional loads and improves physical and mental health. Surround yourself with things that make you smile or laugh: have a comedy movie festival at your house, and buy stupid-joke books. If humor is a part of everyday life, it will be easier to activate it when you (or your child) are feeling at your worst.

CHAPTER 9

THE LAW

A Good Lawyer Can Help

Margie, mom of a ten-year-old child diagnosed as bipolar two years before, was in tears. The school had just informed her that her son was suspended indefinitely because he had threatened to "burn the school down" and "blow up the teacher." She was at her wit's end when a friend handed her the telephone number of a nearby educational attorney. He quickly informed her that her son could not be suspended indefinitely. It was against the law. Furthermore, since his threats were within the realm of his disability, the entire suspension could be challenged. Margie brought in the lawyer, who was able to get her son back into school and purge the suspension from his record.

Galen, mom of a fourteen-year-old bipolar girl, was beside herself when her former husband refused to give her daughter her medication during her visits with him. His religious group was strongly against them. He confiscated his daughter's medicine, assuring her that she would be fine. After an extended stay over Christmas break, Galen's daughter tried to slice her wrists open with a pair of scissors and was rushed to the hospital. Galen worked with a lawyer and her daughter's law guardian to ensure that Galen's father's visitation rights were terminated.

As the parent of a bipolar child, you never know when you might need the services of an attorney. Legal issues can include educational concerns, not-so-simple custodial issues, financial issues, malpractice, or juvenile justice problems. This chapter introduces you to the professionals who can help you address legal issues that may arise and provides resources and interview questions for when you do decide to seek legal support.

Begin by collecting good referrals before the need for an attorney arises. The best way to find a good lawyer for your needs, according to Mary Giliberti, an attorney with a legal issues advocacy group, the Bazelon Center for Mental Health Law, is to network with other parents at local health affiliates of NAMI or Federation of Families. This will also put you in touch with other parents to call on if and when a crisis happens. More important, connecting with advocacy groups gives local affiliates the power to lobby for changes in your local laws and your mental health care system.

The Education Attorney

We had to attempt to sue the school to get them to provide an IEP. We're very happy with our current school and placement. Pamela, mom of a bipolar daughter diagnosed at age fourteen

School districts are usually focused on saving money and on ensuring families that accommodations are in place for their child—priorities that sometimes work at cross purposes.

An educational attorney specializes in ensuring that school districts comply with state and federal education laws when dealing with your child. If a case requires due process and goes to an independent hearing, be aware that this is the same as going to court. There will be subpoenas and expert witnesses, and court procedure is followed.

If you decide to use an educational attorney to help you get what you need, you must inform the school ahead of time. Do not be surprised if the school calls on its own attorney and the special education meetings begin to sound like a courtroom instead of a parent-teacher conference.

In certain circumstances, an attorney's fees can be recovered from the school district after an appeal to the state. When choosing an educational attorney, look for one who is familiar with the players in your school system, specializes in educational law and advocacy, and understands exactly what ammunition you will need in your arsenal to get your child the accommodations she needs.

The Labor Attorney

I lost my job because I was constantly getting calls from school. I had to leave work and needed to be there when my son was hospitalized. I missed several meetings. Finally the boss just let me go.
Bernadette, mom of a bipolar son diagnosed at age eight

When parents of a child with bipolar disorder lose their jobs because of problems relating to their child's illness, the situation is doubly distressing: not only is their family without an income, but their child's medical care could become compromised. Laws are in place to protect employees from wrongful termination, and in most cases, the parent would be wise to consult with a labor attorney. Litigating for violations of two of the laws in place, the American with Disabilities Act (ADA) or the Family Medical Leave Act (FMLA), is not easy, according to Thomas Apple, a labor attorney for Itochu International, but both do offer limited protections for parents with a child with bipolar disorder.

The ADA offers protection to disabled employees. In addition to protecting employees themselves from discrimination, the law defines discrimination as "excluding or otherwise denying equal jobs or benefits to a qualified individual because of the known disability of an individual with whom the qualified individual is known to have a relationship or association." In some cases, the inequity is clear—for example:

- Someone else in the company in the exact same circumstances was treated differently.
- You were discriminated against because the employer found out that the health insurance benefits for your child would increase rates company-wide
- You were denied a promotion or initial employment because the employer felt you might not be able to work and take care of your mentally disabled child.

The first attempt at resolution of such cases should be internal since you are fighting to get your job back. If you make a ruckus but are subsequently retained, you may find yourself in a very awkward situation. If your internal attempts at resolution have failed, you may want to consult with an attorney who specializes in labor law. Ask her if it makes sense for an attorney to intercede. Because labor lawyers often work on contingency, they will work for a percentage of the settlement you receive and are not likely to take the case if they feel it has no merit.

Engaging an attorney may show the employer that you are serious. A lawyer's recourse might be to call and see if he can negotiate a quick solution. If he can't, the next step would be to file a complaint with the Equal Employment Opportunity Commission (EEOC), which must be done within three hundred days of the discriminatory act. "Don't expect huge settlements," explains Thomas Apple. If all goes well, you will get paid for time that you were wrongfully terminated and be re-instated at your job.

Malpractice Attorney

The hospital had another doctor do an evaluation on Daisy behind our back. They refused to give her Ativan at night to help control her panic attacks. A doctor ordered another drug. It made matters so much worse. We spent every moment of the day advocating for her proper care. Finally, on day 4, we pulled her out. Her doctor agreed that the nurses were being terrible. We discussed filing a lawsuit but agreed we were exhausted at the prospect and couldn't afford it anyway.

Carla, mom of a bipolar daughter diagnosed at age three

The words of the psychiatrist who berated the obstinate insurance gatekeeper on my son's behalf still linger in my memory: "If you refuse to pay for this child to be hospitalized and this child harms himself or someone else, I will personally bear witness in the malpractice lawsuit when this family sues you in court!"

Negligent behavior on the part of a mental health professional or institution can lead to malpractice. When a child is subjected to a less-than-standard level of care or the professionals treating him do not conform to a prudent level of care, the results can be disastrous. Negligence can lead to inadequate or overmedication, potentially damaging to the child and anyone he might hurt during a subsequent outburst. With managed care limiting hospital stays and reimbursables, there is a high level of misdiagnoses and mistreatment associated with bipolar disease in children. Side effects and cycling triggered by the wrong medications and suicides that can result from neglect can also lead to malpractice suits, according to Bryant Welch, Ph.D., J.D., an attorney and psychologist who specializes in litigating such cases in the Washington, D.C., area.

Psychiatric malpractice suits represent only a small percentage of malpractice cases, according to John J. Lucas, M.D., clinical assistant professor of psychiatry at Weill Medical College at Cornell University, and expert witness in malpractice cases. In his opinion, litigation can cause families undue stress.

While it may be quite stressful to sit through court proceedings after a medical battle with your child, when you have been wronged, the stress is already there. Sometimes legal means are the only way to effect proper treatment. "If a parent questions whether a child has been mistreated, misdiagnosed, or neglected, they should get a second medical opinion immediately, and consider seeing an attorney," explains Bryant Welch. According to Welch, consult with a malpractice attorney if:

- You feel that your practitioner may be capitulating to managed care guidelines at the expense of your child's welfare.
- You feel that a hospital or residential care facility is releasing your child too soon.
- You sense that your child is not getting any better in spite of your doctor's efforts.
- The doctor doesn't acknowledge the range of diagnoses that might be affecting your child (e.g., bipolar disorder).
- The doctor scapegoats you as a parent and threatens you with court action. Mothers who attempt to have

their child diagnosed with bipolar disorder may be accused of Munchausen by proxy, a psychiatric behavior in which a mother "induces" symptoms in her child.

Welch suggests that you find an attorney with a firm specializing in psychiatric malpractice.

Defense Attorney

He was at a special needs day camp. He wanted to paddle and steer a canoe by himself. The counselor needed to do it. He took large rocks and began throwing them toward shore. The other children had to be evacuated from the area. He broke two large windows of the special needs camp. The counselors didn't have the emergency phone numbers for us with them. They called the police, he was handcuffed, and they kept him for three more hours in the police car until we arrived to pick him up.
Cindy, mom of a bipolar son diagnosed at age eight

In these days of zero tolerance, an errant word or threat can bring the bomb squad to your door, and when a child with bipolar disorder is acting impulsively, crimes and misdemeanors occasionally occur. When it happens, you had better have some idea of how to navigate the legal waters. In juvenile proceedings, parents have the right to hire a defense attorney for the child if they are not happy with the lawyer assigned by the courts and can afford one. The judge may order a separate psychiatric evaluation in those cases.

Susan Brofman, a family attorney in New York State, says that when your child is being accused of something, call an attorney promptly. In most juvenile cases, the matter is remanded to family court, but depending on the age of the alleged perpetrator (your child!) and the nature of the crime, children are sometimes tried as adults. If your child is being tried as an adult, it is advisable to seek representation by a criminal defense attorney.

Irene Ratner, a Westchester County, New York, court judge, advises parents that if the police show up on your doorstep, don't invite them in. If they want to search the premises, they need a search warrant. If you are served with a warrant, read it and allow them to search only in areas specified in the warrant, keeping in mind that anything illegal that is in plain view may be considered evidence. If they want to question your child, you must be present. Do not make any statements, or allow your child to make any statements or answer any questions without an attorney present.

If your child is arrested, meet with the assigned attorney and determine whether he or she seems to have an understanding of your child's disability. See if your child seems to like the attorney.

Although the nature of the legal remedy will vary from case to case and state to state, it is important to remember the nature of your child's disability and protect his rights. Whether you choose a family or a criminal attorney, look for someone who has experience practicing in juvenile court and experience defending juveniles with mental illness. The more precise your attorney's specialty, the better. If your child is arrested and you don't have the money to hire an attorney, your child will be assigned a public defender.

Family Law Attorney

My son is quite the storyteller. The first night at the hospital, he told the staff that I beat him across the face with a belt nightly. I don't even own a belt, let alone abuse him with one. Of course, the nurse was hypervigilant about leaving me alone with him when I came to visit the next day.
Carrie, mom of a bipolar son diagnosed at age seven

Cheryl, mom of a twelve-year-old bipolar girl, got the call at her workplace. Her daughter had a "routine" fight with her sister after school. The sister called the family therapist, alleging that her bipolar sibling had attacked her. The therapist informed Cheryl that she was obliged to call in Children's Protective Services (CPS) and inform them of a potentially dangerous situation. Cheryl understandably was alarmed at the possibility that CPS could allege neglect and remove her child (or children) from the home. Before she panicked, she called a reputable family court lawyer to help advise her of her rights and negotiate the situation legally.

A family court lawyer is equipped to handle custodial issues, whether they center around a husband and wife (or formerly married couple) arguing over the treatment of a bipolar child or a family that is fighting CPS. An allegation of neglect can happen if a hospital decides that a child should be admitted and the parents object to the admission, or if a child being admitted to a hospital alleges that he was abused. Most states mandate that alleged abuse be reported within twenty-four hours. Usually an investigation follows. If evidence supports the allegation, the agency in charge could file a petition, and a law guardian might be assigned to the child. If your child alleges abuse in your home and you refuse to allow him to be examined by CPS, the agency may remove him from the home.

Another custody issue, relinquishments, is an unfortunate by-product of a failing mental health system. When children with mental health needs cannot get the services they require because of limited insurance coverage or because their home state doesn't federally mandate Medicaid services, a family may be forced to choose between maintaining custody of their mentally ill child or relinquishing it so the child can obtain the needed services. Child welfare systems require custody relinquishment for children in residential care. That way, the state can qualify for matching funds from the federal government. A happier arrangement for everyone is a voluntary placement agreement, which enables the state to provide treatment for children in residential settings, leaving the family with custody of the child.

Some couples divorce solely to lower the family income enough to qualify a child for Medicaid or other support services. According to a 1999 NAMI report, almost one-quarter of all parents of children with severe emotional disturbances who responded to a national survey were advised to relinquish custody so that their children could have access to mental health services. One in five of those families actually did so.

Families should try to stay together if possible. Before making these sad and difficult decisions, parents should explore all other available options and consult with an experienced family attorney to ensure that their rights are protected.

Law Guardian

According to Andrew H. Kulak, a practicing attorney in New York City specializing in mental hygiene and guardianship law, children are viewed as "incapacitated" by the courts by virtue of the fact that they are minors. For some court proceedings, a law guardian—a lawyer who represents the child—will automatically be assigned, free of charge, to a child. This can happen during custodial proceedings if parents are fighting over who should make treatment or handling decisions for the child; in retention cases when a hospital wants to retain a child but the parent wants the child to come home; and in cases of suspected neglect or abuse. Parents may retain lawyers for themselves, but they probably can't choose who will represent their child. Depending on the age of the child, the law guardian may or may not espouse the precise views of the child.

Once a law guardian is assigned, it is difficult to get the guardian removed, as parents are viewed as partial and not necessarily acting in the child's best interests. Guardians can also be appointed to manage assets and awards.

Finding the Right Attorney

Although no one relishes the thought of going to court, it is important that when you do, you feel confident that you are getting the very best representation. Once again, preparation is important. If you have the opportunity to network and research before you are in crisis, you will have more choices and be able to make them in an educated fashion. Sometimes you may not have a choice. If all you can afford is a legal aid attorney, you may want to offer to help with the legal legwork to expedite the case.

The best way to find an attorney is by referral from people you know and trust. Ask attorneys you know with other specialties to make a recommendation. If you can't come up with possibilities that way, there are on-line referral sources like

Martindale-Hubble (www.martindale.com), which enables you to identify lawyers by expertise, location, and other criteria. If you can't find anyone through a direct referral, contact NAMI or the Bazelon Center in Washington, D.C., for information on referrals. Interview prospects carefully to find out about their experience and to get an idea of how they can help you.

The following questions are meant to open a dialogue with a prospective attorney. Keep in mind that you are going into this relationship with very specialized needs. Focus your questions on the issues to be addressed. Use the specifics of your own case to formulate additional specific questions:

- What are your areas of concentration?
- Have you ever dealt with children with bipolar disorder? If so, how many cases have you handled?
- Have you ever served as a guardian for a child?
- When doing a legal examination, what do you look for in a child's behavior that would indicate anxiety and depression?
- Are you familiar with the different forms of treatment for this disorder?
- Do you feel that the child has to be an inpatient to receive treatment?
- Are you familiar with the hospitals and facilities that treat bipolar illness?
- Do you have any objection to representing a child with bipolar disorder?
- Do you have any personal experience with bipolar disorder?
- How do you get paid?
- What continuing-education courses or panels or workshops have you taken in the area of child growth

and development and childhood and adult mental
health issues?

Compensating an Attorney

Legal representation is costly. With some attorneys (educational, defense), you will likely be asked to put down a sizable retainer that represents a set amount of hours that the attorney expects to work on your behalf. You will be paying for the lawyer's telephone time, travel time, time spent writing on your child's behalf, and meeting time, so use any time with your attorney expeditiously.

Labor and malpractice attorneys often work on a contingency fee basis. Excepting expenses, which they likely will ask you for periodically, you pay them only after they have settled or won your case. At that time, they will usually take around one-third of the settlement or award.

Notes from the Couch: A Psychiatrist's Point of View

Hit lists, bomb threats, and assaults are just a few of the behaviors I have seen in children with bipolar disorder. These are serious and scary allegations that can send families into chaos. Stay focused on the techniques you have used before for getting through the worst of it, and try to devote whatever energy is left to solving the legal dilemma. If the family system goes into meltdown over these allegations and behaviors, there will be no energy left to problem-solve and move forward. Get good help—the best you can afford. These problems take your child's difficulties to another level. You will need good advice.

I rarely show my temper to my patients, but in cases of nasty and drawn-out custody battles, I sometimes lose my cool. These situations inflict unnecessary and deeply hurtful wounds on all children, but with kids with bipolar disorder, the damage is far worse. Yes, divorce happens. But the raging, toxic venom that is spewed during the legal wrangling would make anyone wilt. Look carefully at what you really need to attend to and what you can let go. These battles are often about the parents' needs, not the child's.

Part Three

Your Family

CHAPTER 10

YOU

Caring for Yourself So You Can Care for Your Child

Being a survivor is not at all the same thing as being a saint. I hate it when people tell me that. I'm not a saint, but I made a promise to a child, and I'll keep that promise.
Lenore, mom of a bipolar son diagnosed at age eleven

We've all heard airline attendants give the speech about how, in the event the aircraft loses cabin pressure, you should put on your own oxygen mask before you try to help your child or anyone else. It all makes sense. If we have not secured our own survival, how can we possibly help the people around us? In the context of caring for your family, it is harder to apply the principle, but it is every bit as important that we follow it.

Even if you have never had an extreme mood swing in your life, it takes only a moment—that phone call from the school to let you know he's suspended, that fight in the grocery store when your daughter punches you and calls you the most vile names you've ever heard—for your own mood to change from reasonably content to devastated. It's hard to avoid self-pity.

As you spend the better part of each day negotiating with schools, sending e-mail updates to doctors, calling the pharmacy for prescriptions, wrangling with insurance companies, or shifting plans midstream to accommodate a raging child, it's ridiculously easy to lose yourself. So much time and attention must be focused on the bipolar child that parents often neglect themselves, particularly the moms who shoulder most of the burden, often without the physical presence or psychological support of a spouse.

"Society says that women should take on any problems relating to children," explains Mary Pender Greene, A.C.S.W. and chief of social work services for the Jewish Board of Family and Children's Services in New York City. "If any child takes ill, mother cares for him. To do it any other way is thinking outside the box."

Even in households with healthy children, it is the mom who typically takes on the overall balancing act and the lion's share of any responsibility dealing with children. Those responsibilities are compounded by a child's illness. Regardless of whether a mother has six degrees and is working full-time as a nuclear physicist, the child rearing and household chores are perceived as her domain in most American families.

The paradox is that the more emotionally and physically draining the parenting challenge is, the more stamina and strength parents need to be at their fighting best. But if you're constantly on high alert, how and when are you supposed to rest? The cycle is all the more debilitating for parents with emotionally disturbed children who need them to be good role models emotionally, mentally, and physically.

Seventy percent of families responding to my survey indicated that at least one parent in the family was on medications for depression or similar conditions. While the congenital link means that these parents could well be suffering from a mood disorder themselves, respondents indicated that they believed that the very act of parenting their bipolar child was often the cause of their depression.

When a mother is emotionally and physically exhausted,

her already suffering children suffer along with her. How can a school principal, a doctor, or a lawyer take a parent seriously when she looks the way she feels—like the milk-soaked clumps of cereal her bipolar child just threw all over the kitchen table? This is why it is imperative for parents to find a way to focus time and energy on themselves each day.

The Positive Spin on Inconsistency

With a bipolar child, the only thing you can rely on is inconsistency—in your schedule, that is. A child who may be on the brink at any given moment and doesn't take well to child care or school translates into career interruptus, canceled trips to the gym, and art classes shot to hell.

Gilda Carle, Ph.D., psychotherapist, professor of psychology and communications at Mercy College in New York, and author of *Don't Bet on the Prince!,* suggests that bipolar children are in fact doing their parents a favor by teaching them that things can change in a heartbeat. She points out that one of the lessons the rest of the world learned from the terrorist attacks on the World Trade Center and the Pentagon, parents of bipolar children already knew from day-to-day dealings with their children. If anyone understands the nature of constant change, it is parents of bipolar children.

Challenged—Not Trapped

On your last trip to the mall, your bipolar child asked for a bow and arrow—not the greatest recreation for a child prone to rages—and you told him no. He hit you with the boxed set and proceeded to punch you as he called you "Whore!" and other horrible names. People stared. You handled the situation with dignity and appropriate strictness, but you were trapped. What had started out as an enjoyable outing turned into a nightmare.

The grim reality that you must now mold your life and activities around your child's ability to handle a place, event, or experience suddenly hits you like a bolt of lightning. Most children become more independent and easier to handle as they get older. Not your child.

How do you fight that trapped feeling?

Dr. Carle reminds us that when tension surrounds you, the change must come from within. Freeing yourself begins with acceptance. She suggests that parents embrace their lot and begin to view it as a mission rather than a burden. "If you look at life as an adventure, it will ease some of the pain," she explains. "The difference between those of us who make it through adversity and those who don't is, in a word, attitude." Here are some attitude-adjusting ideas:

- **"What I've Learned."** On a sheet of paper, write at the top, "What I've Learned." Then make a list of all the things you have learned or gained as a result of having a special child.
- **Photo album.** Use family photo albums to jog your memory. What other challenges have you encountered and conquered over the years? Did you climb a mountain? Raft the rapids? Sing an aria or speak in front of others? Use those victorious moments to help you recall your strengths and steel you for challenges that lie ahead.
- **Change your vocabulary.** Don't refer to your child as a "bipolar child," equating him to his disease. Instead, think of him as a "child with special needs." By focusing on the positive instead of the negative—the chal-

lenge of meeting your child's particular needs rather than the stigma of his illness—you can help change your attitude, and those of others, for the better.

Focus on Simple Abundance

The first step in reclaiming yourself, according to Mary Pender Greene, is to scale back your family's way of life to include only what is truly necessary. Make sure to include your own needs. Lots of things can be dropped from the equation, but the parent of a bipolar child must never, ever do away with time for self.

When I began reclaiming my life, one of the first things I did was sign up for Pilates classes, a delicious yoga-like exercise regime that helped strengthen my body and relax my mind. There were times when my son was unexpectedly home from school, but that Pilates class was sacrosanct. No one was going to take it away from me. At times, that meant finding someone to stay with my son at home or bringing him along to sit on the couch and watch me exercise. I scaled back on certain chores around the house and other distractions. My Pilates class was as important as my daughter's after-school club, my son's therapy appointment, and my husband's after-dinner walks.

"Getting your nails done, attending a yoga class, exercising on a treadmill, or going out with a friend for coffee is not a waste of time," confirms Pender Greene. "It is essential time spent replenishing yourself. Give yourself time to recharge every day." Here are some suggestions:

- Healthy eating. It takes a conscious effort to eat right in the midst of a crisis, but it can be done. Eating the salad first reduces the chances you'll crave dessert.

- A simple cup of tea or a quick visit to a nearby coffee shop can be a delightful and easy getaway. Call a good friend to join you.
- Water, water, water. Buy a water cooler and indulge in ice-cold water all day long. Not only will it keep you hydrated and healthy, but your children will get used to drinking water instead of sugar-laden drinks.

The No-Martyr Zone

Many parents of bipolar children, more often moms than dads, adopt the role of the martyr, a condition that sets them up for a self-perpetuating cycle of disappointment. Martyr-dom thrives on Mom's being essential to everyone. No one else can do what she does. There is some satisfaction in explaining, as she shrugs off a dinner engagement with a friend, that she can't possibly leave her raging son home with her clueless husband. Being the sole person who can care for this needy child gives her life purpose and meaning.

But the more her family leans on her, the more she must swallow her own feelings. She may not realize the situation that she is setting up by giving, giving, giving and getting little or nothing in return, but little by little, resentment sets in. She may suppress her anger, which can lead to depression or illness. When she can't keep the lid on her emotions, she may well unleash on the person to whom she is trying so hard to give the best care: her bipolar child. A depressed mom is no better than an angry one. Scientific studies show that when a mom is depressed, her offspring are more likely to suffer from mood disorders, social problems, and psychiatric conditions.

"Martyr Mom must come to the realization," Mary Pender Greene explains, "that the only way she can really be there for everyone else is to cross the bridge from martyr to human be-ing. She can enjoy dinner with that friend without putting anyone's life at risk. And the better she takes care of herself, the more her family benefits."

While Dad may not cook dinner or get the kids ready for bed exactly as Mom would have done it, it *will* get done. Take heart in the knowledge that no one on the planet can care for that child as well as you do, but she will be even better off if you take some time for yourself. A mom who routinely takes time to refresh and rejuvenate is a better mom. This means making time for exercise—no matter what. It means taking time to dress up for the school meeting, and arranging for someone to care for your children so you can still meet your dear friend for lunch. The key is systematically and selfishly factoring in time for yourself. In doing so, you ensure that your child's primary caretaker is strong, healthy, and mentally fit enough to give your child the best.

Girlfriend, you deserve every ounce of strength you can muster! Take it whenever and wherever you can get it!

A brisk walk, a Pilates class, an hour of yoga, or a bike ride can free the mind and rejuvenate the body. This is especially helpful on those days when you get called to pick up your child at school. Try aromatherapy baths. This works for children in agitated states, but hide your own stash of mood-boosting bath oils for yourself. Naturopaths rely on lavender for its stress-relieving properties and rosemary for rejuvenation.

Fighting Isolation with Community

While moms are prone to martyrdom, dads more often fall into patterns of isolation. As discussed earlier in this book, we're often hard-pressed to explain our children's public behavior. We avoid certain social situations because the environmental stimulation can trigger the worst kinds of behavior in our children. While women often reach out and find one another, men keep their problems, emotions, and family history to themselves. A case in point was my on-line survey in which the vast majority of respondents were moms. Their written answers were copious and emotionally laden. The few responses I got from dads were curt. Moms flood listserves and electronic bulletin boards with questions and concerns, far outnumbering the occasional dad's voice.

Poor Dad, suffering in silence. While women talk about their flaws, disappointments, and anxieties, men are conditioned to bury any such talk. How often do you overhear a man complaining about going off his diet or gaining a few pounds after arduous and passionate debate with the Special Education Committee? Moms of bipolar children do it all the time.

"The male model is different," Mary Pender Greene points out. "'If I can deny it, then I don't have to work on learning to live with it.' That's the way his thinking goes. He tries to hide his family away from the rest of the world." What these dads don't understand is that reaching out can be a kind of salvation and can bring emotional, physical, and financial support into the household. One survey respondent reported that thanks to her church group, her child's doctor bills were paid in full. Another said that her involvement in the PTA has raised awareness of emotional disorders in the community and brought new and improved services to her school.

Community involvement requires give-and-take. It is more than just building a social network. It's a valuable resource and a method of creating a support base where there was none.

If you are part of a close community but are uncomfortable discussing your child, then you still may be suffering from isolation. Seek out other parents with issues similar to your own. Ask how to handle behavioral issues, spousal problems, time concerns, and other pertinent issues. Find a group that is conducive to sharing—perhaps a NAMI support group or an on-line forum for parents of bipolar children on the Child and Adolescent Bipolar Foundation (CABF) Web site at www.bpkids.org.

Make a Friend

It isn't as easy for parents to make friends when others deem their child asocial. That is why just one good friend can be a lifesaver. Here are some tips for making friends:

- Join a support group for parents. If you can't find one for parents of bipolar children, find one for parents of kids with all kinds of disabilities. You'll be surprised how much in common you have with, say, parents of hemophiliacs or parents of autistic children. Reach out!
- Join CABF (www.bpkids.org) and make an on-line friend.
- Join a church, synagogue, or mosque and see if it has any groups for parents of children with disabilities. If it doesn't, start one.
- Join the PTA, and make it your mission to educate the community about bipolar disorder in children.
- Start a scout troop. Working with nonbipolar children (other than your own) will give you an interesting perspective on what is "normal" and what is not. Scouting is a terrific way to make new friends and rediscover a part of yourself.

- Take art classes at a local Y or adult education, and find people to whom you could pour your soul out.
- Take up knitting, quilting, or some other craft. Local craft shops often sponsor evenings where crafters gather to work and talk.
- Join a book club.
- Bake cookies for local events and functions.
- Join NAMI, and become an activist for causes relating to your child.

Notes from the Couch: A Psychiatrist's Point of View

I can't stress enough how important it is for parents to take care of themselves so that they can take care of their children. Nourishing yourself mentally, physically, spiritually, and emotionally allows you to keep your own emotional reactivity under control. This is a key to a calmer child. This nourishment also enriches your child's life and teaches her the importance of self-care.

I often talk with my patients' parents about learned optimism and changing negative perspectives to more positive ones. These skills, documented by top-notch scientific research, are powerful tools for navigating life-changing events, as well as day-to-day challenges. My mantra is, "There are no crises, only opportunities for growth."

CHAPTER 11

RELATIONSHIPS

Meeting the Challenge Together

*I think we are closer right now than ever before. We went
through really tough times not being able to get pregnant,
and that brought us together, but over the years, kids and
work have put some distance there. We are now, again, working together to get through this. We hug a lot and are there for
each other. My husband tends to take on too much load and
then blow up emotionally, so I am trying to watch out for
him, but I am having a very difficult time with all this.*
Sarita, mom of a bipolar daughter diagnosed at age seven

*Dealing with our son's illness has made us more understand-
ing of each other's breaking points. We are like a tag team.
We both like to bring humor into it as often as possible.*
Leslie, mom of a bipolar son diagnosed at age three

She says, "He's manic," and he says, "He's just a little overtired."
She says "depressive," and he says, "I used to cry like that all the
time." Add a few overdue medical bills and subtract one
spouse's income, and you have the recipe for marital disaster.
The vast majority of respondents to my on-line survey indicated that their child's condition was a major source of conflict.

Although relationships are greatly affected by the day-to-
day pressures of parenting a bipolar child, there is a silver lining in this particular cloud. Some of the couples answering my
survey indicated that, after some work—often quite a lot of

work—when they got it right, their marriages became closer as a result of parenting their bipolar child.

Sharing the tears, fears, trials, tribulations, and working together to nurture a family can be the most intense and wonderful thing that could ever happen to a marriage. While having a bipolar child can be tremendously stressful, working together to fight the bipolar demons can be a unifying experience. When you realize that you have met the enemy—and it is not you, your spouse, or your child, but rather the disease that your child is fighting—then you can all work together to make changes in your family and your lives. But most parents with a bipolar child don't start out that way. This chapter will describe some of the land mines littering the relationship landscape, from bipolar spouses to partners in denial, and will give you solutions.

Dad's Blue Eyes/Mom's Blue Moods

I protected him from his bipolar dad when he was young. We are divorced, and I've encouraged them to have a relationship. I keep them apart when they're both cycling. It's hard.
Kelly, mom of a bipolar son diagnosed at age eleven

Since I am bipolar, I understand the highs and lows. It's easier for me to empathize with him, which in turn makes dealing with him easier. Of course, it can still be a trial when he's being oppositional and defiant.
Jessica, mom of a bipolar son diagnosed at age six

One well-known psychiatrist told me that a bipolar child is often just the tip of the iceberg when it comes to the family's history of mental illness. It's not uncommon to find that one or both parents suffer from an undiagnosed bipolar condition. For these parents, confronting the truth about their child forces them to confront their own condition, a frightening situation. An undiagnosed bipolar parent, because of his own mood swings, may forget, or just decide to ignore, the child's treatment needs, not to mention his own.

Undiagnosed, untreated bipolar parents can be dangerous in their most severe moods and unreliable in their more moderate stages. A parent with the disorder may have moods that render her unable to function, leaving the healthy spouse to manage everything. Bipolar moods playing off each other produce anxiety and arousal, not just for the bipolar parent and child but also for the unaffected spouse and siblings.

If you suspect that you or your spouse might be suffering from bipolar disorder, the best thing you can do for yourself and your family is to find a good mental health professional and seek treatment.

For the self-aware bipolar parent of a bipolar child, the guilt associated with passing on this illness can be painful. The nonbipolar parent will need to guide his spouse to psychiatric help and at times protect his bipolar child and spouse from each other.

The positive aspect of a well-informed, well-treated bipolar parent parenting a bipolar child is that the parent truly understands the nuances and rhythms of the moods of the child in a way that no one else can. Although there will be differences in how each person is affected by the disorder, the level of empathy and understanding is heightened when a parent has stood in his child's shoes. Then again, there will be times when two bipolar moods meet and clash. Those times call for lots of personal space and ready access to a competent professional.

Stuck in the Grief Cycle

When parents first hear about the bipolar diagnosis in their child, they enter a cycle that mimics Elisabeth Kübler-Ross's five-stage process of grieving: denial, anger, bargaining, depression, and acceptance. With the diagnosis of mental illness, a parent must grieve for the way things might have been without the illness. Knowing that the child who was once your sweet infant will forever be battling this illness is difficult to accept.

Grief has a way of creeping into a parent's life. Parents feel special pride when they can bask in their child's success. Couples with a bipolar child, however, may have to redefine success before they can enjoy it. Before the diagnosis, many parents dream of their child hitting a home run in Little League or becoming an honor student. Parents with a bipolar child may have to fine-tune their expectations and take pleasure in less sweeping accomplishments.

Parents dealing with a bipolar child must come to grips with their own aborted dreams. While bipolar children can be outstanding achievers, the realization that those achievements might be more challenging for them is a sobering one. And no matter how positive a thinker a parent is, that can be one tough pill to swallow.

A typical grieving process is described below:

- **Denial.** Refusal to believe the diagnosis no matter how many psychiatrists, psychologists, educators, or therapists try to tell you it is so. A parent in a strong state of denial may swear that the mental illness is fabricated and disavow the basic science of brain chemistry.
- **Anger.** Anger can translate into blame and can be directed at the child, the spouse, or the diagnosing pro-

fessional. Anger can be turned inward at yourself for "letting this illness strike your child."

- **Bargaining.** This involves turning to a spiritual entity or the medical establishment and trying to reclaim some semblance of normality for your child and your life in exchange for being a better parent, being around more often, or any other condition that you think will "reverse" the diagnosis.
- **Depression.** The realization that this is real and you can't change things hits hard and fast. Parents can find themselves depressed in response to the gravity of the diagnosis or crisis.
- **Acceptance/Advocacy.** In this final stage, a parent realizes that she cannot change the situation but can learn to live with it and can become an advocate for her child and others like him—in school, on the playground, and throughout life.

Some parents move through the cycle faster than others. In fact, it's rare when parents move through the cycle together. So communicating with your partner when you are depressed and he is still stuck in denial can be a tricky and painful endeavor. The unfortunate reality about this grief cycle, unlike grieving a death, is that it tends to repeat whenever the child has an episode or setback. You and your partner can spend an awful lot of time on different stages and pages. At times it feels like the movie *Groundhog Day*, a never-ending work in progress.

Dealing with Denial

After getting the bipolar diagnosis for her child, typically a mom reads every book on the disorder in children. She's traced familial links on both sides of the family. She is armed and educated and poised to use her newfound knowledge to help her child navigate the world. But wait a minute! Where's Dad?

She has given him the books and encouraged him to meet the child's doctors but still he chooses to get the information secondhand. When confronted with the behaviors, his response is, "It's not mental illness. He's just being a boy. He hates school. What does that prove?" Dad withdraws when she tries to let him know what she's learned. He discards the books. Worst of all, the disharmony is making the child's condition worse. The child is caught in a matrimonial tug-of-war. What is a loving spouse and parent to do?

Before you try to do something about denial, it is important to understand where it is coming from. Denial is a normal and necessary part of the grieving process that ultimately leads to acceptance that your child has an incurable disease. Sheila Brown, O.B.E., a special needs family counselor with the organization Birth Defects Foundation, the U.K. equivalent to the March of Dimes, and a mother of two children with birth defects, has seen parents grapple with acknowledging their child's birth defects. Often, she says, they get stuck at one stage of the grieving process. "Mothers tend to move more quickly through the process," she explains, attributing this progress to the practical parenting tasks most moms tend to each day. She says that for many men, the most pressing question is "Why?" They want to understand cause and effect. If the answer is that the condition was passed on through Dad's genes, it hits them pretty hard.

Mothers and fathers have very different reactions to the parenting experience, and accepting the diagnosis, acknowledging each other's grief, and appreciating the efforts of a spouse on behalf of a bipolar child are very important if the relationship is to survive. Getting stuck in any of the grief cycle phases will limit the ability to cope with the realities of dealing with a bipolar child.

Confronting a spouse in denial or one who is crippled by another stage of grief is difficult and shouldn't be done alone. If your partner is willing to go into couples therapy, that is probably the best way to mend your marriage. If your partner is resistant, don't hesitate to go into therapy on your own.

My mother-in-law used to say about my father-in-law, who was diagnosed with bipolar disorder, "One ill person can make an army crazy!" Conversely, one well person can make a whole family better. If you are the spouse helping your child through this mental illness while your partner is unable to accept the diagnosis, remember that support services are available to you. Clinics with sliding fees, with costs adjusted according to income, are out there. NAMI has a help line and affiliates to give you support and advice. Even if you've had it with psychiatrists, psychologists, and social workers, seeing a therapist for your own support needs can be enormously helpful in teaching you to negotiate the relationship issues that come up when dealing with a grieving spouse and a bipolar child.

Anger and Blame

It is easy to fall into "The Blame Game" when confronting mental illness, because nobody, not even the most respected professionals, has figured out exactly how and why mental illness affects some people, while others in similar circumstances, situations, and families emerge unscathed. Blaming your spouse for her bad parenting or your grandmother for her bad genes doesn't help solve the problem. There is no definitive answer to the question why, and blame is often leveled, consciously or unconsciously, when someone just can't let go of the need to control an uncontrollable situation.

Blaming a spouse doesn't make anyone feel better and will not help your bipolar child. Worse than blaming a spouse for a bipolar child's illness is a parent who blames herself. Both spouses should be looking forward instead of backward and must commit to working together to figure out how best to serve this child.

If you want to turn "your fault" arguments into "no fault" ones, let your partner scream, Dr. Gilda Carle suggests, but find an opportunity to tape him. Later, when he's calm and receptive, rewind the tape and say, "I just want you to hear this. I don't think you would want to be talked to like this." When the tape is done, turn the conversation to your child, asking your spouse how he suggests you handle the situation together.

Know Your Negotiable Limits

Mary Pender Greene describes a healthy relationship as one in which each partner sees the other as self-fulfilled. A healthy and happy individual counts on no one but him or herself to make them whole but leaves plenty of room for someone else. Partners exist side by side without eclipsing the other's needs with their own. When parents disagree, Greene advises them to ask themselves, "What is my negotiable limit?" Every relationship involves compromise. The two individuals who make up the couple learn along the way what is negotiable and what is not. "As issues arise, ask yourself how important the issue is to you on a scale of one to ten. Sometimes you give in, and sometimes you get your way. But never, ever let your gas tank drain completely."

Knowing your negotiable limit also means setting strict

boundaries. A spouse who treats another badly—constantly blaming and complaining and even abusing—is acting beyond the negotiable limit. Women buy into abuse because they feel that the abuser is taking care of them in some way. If they have serious self-esteem issues, they may even feel lucky that their husband is willing to live with them and their bipolar child. Abusers also suffer from low self-esteem. Men who abuse are often locked into a dependent relationship and angry at themselves for feeling so dependent.

Letting your spouse rant and dismissing him or her as a stark, raving lunatic is not the answer either, Pender Greene asserts, because it leaves you with a void in your life and with the lion's share of responsibility—responsibility that in a good marriage, couples share.

The United Front

My husband has finally accepted that this is Danny's problem and we need to be a team, together in purpose, to work with him.
Lenore, mom of a bipolar son diagnosed at age ten

"His father is a real SOB," one mother of a bipolar teen told me as her teen son stood by nodding his head in agreement. "Dad's a jerk," he verified.

There's nothing more counterproductive than parents who can't agree on a child-rearing issue. Whether a couple is married, separated, or divorced, they have to be able to present a united front for all children, but especially for bipolar children, who will seize any opportunity to divide and conquer.

Disciplinary rules should be hashed out and established far away from the child. Discuss and decide on strategies for crisis situations before one arises. If you adopt a proactive rather than reactive disciplinary approach, your children (bipolar and otherwise) will learn that the rules you make will be enforced. If you don't have a game plan and instead contradict each other publicly, the child will take advantage of the discord, driving a greater wedge between spouses and generally wreaking havoc.

One mom of a bipolar adolescent tried to tell her husband over the phone why her son was suspended from school, while her son did everything he could to interfere. He whined as she whispered to her husband. He picked up the extension but refused to acknowledge he had, disobeying orders to put the phone down. When she pressed on, he pulled the plug. It is no wonder that this mother was beset with anxiety. Her child knew no boundaries. He routinely crossed lines, wandering into adult matters and placing himself where he didn't belong.

Another mom once sheepishly confided that her bipolar son wouldn't take no for an answer. I thought about it for a minute, then asked, "So, if he decides to follow you into the bathroom and watch you relieve yourself, you'll let him?" Her answer was an emphatic "No!" "So, he does respect some boundaries," I pointed out—and it was high time for some new ones.

In every household, even one with a bipolar child, there must be boundaries, and parents must work together to teach children to respect them. Privacy is a major issue, and setting boundaries in terms of what is off-limits to whom is essential. A child must understand that before entering someone's bedroom, he must knock and receive permission to enter. In exchange, he will be awarded the same courtesy. With these boundaries, a child will feel cared for, and parents will have privacy as well.

Parents who don't set boundaries struggle to find time to

nurture themselves, and their marriage suffers. If your child doesn't respect a locked door or feels entitled to insinuate herself into your adult conversations, it is high time to let her know that while you love her, she must respect your privacy and observe the boundaries you've set forth. There is no better way to teach this than to do the same for your child.

Tag Team Parenting

Your child has been raging for two hours straight. Just as you're about to lose your mind, in walks Dad, and suddenly her mood tapers off. He issues a few curt commands, and she snaps to attention. With an exasperated look, Dad poses the infuriating question, "Why is it that whenever she's with you, she goes nuts, but when she's with me, she behaves?" Is there a "Mom Factor" that causes Mom to bear the brunt of a bipolar mood?

According to many experts and the testimony of parental interviews, the Mom Factor is clearly evident in many families, for the following reasons:

- Mom is usually the primary caregiver and thus present to witness more of the child's behaviors, both good and bad. Dad is around the child less and thus less likely to witness the worst of the child's moods.
- Mom is not as strong, scary, and physically intimidating as Dad.
- Mom is more likely to be empathetic and unconditionally loving.
- Dad is a "novel stimulus." When he walks into the room, his presence and voice change the dynamics of the situation. He distracts the child from the focus of his rage or paranoia and redirects his thoughts.

Unfortunately, Mom is also more likely to be verbally and physically abused by the bipolar child. She's often the one who gets hit or punched by a child who wouldn't dream of assaulting Dad. The Mom Factor is seldom a reflection on Mom's parenting skills, as some dads would like to believe. Any dad who wants to test the theory can send Mom on a two-week vacation, leaving the bipolar child to him. Mood free? Not for long.

Once again, the key to having a happy marriage is taking that time to nurture yourself and yield some of the responsibilities to your partner. Unhappy marriages come from partners feeling overworked, unattractive, and uncared for.

"What you expect, you teach," preaches Dr. Gilda Carle. "If you don't expect to share responsibility and instead tackle the problem on your own, you are unwittingly teaching your spouse that you'll always take care of it. Why are you doing it? Taking on the lion's share is not productive or healthy and can harm the relationship."

For everyone involved, communications skills are vital. When dealing with a difficult spouse, try to understand and appreciate that your spouse may not have the same level of understanding about mental illness that you have. Make him part of the team. Instead of saying, "You are in complete denial. You didn't give him his medicine today. What were you thinking?" try expressing yourself in nonaccusatory task-oriented language. Start with an "I" sentence, like, "I need your help caring for him. He needs his medicine on time."

Keep in mind what Dr. Carle has labeled the "Condominium Approach": once he's done some of the work—from doing research on the Internet, to taking your child to doctors—he owns a piece of the problem. If he owns some of the problem, it will be harder for him to remain in denial.

A Time for Your Marriage

After you have learned to take time for yourself, it is time to reclaim your marriage. Just as it is essential for the parent of a bipolar child to earmark time alone, it is equally important to set aside time for your spouse. In order for the marriage to succeed, a couple must create quality time together. Stealing away one afternoon every couple of weeks while the kids are at school to go shopping, have lunch, or catch a movie will do wonders for the relationship. The key is to find some kind of support or respite that will leave the child out of sight and away from your consciousness so you can strengthen your relationship.

Communicating Through Divorce

Too often marriage is the unfortunate victim of circumstances when bipolar disorder is involved. The stress of being bipolar, being married to someone with the condition, or having a child with the disorder is enormous, and any variation of the two (bipolar parent plus bipolar child) can be even more difficult.

Once parents have made the decision to divorce, they have a whole new set of stressors and circumstances to deal with. According to Christie, the bipolar mom of a bipolar son diagnosed at age ten and two other nonbipolar children, some of those stressors include treatments that tax her already limited finances, shifting child care arrangements, disrupted schedules, employers who get testy over her unexpected absences, and finding time for herself when her child needs her 24/7. Although Christie's ex-husband would like to lend a hand, he lives in another state, so she has surrounded herself with friends who are a phone call away, her parents who are nearby, her sister and her family, an Internet support group, a therapist she can always ask for support or advice, a psychiatrist she trusts with her son's sanity, a school caseworker, and, most important, she says, a sense of humor.

Christie's son sometimes takes on the role of caregiver with his mother. They take turns caring for each other in dealing with the illness they share and with the divorce. Christie left her husband, whom she felt was "oppressive" and not working with her to deal with her son, who had recently been diagnosed. Her son reminds her to call her doctor when she is depressed or he'll chide her if she seems to be getting too manic.

Because rage and disharmony will ratchet up the emotions in any parenting relationship and because rage and disharmony can prevail when two people are divorcing, it is extremely important that parents focus on their child with bipolar disorder during the transition period. This means that parents must swallow the tendency to turn inward or become self-absorbed, not an easy thing to do when you are dealing with the overwhelming task of sorting out legal, financial, and tremendously emotional issues.

If being available for the children becomes challenging, it is important to find someone else to spend time with them, particularly the one with bipolar disorder. Depending on which state you live in, divorces can take a long time. For transition-sensitive bipolar children, the process can seem endless.

Support for Singles

The key to succeeding as a single parent of a bipolar child is to find logistical, financial, and emotional resources. Networking and making connections with sympathetic people is essential. NAMI offers Family to Family classes that educate and support families of people with mental illness. The Internet also offers family members networking opportunities.

After the smoke clears from the divorce and both parent and child have recovered from it, a parent may want to begin dating. For the bipolar child, this represents a new transition to deal with, and for Mom or Dad, disclosure issues come to the fore.

Here are some dating ideas for parents of children with bipolar disorder shared by Anne, the single mom of a sixteen-year-old with bipolar disorder:

- Start with a friendship based on mutual acceptance and respect rather than a chemically charged attraction.
- Watch out for excess baggage. When parenting a bipolar child, you don't need extra complications and emotional drain. If the other person is divorced, ask why. Find out if the person has kids and what those relationships are like. Does there seem to be resentment? Guilt? If so, beware.
- Get to know each other away from the family at first. Focus on shared interests and good conversation.
- Be open from the start about your child's special needs. Your child's needs may affect the amount of time you can spend with this person.
- Watch how this potentially special person relates to your child. Friendly? Neutral and patient? And what about handling that obnoxious "attention-getting" behavior?
- Because time is frequently a problem for parents of bipolar children, learn to appreciate short visits, telephone conversations, and quick coffee dates.

Being parents to children with bipolar disorder makes us very special people. We learn immeasurably just how much strength and wisdom is possible when we begin with love. We also deserve to be appreciated as the special people we are—no change required!

Notes from the Couch: A Psychiatrist's Point of View

Recently, I had back-to-back parent meetings about children with mood disorders. The first couple came into my office raging, judging, and criticizing each other. I did my best to find some emotional space to work in, but mostly I felt paralyzed and rather hopeless. The next couple I met with entered the room with a completely different demeanor. They spoke kindly to each other, listened carefully, and stayed focused on their daughter's well-being. I was able to relax and engage in the discussion in a meaningful way, and we problem-solved some specific issues about their little girl.

Now imagine a child in a room with these two different couples. Even with my training and professional experience, I felt overwhelmed with the emotion in the room with the first couple. Imagine the response of a vulnerable child. How can we ask a child to be on her best behavior when the conflict between the adults is so powerful?

You might be curious to learn how long those two couples had been together. The first had been married twenty years. The second couple was divorced for two years. The legal status of the relationship was far less important than the way it functioned.

CHAPTER 12

SIBLINGS

Parenting the "Normal" Ones

My children have a very poor relationship. My son Jim does not respect my other children's space or property. In turn, they pretty much want nothing to do with him. They constantly nag him about every little thing he does. They are always fighting. Every year I ask for the same thing for my birthday and Mother's Day: one day when my family acts like—and actually does—love one another.
Cleo, mom of a bipolar son diagnosed at age ten

Children with bipolar disorder often have intense relationships with their siblings. Some are embarrassed by their mentally ill sibling and isolate themselves from friends. Others resent the bipolar child who isn't able to fulfill her share of responsibilities, and another group takes on caregiving tasks, nurturing both the bipolar child and the beleaguered parents. Especially disconcerting for parents are siblings who act like copycats, imitating the worst of their mentally ill sibling's behaviors.

Having a bipolar child for a sibling can result in a fast-forward maturity process. Siblings need to develop special coping skills. With time and a thorough understanding of the illness, they can recapture their own lives in spite of their bipolar sibling.

The First Step Is Understanding

A sibling falls into the category of people who need to know about your child's bipolar diagnosis. While you can't expect your other children, especially very young ones, to understand all about the condition, lying about it usually doesn't work. Likewise, advising a sibling to cover up for the child with bipolar disorder doesn't work either.

Offer your children a careful and thorough age-appropriate explanation of the condition, and assure them that their sibling is being treated and will get better. The older a child is, the more detail you can expect her to absorb. Here are some age-appropriate explanations:

Preschool: "Johnny is not feeling well today. He is in an angry mood and can't really help himself feel good. Tomorrow we hope he will feel better. If something he says or does bothers you, you can talk to me."

School age: "Johnny has a brain disorder. That means that sometimes chemicals in his brain don't work the way they should, and that puts him into different moods. We all get angry sometimes, but Johnny has trouble getting back into good moods. We hope that, with medication, Johnny will feel better soon. In the meantime, if he does something or says something that you want to talk about, I want to listen. I am always here for you."

High school: "Johnny has bipolar disorder, which is also known as manic-depression. That is why he sometimes seems low energy—or high energy." (Refer to Chapter 1, which your high schooler may want to read for himself.)

Explain that it's the family's responsibility to take special care of your bipolar child, but that there is always someone they can talk to if things get unpleasant or upsetting. Designate a family member, close friend, or family therapist who does not bear responsibility for the bipolar child as the point person for nonbipolar siblings. Pick someone she feels comfortable with and trusts enough to confide in. Make sure she has the phone number where this person can be reached in case of an emergency.

Tell siblings that while the diagnosis is not a secret, certain things should not be discussed at great length outside the family. If people ask questions, siblings can direct them to a parent. Some role playing and coaching may be in order, especially for younger children.

Copycat Behavior

"Why does *he* always get more time with you than I do? I'm sick of having him for a brother. He always ruins everything. He's ruined my life!" Those are the words my nine-year-old daughter chose to describe her older brother as she kicked a hole in the wall! She does not share his diagnosis, but sometimes her attention-getting tactics mimic his. And who can blame her? He's become quite the expert at turning heads with bad behavior.

Imitative episodes can make a parent's hair stand on end. Could it be? Another bipolar child? One bipolar child is difficult. Two are doubly difficult. Bipolar disorder is known to run in families, so how do you know if a sibling is truly suffering from bipolar disorder or simply imitating the behavior of an older or younger sibling to get attention?

Copycat behavior looks an awful lot like the real thing—with one significant difference: a healthy child who copies the behaviors of a bipolar one often gets bored with it after being consistently called on it and suffering the consequences. A healthy child will quickly understand that the "payoff"—a moment or two of an angry parent's attention—isn't worth it. Children with bipolar disorder are so directed by their moods that they aren't always able to make this connection. Even if they do, they may be unable to stop themselves. A sibling whose poor behavior goes on for weeks *and* who appears to be having mood swings should be evaluated by a mental health professional.

Before you jump to any conclusions, remember that children naturally imitate others' behavior, especially when a child observes that the result is a parent's focused attention.

It's Not FAIR!

When he is doing well, he has a great time with his siblings. When he's cycling, the others are sometimes afraid of him or don't want to be around his obnoxious and aggressive behaviors.
Tricia, mom of a bipolar son diagnosed at age seven

Any parent with more than one child has heard a plaintive "It's not fair!" countless times, but if you have a special needs child, chances are your ears ring with those words as you read these lines. The truth is, there will be times when a bipolar child is cut a ridiculously lenient deal. When you discipline a sibling for imitating a brother or sister with bipolar disorder, what they see is a double standard: the bipolar child gets away with behavior they can't. It is therefore important that parents reevaluate the reward and punishment mechanisms in place for the entire family to see if things are working.

Make sure that your discipline is as consistent as it can be from child to child. When my son came home from the hospital, we adopted its points behavioral system. Inpatients were given a small amount of money to visit the hospital gift shop in exchange for their good behavior. We decided to incorporate that into our system too, but it seemed off balance to exclude our daughter. Eventually "Gift Shop" evolved into an allowance system contingent on good behavior: good behavior was rewarded with cash and the opportunity to spend it. Negative behavior "debited" their account. We made it as even-handed as possible.

As parents, we must choose our battles. It isn't always productive to enforce punishment for a behavior our child can't control. And, yes, this is definitely unfair to siblings, who are asked to comply simply because they're able. "Why do I have to make my bed, while he gets away with throwing a tantrum and avoiding it?" If you have an allowance system like ours in place, you have an answer for that: "Because he is not able to do it, and you are, which means you're the one with the nice, neat room *and* you will get your allowance this week because you stayed on task!"

There will be times when we reward behavior in our bipolar child that would banish his sibling to her room for a week. Equity is a tough concept when you are parenting children with different needs. The best we can do is listen and let siblings know that while we understand that it isn't fair, we also have to make decisions that take the bipolar child's circumstances into account.

If you decide to reward your bipolar child for specific tasks, do it with a game or toy that can be shared with other siblings. Board games like Moods or Scrabble or a puzzle are rewards that siblings can work on together. Even though their reward systems may not be identical, when a reward is earned, all can enjoy it.

Sibling Caregiver

My son sits at the dinner table refusing to eat. He has bitten his fingernails bloody, then rubbed streaks of blood on his face. Now he stares sullenly, mumbling incoherently to himself. My daughter sets a plate of spaghetti in front of him and kisses him on the forehead. "I love you," she coos, and his mood softens.

While I am touched by the fact that a kiss from his sister can calm my son as few other things can, I wonder if she will always feel the need to be his caregiver and how that will affect her life.

Celia, a forty-year-old woman, recalls her experiences "caregiving" for her older brother, who was first diagnosed bipolar at the age of fifteen: "From the age of four or five, he was painfully shy, so I would talk for him at the candy store and in the schoolyard." Celia went on to do all her brother's homework, read books aloud to him, and write all his school papers. When her brother failed algebra in high school, Celia went to summer school with him, even though she had more than passing grades in all her subjects. She took driver's education and a typing class and accompanied her brother to and from school. At one point, their parents took them to a restaurant and announced that they were planning to divorce due to the stress of dealing with the budding bipolar diagnosis. Celia teamed up with her brother and threatened to run away if they went through with it. "I didn't resent taking care of my brother," she recalls. "I thought it was my duty. Once I got out of the house and was no longer with him, I was able to figure out who I was. For once, I was not preoccupied with him."

Caregiving can be worrisome if the sibling isn't developing healthy friendships outside the family. Optimally, both siblings should be encouraged to have their own sets of friends. Parents should do what they can to help.

Be careful not to lean on your nonbipolar child. Remember that this child has needs as well. Try to give him as much attention as possible, even when your bipolar child is having hard times. Be sure to take respite time to be with each nonbipolar sibling, and when you do, steer clear of conversations about your bipolar child. Focus instead on the child you're with and his unique talents and gifts.

Making Friends and Keeping Them

Jed can be irritating, stubborn, and insist on having his own way. Our daughter has a hard time being around our bipolar son and is embarrassed to have her friends near him.
Teresa, mom of a bipolar son diagnosed at age seven

The child with bipolar disorder may need more guidance in finding and maintaining friendships than his siblings do. While some children with bipolar disorder manage to maintain friendships of their own, it is often difficult for them to make and keep friends. Being part of a greater whole—a baseball team, the school band, ballet class, or scouts—may be especially difficult for them. Meeting group standards can be daunting for bipolar children who may be unstable at times. Public meltdowns during unstable periods may make them ashamed to return to a group activity they once enjoyed.

Finding friends one-on-one, particularly if they have special school accommodations, can be difficult. It is incumbent on parents to make sure that each of their children enjoys activities and the company of friends as frequently as they can orchestrate it. The bipolar child needs her own life, and her siblings need theirs.

If a bipolar child is interacting with other emotionally disturbed children, a parent may need to help manage the responses that take place during unstructured playtime. If the bipolar child is playing with nonbipolar children, a parent may need to intervene to help preserve the friendships when the bipolar child has a paranoid period, a manic episode, or an extreme meltdown.

Because it is harder for them to make friends, it is no surprise when a child with bipolar disorder depends on a healthy sibling to be his best friend. In a best-case scenario, the child with bipolar disorder may draw on the relationships developed by nonbipolar siblings. In other cases, he may resent them—and even try to sabotage them.

Mood-driven antics can be a source of embarrassment for siblings and can drive that child into isolation. Preparing the bipolar child for the social agenda of the nonbipolar child is important. If the nonbipolar sibling will be entertaining a guest, tell the bipolar child ahead of time, and plan a special activity just for him. Have him bake cookies or make play dough—anything to keep him distracted and amused.

Accommodations

Here are some accommodations you may have to make in order to ensure that nonbipolar siblings are getting what they need:

- Keep your bipolar child occupied with games or a project when siblings have friends come over.
- Reward the bipolar child for initiating and sustaining friendships on her own and for staying away from siblings during play dates.
- Support extracurricular activities for all your children as best you can.
- Make sure that chores are shared in as equal a manner as possible. If one child assumes more responsibility, reward that child appropriately.
- Whether it's friends, goals scored, or school grades, try not to compare the bipolar child to his sibling. Be generous with compliments for everyone and stress that cooperation comes in many different forms.

Abuse

My bipolar son is viciously mean to our six-year-old and gentle as can be with the baby. My six-year-old is afraid to be in a room alone with my bipolar son. He won't shower alone, and he begs to be in after-school care because his brother can't get at him there. He doesn't feel safe in our home. It breaks my heart.
Eleanor, mom of a bipolar son diagnosed at age ten

In a family that has a child with bipolar disorder, as with any other family, there must be a zero-tolerance policy when it comes to abuse. No child should ever be afraid to come home. Nonbipolar siblings are entitled to feel safe at home. If this means removing the abusive child from the home, start researching options discussed in Chapter 7. A 1997 study by

Middle Tennessee State University showed that even victims of severe abuse—people who were kicked, bitten, hit with a fist, or choked at the hands of a sibling—did not perceive the violence as abuse. Where do you draw the line between normal sibling fights and abuse? This is a subjective matter and often influenced by culture. One family's loud dinnertime sibling sparring may be perceived as abuse by a family accustomed to a whisper-quiet household. Every family must develop behavior standards to determine the line between sibling rivalry and abuse. In our home, it is abuse if:

- Weapons are used. A child uses a paperweight, knife, slingshot, or anything else as a weapon to threaten or attack a sibling.
- The period of anger is intense and long in duration. A child has prolonged periods of intense emotional or physical tirades against a sibling.
- There is an overwhelming physical advantage. The aggressor is bigger and stronger.
- Injury is sustained. A child suffers an injury as the result of a sibling fight.
- Cruel behavior is exhibited. A child is attacking another in a cruel manner. This includes emotional as well as physical cruelty such as extreme name-calling.
- A child feels threatened. One child feels defenseless and perceives a behavior as specifically threatening to her body or psyche.

The bipolar child must understand that a parent will protect himself and other family members should she be unable to control her impulses. A sibling must be given a "safety plan"—a room with a lock on the door that she can escape to and the phone number that she can use to summon help if she feels unsafe when alone with the bipolar child.

If the bipolar child needs to be hospitalized or if authorities must be called in after a sibling fight, a parent, not the sibling, should make that call. This will alleviate the inevitable guilt that a sibling is likely to experience from putting his sister in the hospital.

Notes from the Couch: A Psychiatrist's Point of View

Sibling concerns are a huge issue for families struggling with bipolar disorder. I often compare their circumstances to those of families with chronically ill or disabled children. One child gets a lot more time and attention from parents. The kids who aren't ill or disabled will have to do more and endure more than their peers. It seems unfair, but you can't say the bipolar or disabled child got a fair deal either.

Ultimately, those who grow up with a sick brother or sister often excel in many areas, perhaps because of the very challenges they faced as children. And if the language of the home is about acceptance of those who are different and helping those who are most vulnerable, those children will be blessed with understanding well beyond their years.

Part Four

Money Matters

CAREER

Balancing Work and the Biggest
Job You'll Ever Have

When I left my full-time software job in July to stay home and work for the agency that is the reform initiative to over-haul the way children's mental health services are provided in the state of Arizona, I told my friends that I loved my new job so much that I finally understood why God gave my son to me. There is so much more to life than having a good paying job. Now when I finish each day of work, I know that I have made a difference not only in the lives of the families I have helped, but in my own as well.
Perry, mom of a bipolar son diagnosed at age eight

My business was taking off like a rocket ship. Six years ago, I was a public relations whiz on a fast-paced career track and loving every minute of it. There was only one thing standing between me and my career advancement: a six-year-old boy who hated school, threw uncontrollable fits, and refused to listen to whomever I left in charge.

I've long since given up working for others. My last job, as a vice president at a large PR firm, didn't work out, as we were forced to switch nannies four times during my six-month tenure. Try as I might, I couldn't find child care that could handle my son. As his behavior worsened and we got the diagnosis,

I was so focused on him that there was no time for anything else.

The solution was to start my own consulting firm. The flexibility inherent in being my own boss enables me to stagger my work hours, accept and reject projects, and put assignments on hold. Unlike moms of bipolar children with nine-to-five jobs and only so many days off, I can keep my head above water—most days.

Keeping a career going when you have a child with bipolar disorder is a serious challenge, and in some cases it may not be worth the effort. There are ways to maintain your career, although some compromise may be necessary. Though the choices aren't many, you do have several, from scaling back to part-time to job sharing, which I'll describe in this chapter. To maintain your career in spite of your cycling child, you will need:

- Superb organization skills—enough to take care of yourself and your child
- Excellent and reliable child care
- Some negotiating power so you can find flexible solutions to help keep your career and your bipolar child going

With dual-career families composing over 50 percent of families with children in the United States and the number of children being diagnosed with bipolar disorder on the rise, careers and families are faced with a whole host of problems, from finding adequate child care and support to dealing with bosses and negotiating absences. Most dual-career families already struggle to achieve balance between work and family. A child who requires special attention, constant monitoring, and sometimes hospitalization, or at the very least regular appointments with a host of professionals, makes matters very hard to manage indeed.

A mother's career typically bears the brunt more than her spouse's, according to my on-line questionnaire. Responses indicated that 75 percent of moms and 36 percent of dads found their careers negatively affected by the rigors of dealing with a bipolar child. Single moms who didn't have the luxury or choice of staying home with their child headed about 25 percent of the families surveyed.

To Work or Not to Work

I deliver the newspaper, seven days a week. I work in the very early morning hours, and I'm self-employed, so I can go home whenever. My bipolar daughter stays with her sister, who is eighteen, but basically they are asleep. I cannot work a day job because she requires so much care. There is no form of child care for her. When she is not in school, I spend all my time with her.
Janice, mom of a bipolar daughter diagnosed at age eight

Parents of a bipolar child may wonder whether it makes more sense for both parents to work or for one of the two partners to stay home. Spotty attendance due to a shifting child care landscape and emergency absences combined with poor on-the-job performance can lead to dismissal. Worse yet, problems may follow a parent to the next job. Every couple has to weigh the particulars of their unique situation to make the right decision for them, but here are some questions to consider:

Developmental State of Your Child
- Does your child's age coincide with her maturity level?
- Can she handle being separated from you for the length of an average workday?
- What sort of adverse behavior does she engage in when you're away for several hours?

Child's Understanding and Awareness of His Condition
- Does your child know how to identify his cycles?
- Can he effectively report his mood state to others?
- Can he identify potential trigger situations?
- Has he mastered effective coping methods?

Your Support Network
- Who will be there for your child?
- Does your child trust them enough to let them know when she needs help?
- Who will you turn to when you need backup?
- Will your support network be able to spot troubling symptoms?

Your Marriage
- Will your marriage benefit from both partners working?
- Have you discussed who will do what if your child needs immediate attention during the workday?
- Who will stay home in that situation?

Job Demands
- Will you be able to negotiate time off when you are needed at home?

- Does company sick leave cover children as well as the parent?
- Can you negotiate other benefits to your bipolar child's advantage?

Disclosure
- If you both intend to work, will one or both of you tell your employer(s) that your child is challenged by mental illness and ask for reasonable accommodations?

Easing the Workload

Before you approach your employer, it is important to sort out exactly what accommodations you need to be productive on the job and keep life with your bipolar child on an even keel. Do you want to reduce the number of hours you work each week? Is it possible for you to work at home? Do you need a leave of absence? Flextime generally tops the list of accommodation wish lists. A leave is usually a subsequent request.

Consult an Expert
Mike Stoltz, executive director of Clubhouse of Suffolk, a Long Island, New York–based psychiatric rehabilitation and support program, suggests that before requesting leave, parents should consult with a labor professional about their employer's policies. A parent who works for a union should consult with the shop steward. Others can call their state labor department for information on how to proceed. If there are still questions, it may be wise to consult with a labor attorney, using your employee handbook or personnel policy manual as a starting point.

Wade Through the Issues of Disclosure

Stoltz says that within the Clubhouse rehabilitation organization, about 50 percent of the participants choose to disclose their child's condition to their employer when asking for job accommodations or a leave. The other half does not. Only you can decide whether it's appropriate. Are you confident that your employer or representative will respect your privacy?

If you do decide to disclose, Stoltz suggests you take the opportunity to educate the employer, laying out exactly what you need and the impact it is likely to have on the job. Some may choose not to disclose their child's condition when requesting a leave. Stoltz warns that those who do not disclose may compromise future legal recourse. Educate yourself about the company's warning, probation, and dismissal process.

The Americans with Disabilities Act

The ADA protects people with mental illness and, in certain circumstances, parents of children with mental illness, from workplace discrimination. The law says that an employer must provide reasonable accommodations for any qualified individual with a disability. ADA also prohibits discrimination against individuals with a known association with an individual with a disability (i.e., parents). Reasonable accommodations are reserved for the disabled, not for their parents. However, if the company is aware of your child's situation and its complaints about your work quality suspiciously correlate with mounting insurance bills, you may be able to prove that the company is indeed discriminating against you because of your child's disability.

The Family Medical Leave Act

The Family Medical Leave Act (FMLA) was passed during the

Clinton administration to protect people in the workplace who are sick or have a sick relative (in-laws are excluded). According to Thomas Apple, a labor attorney with Itochu International, you can invoke the FMLA only when the company you work for has over fifty employees and you have worked at the company for at least one year *and* for at least 1,250 hours.

If both employer and employee are qualified, then the employee is guaranteed up to twelve weeks of leave (with notification). The leave can be intermittent or consecutive, depending on need.

Exiting the Workforce

When your child is cycling, going through a particularly tough time as you search for the right school situation, and you don't have cohesive support systems to help you manage work interruptions, the most logical solution might be to take a temporary leave from the workplace.

According to my on-line survey, moms were more likely than dads to leave their jobs and stay home with a bipolar child. Leaving your career is jolting, even in the case of a planned retirement. When you are forced to give up your career and income, albeit for the best of causes, you're bound to experience some resentment. While therapy is often helpful during this difficult time, how do you pay for it when your income is affected? It is important for women exiting the workforce to find some form of self-nurture. Finding a sense of purpose—for example, through volunteer work or part-time home-based work—is essential. A happy mother generally means a happy child.

Reentering the Workforce

I now work for my mother's real estate business. My hours are flexible, and I've got a very understanding boss.
Judy, mom of a bipolar son diagnosed at age three

I currently work for a nursing agency, where I have complete control of my schedule, and my bipolar son is in RTC. Before I found this position, the only work that fit with my scheduling needs was part-time work at minimum wage, which does not pay the bills!
Eliza, mom of a bipolar son diagnosed at age eight

The nature of the bipolar condition, especially in children, is ebb and flow. While problems do crop up periodically, solutions arise as well. A medication switch, a new school setting, an intensive hospitalization period, or a residential placement may make a radical difference in a child's behavior and overall stability. When your child has stabilized and you have found effective care, you may feel that you are ready to reenter the job market. Thanks to years of deflecting and defusing rages, you have excellent people skills, but where does that go on a resumé? Going back to the traditional workplace may seem like a formidable task after staying home with your child. Should you resume the work you left behind or seek a new career path?

Career counselor Nancy Collamer (www.jobsandmoms.com), a human resource professional who specializes in helping people scale back their jobs and reenter the workforce, suggests that parents of bipolar children consider their choices carefully but ultimately let their passions guide them. Rather than seek full-time work, she suggests parents look for flexibility. While this might limit your choices, it will almost certainly be easier to maintain over time. "Trying to find flexibility in the job market is not just a problem for parents of bipolar children," explains Collamer. People with ailing parents or disabled spouses also have serious limitations. No matter what the root cause, finding work when dependent care is a challenge is no easy feat.

Before you reclaim an office cubicle, you may need to reclaim your self-esteem. According to Collamer, there is an immediate drop in self-esteem when women (or men) stay home to be with a child. It is important to find a way to restore it before you begin job hunting. It will help other people take you seriously; more important, it will help you take yourself seriously. "When people are ready to resume careers after full-time parenting, their self-esteem may not be completely in the toilet, but it certainly isn't what it was when they were working," she explains. "I'm a huge believer in going back to school to familiarize yourself with current technology or update your skills. Getting an A on a paper does wonders for self-esteem!"

Volunteer work is another possibility. In addition to building self-esteem, it could even evolve into a career option. Stay away from making cupcakes for the school bake-a-thon or giving out books at a PTA book fair, Collamer warns. The idea is to get your feet wet in a more professional realm, such as fundraising, Web design, bookkeeping, writing, or public relations work.

Explaining Career Interruptus

Once you have put your resumé together and started seriously job hunting, you face the problem of explaining your absence from the workforce. It's one thing to say you were laid off and out of work for a couple of months, quite another to explain that you've spent the better part of the past five or ten years driving your child to therapy, attending school meetings, and possibly even bailing your child out of jail. Sure, the skills you've picked up over the years are myriad and diverse, but how do you combat the less-than-reliable impression your spotty employment history creates?

"Don't lie, but don't volunteer any extra information," advises Nancy Collamer. "The key is to impress the employer so much that they're willing to take a chance on you. Explain the gaps as best you can, avoiding details. For example, 'I had issues at home that I needed to attend to.' If they are under control, be sure to let the employer know that too."

Mike Stoltz concurs. "Do not say, 'I've spent the last few years being an advocate and caregiver for my special needs child.' The employer's first response is likely to be, 'If that's so, is it really possible that it's over?'" He suggests that parents planning a return to work make time every day for professional nourishment and transition activities. Your child will take notice and begin to make adjustments too.

Your transitional activities should include taking undisturbed time for yourself. When your child sees you working from home, he will learn something about work ethics, but he may also be jealous. With the help of your child's therapist, prepare to deal with it and to work with your child toward acceptance. Both parent and child have to learn to detach, not an easy feat for parents and especially not for bipolar children. That's when solutions like flextime and partnering can be your salvation.

Creative Solutions

When a full-time career is not the answer, creative alternatives enable parents to work and parent a bipolar child.

Partnering

If you've run your own business before and are contemplating hanging out a shingle again, ask yourself if a new business is likely to thrive when you aren't around full-time to tend it. Businesses, like children, need nurturing and can go through growth spurts that require more than a peripheral commitment. Consider partnering with someone. That way, there's someone available to pick up the pieces on the days when your child is acting up. Finding a good partner is the next best thing to cloning yourself. Be sure your partner knows and understands your child's situation and that you draft a formal agreement that protects you from an enterprise gone awry.

Job Sharing

Job sharing is a terrific way to split a job in half and works really well with line jobs in big companies or sales jobs. The work is divided, and the job-sharing partners split the salary, benefits, and work hours. Finding a job-sharing partner can be done through an agency that specializes in pairing people or by finding someone with similar skills to yours and going on job interviews together. It is also a flex option that can be negotiated if you find that you have to scale back your hours and you've established a good rapport with your superiors. Both major corporations and smaller companies seeking to retain quality workers employ job-sharing partners for a variety of positions, including bookkeeping, sales, and executive assistants.

There are no rules to splitting the workload. Some people split the day; others split the workweek. Some have an overlapping day, and others alternate weeks. For more information on job sharing, visit www.sharegoals.com, a Web site produced by two job-sharing consultants, Shari Rosen Ascher and Maggie Sisco.

"Home" Work

If you work at home, use a kitchen timer to show your child just how long you will be working. When the timer dings or beeps, call it a day, end that conference call, and do something with your child. After your shared activity, set your child up with another activity, reset the timer, and log another stretch of work time. The timer translates your time into a an easy-to-grasp period for your child and represents a two-way contract: when the timer goes off, you will become available for him; while it is on, he has agreed to allow you time to work.

Notes from the Couch: A Psychiatrist's Point of View

I recently read in the newspaper that a survey of top female executives indicated that more than half of them had remained single or childless. Even without the challenge of bipolar illness in a child, combining parenting and a career is a high-wire act. There is little margin for error, and it requires constant adjustments.

The pressures are enormous, and it can overload the most energetic moms and dads. Keep a close eye on your own "overload meter," and make changes accordingly. That might mean working less, changing careers, or not working at all. Sometimes it might mean working more—to get needed funds or needed mental breaks from the bipolar parenting experience. Needs will change as your child and family grows. Flexibility and openness to creative solutions will be invaluable.

CHAPTER 14

FAMILY FINANCES

Paying for Special Needs Now and Later

*At this point, I have no way of maintaining a steady in-
come! I took a leave from work but can't take any more time
off. We live on credit cards, but I've reached my credit limits. I have no cushion for the times when my son needs me
at home, and I can't work.*
Katy, mom of a bipolar son diagnosed at age seven

Financial issues haunt parents of children with bipolar disorder throughout the parents' lifetimes. The costs associated
with caring for a child with bipolar disorder take a bite out of
the family bank account. A steady income may elude you, special programs and supplemental education are costly, and
most insurance policies cover only a fraction of the bill. For
the uninsured, it's even worse.

You may be surprised to learn that insurance coverage for
mental illness and hospitalization is far from comparable to
the coverage you receive for physical treatments. According to
Dr. Jeanne S. Ringel, Ph.D., associate economist with the
RAND Corporation, a think tank, if there were parity, children would be the biggest beneficiaries. Besides dictating
treatment reimbursements, your insurance plan may limit you
to particular practitioners, refuse to pay for hospitalizations, or
cap the number of therapy visits.

In too many cases, practitioners simply refuse to deal with

insurance companies. They will give you an invoice, and it is up to you to pay and then secure reimbursement as best you can. While some insurance plans reimburse for medications, often the newer the drug, the less likely you'll be reimbursed. Visits to alternative practitioners and treatments like omega 3 fish oil capsules are rarely covered. Parents are typically left with sky-high treatment bills.

The sad facts, according to data collected by the National Survey of America's Families, are that a substantial share of children who could benefit from mental health services do not receive any. Furthermore, over 80 percent of uninsured children with mental health needs receive no care at all. The total pharmaceutical costs alone are estimated to be over $1.1 billion each year.

That is why it's so important for you to understand where and how you can get a financial break. This chapter will teach you how to get the most out of your health care dollars, find programs to help you pay for care and medications, and manage your finances in anticipation of future needs.

Financial Health Care Choices

When choosing your health care practitioner, you will be faced with choices ranging from psychiatrists, psychologists, and social workers in private practice to those affiliated with clinics. Clinics may be run by community service organizations with funding from philanthropic and government sources or by hospitals as part of larger teaching programs. The quality of the care you choose may well reflect how much you pay for it. While clinics usually operate on a sliding-fee scale and may provide access to top-notch practitioners who are in private practice elsewhere, your access to them will be limited and your time with them closely monitored. You may well be left without support in case of an off-hours emergency.

Alleviating the Cost Burdens

Negotiating Treatment Fees

Keep in mind that psychiatrists' and therapists' fees are almost always negotiable. Figure out what you can realistically spend each month on therapy and medication for your family. Explain to your provider that you have financial constraints and would like her to consider lowering her fee. Then wait for her to throw out a number. If the best price she says she can offer still exceeds your budget, tell her what you have allocated for treatment. Hopefully, you can agree on a fee you can both live with.

It's Deductible!

The silver lining in the thundercloud of your medical expenses is that those not covered by insurers or by your medical savings account plan may be deducted on your tax return as itemized expenses (Form 1040, Schedule A). Deductible items include prescription medications, medical insurance premiums, doctor fees, and more. The total deductible is limited to a percentage of your adjusted gross income. There are a number of further restrictions, so discuss this matter with your tax adviser. TurboTax or similar software can help you identify and track these deductions.

Medicaid

Medicaid is a federal program that requires states to provide medically necessary services, including mental health services, to the needy. Because the program is state driven, whether your child gets help or not may depend on your home state's administrative services. Medicaid is reserved for children from low-income families and is unavailable for middle- and higher-income families. Sadly, many doctors don't participate in the Medicaid program, perhaps because the reimbursements tend to be significantly less than those offered by private insurance companies.

A child from a middle- or higher-income household could qualify for Medicaid if he is in a hospital or residential setting for a certain amount of time. In almost half of all states, these children can apply for Medicaid benefits even if they don't live in a residential setting. If your child is in a hospital or residential treatment facility, ask his social worker to help you find out more about the program. In Kansas, Vermont, and New York, there are a very limited number of home- and community-based waivers that enable a state to provide mental health services through Medicaid to children who would otherwise be ineligible due to their parents' income. You can apply for a waiver through your state or county mental health association.

Social Security and Disability

Depending on the state you live in and your family's income, your child may be eligible for social security or disability payments. For a child to qualify, she must be disabled, and the family and individual income must fall below a certain level, which varies from state to state. To find out if your child is eligible, visit your local social security office. Make sure to bring your child's birth certificate, proof of identity, and a letter or other documentation of your child's disability from the doctor. You'll be asked to fill out some forms, and this will start the application process. Afterward, you may be asked to provide further documentation to determine whether your family income and the child's income, as well as your family's resources, exceed the social security and disability requirements in your state. For more information, visit www.ssa.gov.

Prescription Drug Patient Assistance Programs

A number of pharmaceutical companies have specially funded programs to assist low-income patients with prescription medications for specific conditions or diseases. These programs work with Medigap, Medicare managed care plans, state assistance programs, community-based programs, and other funding sources. For more information or to find out if your child is eligible, visit www.phrma.org.

Planning for Your BP Child's Future

While some bipolar children will undoubtedly find success and good fortune in life, the disease is so variable and the diagnosis so relatively new that there is no longitudinal data available on how those diagnosed as children will ultimately fare. And if that doesn't say enough about the lack of predictability of life, we have no idea how long we will remain on this planet, fit and able to care for a child who may rely on others far longer than nonbipolar siblings.

Bipolar adults who refuse medication or are resistant to treatment may end up unable to care for themselves financially as well as physically. The hope is that early treatment and intervention will enable our children to live productive and stable lives, but there's no question that some adults with bipolar disorder are victims of their mood swings, unable to manage money or treatments.

In planning for their bipolar child's future, parents should take into account how much money and property is available, whether either parent is physically and emotionally able to care for the child should the other die, and who is available as backup coverage.

Ask yourself about the nature and degree of your child's problem. What abilities are affected now, and which are likely to be affected in the future? Is it likely that your child will have difficulties managing money or making decisions on his own behalf? What about the tasks of daily living? While no parent has a crystal ball, and it's painful to think that the child you are raising may have such serious impediments, you should nevertheless consider your child's situation carefully and consult with your psychiatrist and therapist to try to get an understanding of his or her long-term prognosis.

Barbara H. Cane, a New York–based attorney whose practice concentrates on estate matters, explains that "an attorney is the person who can help you sift through the issues and plan for your child's long-term care if you're not around. If you don't write a will, you've lost your chance to name the person most appropriate to care for your bipolar child, and you've lost all say in how that child will be provided for."

When you visit an attorney, she'll ask questions about your family and resources and help you make a plan that satisfies your current and future family needs. Wills, trusts, and power-of-attorney documents may periodically need to be amended to reflect changes in your situation, but the goal is to build flexibility into your documents from the beginning.

Guardianship

First and foremost, you will have to name a guardian. Should you and your spouse die, a guardian would take charge of the physical care of your children and make decisions for them until they're at the age of majority, which varies from state to state. In choosing a guardian for your bipolar child, clearly you want to give the matter serious and measured thought. Who understands the bipolar condition and will be able to advocate for your child as you do? Who does your child like and respond well to? Remember that your child's guardian will be helping to make medical decisions, ensure she stays on her medications, and care for her on a daily basis until—and possibly beyond—the age of majority.

The "duty to support" age varies from state to state and may even stretch long past the child's twenty-first birthday. Guardianship proceedings may be necessary if a child is legally an adult, but in fact cannot make decisions about her health care or other matters. Some states have guardianship statutes that tailor a guardianship to the needs of the adult child so that it is a minimally intrusive legal agreement.

Dividing Up Resources

Most families divide the resources among the children equally. If the parents die while the children are still young, often the money is kept in a fund until they all reach a certain age, at which time it is distributed equally. Generally, a fixed amount of money is available for the trustee to give to the guardian for the children on an as-needed basis.

When one child has special needs, her basic care may simply cost more, and the parents' estate plan should reflect that. As you begin making such plans, consider the following:

- Is your bipolar child in a residential treatment facility? A government-funded program or group home? What impact will inheritance money have on her public entitlements?
- Can your bipolar child be trusted to make judicious monetary decisions?

- Is your bipolar child independent but likely to need more money than his nonbipolar siblings?

These factors will influence how you will distribute resources. Obviously, if a bipolar child cannot be trusted to manage his own money, leaving an inheritance in his hands is a mistake. Consider too how his current treatment is funded. A bipolar child who is on public entitlement and ensconced in a steady and satisfying residential situation can be knocked out of his residential treatment center or group home as the result of a lump-sum inheritance.

Trusts

One way to ensure your child will have money when she needs it without jeopardizing governmental entitlements is to put the money in trust for her. State laws on trusts vary, so it is essential to get a competent professional to draft an agreement for the type of trust most appropriate for your situation.

Supplemental Needs Trust

Supplemental needs trust money is put in trust for the child who is receiving government entitlements but requires additional funds for things such as vacations, recreational activities, or a car. The idea is to protect your child's entitlements while providing a better quality of life for her.

Discretionary Trust

Another approach is to create a discretionary trust for one or more of your children. As the name of this type of trust implies, the trustee can give each child what she needs as she needs it, and decisions are based on the trustee's discretion.

Because the trust belongs to more than one child, the bipolar child's financial eligibility for public entitlements is preserved.

Community Trust

In some cases, parents have no one to entrust with the care of their bipolar child. UJA-Federation of New York, a nonprofit organization, developed the community trust for this situation. A certain amount of money is put in trust for the child, and an advocate is assigned to work with the child to ensure he gets the services and entitlements he needs, supplemented by funds from the trust. Some people find that using a knowledgeable advocate coupled with a professional money manager makes more sense than burdening a sibling or family friend with these responsibilities, according to Morton Asch, director of planned giving initiatives for UJA-Federation of New York. The inheritance will not affect the person's entitlements but is only for adult children. Until your child reaches the age of majority, the money would have to be protected in another type of trust, but at that time it could be turned over to the community trust. The bipolar adult would then be assigned an advocate with F.E.G.S., one of the largest human service agencies in the United States. This caseworker would help your grown child make decisions and manage his life.

There is a $25,000 minimum to open a trust, which can be financed through a will, insurance policy, or pension plan. A trustee at UJA-Federation of New York distributes the resources. The money can be used to augment food, clothing, and shelter monies provided by government entitlements, but also for "extras" like a vacation, television, or private dentist that may not be covered by entitlements. The trustee will judge whether the request is appropriate and if it's in line with the monies available in the trust fund. If the beneficiary outlives the income and principal of the trust, the agency still cares for the individual throughout his lifetime. The UJA-Federation program has become a model for others across the country. If you are interested in finding out more about this program, call your local UJA-Federation office and ask about the supplemental needs trust.

Disabled & Alone, Life Services for the Disabled, is another nonprofit corporation that works with parents to create complete care plans based on an individual's disabilities and interests.

The Trustee

It's possible that the person you've chosen as guardian for your child is also great at making financial decisions, in which case you can name him trustee as well. Otherwise, you will need to find someone else to responsibly manage the resources you have left. The trustee should be someone with excellent financial judgment. It needn't be a friend or family member. Many people name a relied-on attorney or accountant. The trustee should be willing to call in professionals when needed to help make financial decisions. For instance, if the guardian feels that the child would benefit from costly mental health services, the trustee might want to pay for a second opinion to evaluate how necessary that service is. A trustee can be an individual (friend, family member, attorney, accountant) or a corporation or nonprofit organization. Corporate trustees are more likely to survive parents than are individuals.

At times, the trustee will be supporting the guardian in ways that will secondarily benefit your child. For instance, the guardian may request funds for a home renovation or to obtain child care.

Other Sources of Income

Barbara Cane suggests that parents discuss and coordinate their financial plans with grandparents and other relatives who may leave money to the child so that generous bequests do not carry the unintended consequence of compromising the child's public entitlements. As you try to get a handle on the big picture, consider your will, as well as custodial accounts, co-owned savings bonds, life insurance policies, pensions, IRAs, and other monies that might eventually pass to the child with bipolar disease.

"My father-in-law used to say, whether you're rich or poor, it's better to have money," states Barbara Cane. "And it is true that the more resources you have, the more care options you will have for your child. But money in the wrong place at the wrong time can be a disaster. Even more important than the absolute number of available dollars is the quality of the planning for the adult child with bipolar disorder."

Notes from the Couch: A Psychiatrist's Point of View

Any marriage counselor will tell you that couples fight more about money than just about anything else. In fact, many people would rather relate their most intimate sexual details than talk about how they handle money. Budgeting, planning, and saving are hard for most people; financial disarray can be embarrassing and appear insurmountable. It's not easy to talk about. The issue is magnified in the light of your child's illness and special needs. Honest communication and tolerating the uncomfortable emotions are the first steps toward successfully resolving these issues.

Financial savvy is not something we're born with. Get help for planning and budgeting. Expert advice usually pays for itself over time.

RESOURCES

Resource Links

The Ups & Downs of Raising a Bipolar Child,
www.parentingbipolars.com
About Our Kids, www.aboutourkids.org
Administration for Children and Families, www.acf.dhhs.gov
American Academy of Child and Adolescent Psychiatry, www.aacap.org
American Academy of Pediatrics, www.aap.org
American Association of People with Disabilities, www.aapd-dc.org
American Medical Association, www.ama-assn.org
American Psychiatric Association, www.psych.org
American Psychiatric Press, www.appi.org
American Psychoanalytic Association, www.apsa.org
American Psychological Association, www.apa.org
American Society of Adolescent Psychiatry, www.adolpsych.org
Animal Assisted Therapy, www.peteducation.com
Bazelon Center for Mental Health Law, www.bazelon.org
Bipolar Resource Site, www.bpdresources.com/supportnons.html
Bipolar Significant Others, www.bpso.org
Bright Futures Health Web Site for Children, www.brightfutures.org
Center for Mental Health Services, www.mentalhealth.org
Center for Treatment Research on Adolescent Drug Abuse,
www.med.miami.edu/ctrada
Childsafe, www.pivot.net/~childsafe/kidslink.htm
The Child Advocate, www.childadvocate.net
Child and Adolescent Bipolar Foundation, www.bpkids.org
Children with Disabilities, www.childrenwithdisabilities.ncjrs.org
Children's Defense Fund, www.childrensdefense.org
The Children's Health Council, www.chconline.org

Child Welfare League of America, www.cwla.org
Connect for Kids—Guidance for Grownups, www.connectforkids.org
Coping.org, www.coping.org
Court Appointed Special Advocates, www.nationalcasa.org
The Cross Cultural Health Care Program, www.xculture.org
Depression and Bipolar Support Alliance, www.dbsalliance.org
Disabled Resources, www.familyvillage.wisc.edu/index.htmlx
Educational Advocacy, www.azadvocate.com
Families Worldwide, www.fww.org
Federation of Families for Children's Mental Health, www.ffcmh.org
Freedom from Fear—Building Bridges from Education to Treatment,
www.freedomfromfear.org
Harvard Medical Library, www.med.harvard.edu
Healthfinder, www.healthfinder.gov
Healthfinder Español, www.healthfinder.gov/espanol/
Hospitals, www.usnews.com/usnews/nycu/health/hosptl/rankings/
specreppsyc.htm
How Children Learn, www.ed.gov/pubs/ReadWithMe/ makconn.html
Job Sharing, www.sharegoals.com
Juvenile Bipolar Research Foundation, www.bpchildresearch.org
Madison Institute of Medicine, www.miminc.org
Medicare/Medicaid, cms.hhs.gov/default.asp?fromhcfadotgov=true
National Alliance for the Mentally Ill, www.nami.org
National Association of Psychiatric Health Systems, www.naphs.org
National Information Center for Children and Youth with Disabilities,
www.nichcy.org
National Institute of Mental Health, www.nimh.nih.gov
National Library of Medicine, www.nlm.nih.gov
National Mental Health Association, www.nmha.org
National Organization on Disability, www.nod.org/cont/
dsp_cont_loc_hme.cfm?locationId=12&locationNm=Home
National Parent Network on Disability, www.npnd.org
No Child Left Behind, www.nochildleftbehind.gov/index.html
Pharmaceutical Company Patient Assistance Programs, www.phrma.org
Psychiatric and Personality Disorders, www.parentshandbook.org
Psychiatric Legal Issues, www.psyclaw.org/mental.html
Safer Child, Inc., www.saferchild.org
SOS High School Suicide Prevention Program,
www.mentalhealthscreening.org/sos_highschool
Stanley Foundation Bipolar Network, www.bipolarnetwork.org
Surgeon General's Report, www.aacap.org/SurgeonGeneral/index.htm

Social Security Administration, www.ssa.gov/odhome
Stand for Children, www.stand.org
Substance Abuse and Mental Health Services Administration,
www.samhsa.gov
Youth Law Center, www.youthlawcenter.org

Books

The Bipolar Child, Demitri and Janice Papolos, 1999, Broadway Books.
Change Your Brain, Change Your Life, Daniel Amen, M.D., 1999, Crown
Publishing Group.
Delayed Posttraumatic Stress Disorders from Infancy: The Two Trauma Mechanism, Clancy D. McKenzie, M.D., and Lance S. Wright, M.D., 1996,
Harwood Academic Publishers.
The Explosive Child, Ross W. Greene, Ph.D., 2001, Quill.
Help Me, I'm Sad, David G. Fassler, M.D., and Lynne S. Dumas, Penguin
Books, 1997.
Living Without Depression and Manic-Depression: A Workbook for Maintaining Mood Stability, Mary Ellen Copeland, 1994, New Harbinger Publications.
The Natural Medicine Chest, Eugene R. Zampieron, N.D., A.H.G., and
Ellen Kamhi, Ph.D., R.N., H.N.C., 1999, M. Evans & Company.
Overcoming Depression, Demitri and Janice Papolos, 3rd ed., 1997,
HarperCollins.
Detour: My Bipolar Road Trip in 4-D, Lizzie Simon, 2002, Atria Books.
Taking the Bully by the Horns, Kathy Noll with Dr. Jay Carter, 1998, Unicorn Press.
When Someone You Love Is Depressed: How to Help Your Loved One Without Losing Yourself, Laura Epstein Rosen, Ph.D., and Xavier Francisco
Amador, Ph.D., 1996, Simon & Schuster.

INDEX

abuse, 247
  of siblings, 263–65
  substance, 14, 110, 118, 120
adolescents, 4, 8, 133, 197, 203, 248
  diagnoses and, 15, 30
  medications and, 110, 116,
    120–21, 123
  mental health care professionals
    and, 39–40, 70
  moods and, 102–4
  schools and, 187, 190
adopted children, 31
advocates, advocacy, 7, 160
  diagnoses and, 33–34
  explaining your child's condition
    and, 208–9
  family finances and, 287, 289
  laws and, 213–14, 216, 224
  schooling and, 180–83, 199, 243
aggressiveness, 2–5, 13, 22, 104, 121
  daily life and, 132, 143
  day care and, 175–76
  helping with, 72, 95
  hospitalization and, 151–52,
    156–57
  laws and, 212, 218, 220, 224
  mental health care professionals
    and, 57–58

parental relationships and, 247, 249
parental self-care and, 229, 231
schools and, 185–86
siblings and, 257–58, 263–65
alcohol, 110, 120
Amen, Daniel, 23
American Academy of Child and
  Adolescent Psychiatry, 32
American Medical Association, 39
Americans with Disabilities Act
  (ADA), 179, 214–15, 274
anger, 2, 4–5, 8, 104, 121, 149, 234
  diagnoses and, 26–27, 31
  explaining your child's condition
    and, 203, 256
  helping with, 71–74, 97, 99, 101
  hospitalization and, 152, 161
  parental relationships and,
    242–43
  siblings and, 256, 258, 264
animal-assisted therapy, 66–68
antidepressants, 6, 25–26, 110,
  113–17, 120
antipsychotics, 111–13, 163
anxiety, anxieties, 42, 105, 117, 171,
  175, 185, 223, 236
  daily life and, 126, 130, 134,
    137–38

anxiety, anxieties *(cont.)*
  diagnoses and, 14, 21, 26
  helping with, 72, 94–96
  parental relationships and, 241, 248
Apple, Thomas, 214, 216
As Told by Ginger, 203
Ativan, 118, 163, 216
attention deficit disorder (ADD), 25–26
attention-deficit hyperactive disorder (ADHD), 6–7, 38, 42, 116
  diagnoses and, 14, 25–27, 30
attention levels, 20
auditory integration therapy (AIT), 69
Austin, Nancy, 42–43, 130
Axelson, David, 65

babysitters, 2–3, 60, 177, 204
  daily life and, 138, 147
  moods and, 84, 86, 89–90, 94
bargaining, 242–43
behavioral meltdowns, 269
  daily life and, 130–31, 136, 143–44, 147–48
  helping with, 72, 86
  mental health care professionals and, 57–58
  schools and, 186, 188
  siblings and, 259, 261–62
behavioral therapy, 42, 79, 104
Bersoff, Donald, 59–60
bipolar disorder:
  definitions of, 14–15, 44
  early-onset, 7, 15, 17, 19–20, 27, 31, 34, 37–40, 62
  future of children with, 285–91
  statistics on, 14, 19, 26, 28, 31, 34, 94–95, 140, 151, 270–71
  types of, 18
bipolar disorder, diagnosis of, 13–36, 196, 285

advocacy and, 33–34
brain and, 14, 16–17, 23–25, 29–33
comorbidity and, 25–26, 42, 48, 51
coping with, 26–28
daily life and, 130, 133, 146–47
errors in, 6–7, 25–27, 105, 216–17
explaining your child's condition and, 31–33, 204, 206–8, 256–57
hospitalization and, 152, 159, 166, 169
laws and, 212, 216–18
medications and, 15–16, 19, 22, 25–27, 31–32, 34, 106–8, 123
mental health care professionals and, 14–15, 17–22, 26–29, 34–36, 39, 42, 48, 51
moods and, 13–18, 20–21, 25–26, 32–35, 93, 103–5
nature vs. nurture in, 28–29, 34–35
parental relationships and, 242–45, 251–52
schools and, 13, 15, 18–19, 21, 32–34, 178, 181–83, 189, 199
siblings and, 256–57, 260
stigma of, 29–32
symptoms and, 13–14, 16–17, 19–34
tests in, 17–25, 34
work and, 269–70
bipolar disorder, symptoms of, 1–5, 7, 187, 218, 272
  in adults vs. children, 14–15
  daily life and, 136–37
  diagnoses and, 13–14, 16–17, 19–28
  explaining your child's condition and, 204, 206
  hospitalization and, 152, 157, 159

medications and, 108–9, 112, 116–19
mental health care professionals and, 37–38, 42–43, 51, 58
moods and, 104–5
bipolar disorder, treatment of, 5–9, 36, 104–5, 204, 241
diagnoses and, 13–14, 16–17, 19–34
family finances and, 281–85, 287–88
goals of, 52–53, 159
laws and, 216–17, 221, 223
mental health care professionals and, 39, 41–44, 48–49, 51–54, 57–70
moods and, 75, 79, 100–101, 104
schooling and, 189–91, 199
see also hospitals, hospitalization; medications; residential treatment centers; therapists, therapy
birthdays, 145
blame, blaming, 3, 245–47
Blanco, Antonio, 150
blood tests, 107, 112, 121–22
Bloomgarden, Karenne, 196–97
brain, 181, 242, 256
daily life and, 137, 148
diagnoses and, 14, 16–17, 23–25, 29–33
medications and, 108, 110, 112, 114, 116
mental health care professionals and, 38–39, 68
moods and, 72–73, 79, 98–99, 103
breathing, moods and, 95, 99
Brofman, Susan, 219
Brown, Sheila, 244
buproprion (Wellbutrin), 114–15

calendars, 77
camps, 195–99

daily life and, 126, 147
medications and, 123–24, 195–96
special, 197–99, 218
Cane, Barbara H., 286, 291
Carle, Gilda, 231–32, 246, 250
Child and Adolescent Bipolar Foundation (CABF), 45, 65, 187, 237
Children's Protective Services (CPS), 220–21
cognitive therapy, 42, 134
Collamer, Nancy, 276–78
colors, moods and, 76–77, 86
comfort zones, 87–88
communicating, communication, 130, 250–52, 291
community trusts, 289–90
confidentiality, 59–60, 70
contacts, 154–55
contracts, moods and, 101–2
convening, moods and, 100
copycat behavior, 4, 9, 255, 257–58
counting, 96
creative therapies, 66
crisis lists, crisis plans, 60, 157, 186, 196
parental relationships and, 247–48
cruise ships, 147
crying, 1–2, 4–6, 9, 201
diagnoses and, 13
helping with, 71, 81, 92
cursing, 2, 128, 175, 201, 229
custodial issues, 212–13, 220–22, 224–25
cyclothymic disorder, 18

daily life, 161, 286
behavioral meltdowns and, 130–31, 136, 143–44, 147–48
day care and, 147, 176
holidays and, 125, 140–41, 143–47

daily life *(cont.)*
  place to go and, 136–37
  rewards and punishments and,
      125, 128–29, 131–32, 134,
      138
  schedules and, 128–29, 138–39,
      141–42, 144, 146, 148
  sick days and, 139–40
  structure of, 125–49
  transitions and, 125–32, 135,
      139, 141
  typical, 132–39
Daily Schedule charts, 141–42
Dannemiller, Linda, 182, 191–92
day care, 37, 175–77, 192
  daily life and, 147, 176
defense attorneys, 218–19
demands, outrageous, 83
denial, 5, 27
  parental relationships and, 240,
      242–45, 250
Depakote, 106, 112
depression, 6, 8, 113–19, 176, 223
  daily life and, 133, 137–38, 140
  diagnoses and, 14–19, 23, 25, 29
  helping with, 80–81, 83, 91–94,
      96–97, 99, 102, 105
  medications and, 110–11,
      113–17, 119, 140
  mental health care professionals
      and, 38, 67–68
  parental relationships and, 239,
      242–43, 252
  parental self-care and, 230, 234
  symptoms of, 92–93
detoxification:
  daily life and, 136, 144, 147
  moods and, 84, 88, 98–99
disability payments, 284–85
discretionary trusts, 288–89
disengagement, moods and, 87
distractions, moods and, 98

divorces, 240, 251–54, 260
dopamine, 16, 112–13, 116
double-blind studies, 63
due diligence, 166–67

earn bonus miles concept, 129
eating, 122, 260
  daily life and, 132, 141
  diagnoses and, 16, 21
  hospitalization and, 160–61
  moods and, 75, 92
  parental self-care and, 233, 235
eating disorders, 14, 18, 115
educational attorneys, 212–14
electroencephalograms (EEGs), 24
emotionally disturbed (ED), 177–78
emotions, 2, 4, 73, 95, 104, 155,
      221
  camps and, 197–98
  daily life and, 128, 130, 136–37,
      140, 143, 148
  explaining your child's condition
      and, 205, 207
  family finances and, 286, 291
  medications and, 108, 110, 112,
      119–20, 124
  mental health care professionals
      and, 41–42
  parental relationships and, 239,
      252–54
  parental self-care and, 230–31,
      234, 236, 238
  schools and, 183, 185, 187, 199
  siblings and, 262, 264
Employment Discrimination Report,
      44
energy, 4, 105–6, 134, 148, 231,
      256, 280
  diagnoses and, 14, 18–19, 21, 28
  moods and, 81–83, 88, 96, 105
epidemiological studies, 62
essential fatty acids, 119–20

exercise, 122, 137, 177
moods and, 98–99
parental self-care and, 233, 235

Faedda, Gianni, 30–31
families, 13, 111
daily life and, 145–46
explaining your child's condition
and, 202–5, 210–11
hospitalization and, 150, 154–56,
164–65, 167, 170
mental health care professionals
and, 49, 53–54, 56, 62, 70
moods and, 85–87, 95
parental relationships and,
239–41, 244–45, 249, 253
parental self-care and, 229–30,
232–33, 235–36
schooling and, 190, 193
siblings and, 255, 257–58, 261,
263–65
work and, 269–70, 280
family finances, 197, 236, 280–91
alleviating cost burdens and,
283–85
dividing up resources and,
287–90
health care choices and, 282–83
laws and, 212–14, 216, 219,
221–23, 286, 288, 290
parental relationships and, 239,
251–52
schooling and, 193–94, 281
work and, 269, 275–76, 280–81
family histories, 7, 38, 62, 236
diagnoses and, 19–20, 26–29,
31–32
parental relationships and,
240–41, 245
family law attorneys, 219–21
Family Medical Leave Act (FMLA),
214, 274–75

Fassler, David, 27, 92, 131
fears, 1, 26, 114, 207
helping with, 84, 94–96
parental relationships and, 241,
249
siblings and, 258, 263
florid, 76
Frazier, Jean, 24–25
friends, 145, 195
behaviors and, 255, 257–59,
261–62, 264
explaining your child's condition
and, 202, 207–8
family finances and, 289–90
hospitalization and, 150, 165,
170
moods and, 84–85, 100
parental relationships and,
251–53
parental self-care and, 234–35,
237–38
siblings and, 255, 257, 261–63

Geller, Barbara, 15, 20
gift giving, 143, 145
grandiosity, 38, 105
grief cycle, 242–45
guardedness, moods and, 91
guardianship, 221–23, 286–87, 290
guests, daily life and, 143–45
guilt, 6, 150, 186, 241, 253, 265

Haldol, 106, 113, 163
health insurance, 4, 6–7, 33
family finances and, 281–84
hospitalization and, 153, 155,
166–67, 172, 281–82, 284
laws and, 215–17, 221
medications and, 121, 282
mental health care professionals
and, 41, 43–46
parental self-care and, 229

herbal preparations, 118–19
holidays, 125, 140–41, 143–47
homeschooling, 193–95
hospitals, hospitalization, 7, 22, 76,
    150–72
  alternatives to, 157–58
  appealing lengths of stays at,
    166–67
  discharge from, 169, 172
  explaining your child's condition
    and, 205–6, 209
  family finances and, 153, 155,
    166–67, 172, 281–82, 284
  going home from, 167–68
  laws and, 212, 214, 216–17, 220,
    222–23
  mental health care professionals
    and, 41, 45–46, 57–58, 60, 62,
    151–53, 155, 158–59, 166–67
  moods and, 82, 151
  need for, 151–52
  questions to ask about, 154–56
  reentry after, 170
  restraint and seclusion (R/S) in,
    161–64, 172
  reward systems of, 155, 160,
    168–69, 259
  safety and, 160–64
  schooling and, 161, 169–72, 181,
    185, 193
  selection of, 152–53
  siblings and, 164–65, 168, 259,
    265
  taking advantage of programs of,
    165–66
  treatment plans of, 155, 159–60
  treatment teams of, 158–59
  types of programs of, 156–57
  visitors at, 160, 164–65, 220
  what to expect from, 158–70
  work and, 271, 276
hotels, 147
hydrotherapy, 88, 137

hyperactivity, 6–7, 116
  diagnoses and, 15, 24–26
  mental health care professionals
    and, 38, 68

impulsivity, 208, 218
  helping with, 79, 84, 103
  medications and, 110, 112,
    117–18
  mental health care professionals
    and, 52, 67
inconsistency, 231
Individualized Education Programs
    (IEPs), 184, 191–92, 195, 213
Individuals with Disabilities Act
    (IDEA), 179, 192
irritability, 105, 116, 176
  daily life and, 125, 133
  helping with, 92, 96–99

job sharing, 279
Joshi, Paramjit, 93, 150–51, 160,
    164, 169

Karres, Erika, 134, 178

labile, 76
labor attorneys, 214–16, 224, 273,
    275
LaFarge, Stephanie, 66–68
law, lawyers, 212–25
  family finances and, 212–14, 216,
    219, 221–23, 286, 288, 290
  schooling and, 179, 181–83, 188,
    191–94, 212–14, 220
  selection of, 213, 222–24
  types of, 212–21, 224, 273, 275
  work and, 214–16, 220, 273–75
law guardians, 221–23
learning disabled (LD), 178, 183
light therapy, 118
listening, 83
lithium, 57, 106, 110–12

diagnoses and, 15, 25
Luvox, 6, 106, 114

MacIntyre, James, 56–57
magnetic resonance imaging (MRI),
    24–25
magnetic resonance spectroscopy
    (MRS), 25
malpractice attorneys, 216–18, 224
mania, manias, 62, 176, 262
    daily life and, 137–38, 143
    diagnoses and, 14–16, 18–19, 23,
        26, 29
    helping with, 80, 82–85, 92–93,
        96–97, 104–5
    hospitalization and, 151
    medications and, 111–17, 119
    parental relationships and, 239,
        252
March, Stella, 202
marriages, 251, 272
matter-of-fact responses, 84–85
Medicaid, 44, 221, 283–85
medications, 5–9, 36, 105–24,
    154–57, 250
    adolescents and, 110, 116,
        120–21, 123
    camps and, 123–24, 195–96
    daily life and, 132–33, 139–41,
        146
    diagnoses and, 15–16, 19, 22,
        25–27, 31–32, 34, 106–8, 123
    dosages of, 58, 61, 64, 106–7,
        109–12, 123, 152
    explaining your child's condition
        and, 205, 209
    family finances and, 282–83, 285,
        287
    forgetting to take, 122–23
    frequently asked questions about,
        121–24
    guidelines for, 108–11
    health insurance and, 121, 282

hospitalization and, 152, 154–56,
    159, 163–64, 170
interactions between, 75, 109–10,
    119
laws and, 212, 216–17
mental health care professionals
    and, 39–40, 43, 48, 51, 54,
    57–58, 60–65, 106–7, 113,
    115, 120, 124
moods and, 75, 79, 100–101,
    103, 106, 110–12, 114, 116,
    118, 120–22
over-the-counter, 109–10, 118–19
parental self-care and, 229–30
records on, 60–61
research studies and, 62–65
schooling and, 123, 177–78, 191,
    193
side effects of, 39, 57–58, 64, 75,
    105, 107–9, 112–19, 121–22,
    124, 140, 146, 152, 196, 217
suddenly stopping, 110–11,
    120–21
types of, 111–18
melatonin, 118–19
mental health care professionals,
    216, 229, 244
changing of, 54–56
confidentiality and, 59–60, 70
family finances and, 281–84
questions for, 48–51, 70
record keeping and, 60–61, 64
relationship between children and,
    47–48, 51
research studies and, 61–66
selection of, 36–70, 282
siblings and, 49, 53, 60, 257–58
your role in helping your child
    and, 56–57
see also specific types of mental
    health professionals
meta-analysis studies, 62
midday, 134–37

mixed states, helping with, 96
Mom Factor, 249–50
monoamine oxidase (MAO) in-
    hibitors, 115–16
mood boxes, 77
Mood Intensity charts, 77–78
mood regulation, 76
mood response, 76
moods, 8–9, 256, 285
    adolescents and, 102–4
    averting and defusing, 82–99
    contracts to avoid conflicts and,
        101–2
    daily life and, 125–28, 130,
        132–33, 135–37, 139–40, 144,
        146–48
    diagnoses and, 13–18, 20–21,
        25–26, 32–35, 93, 103–5
    helping with, 71–105
    hospitalization and, 82, 151
    learning about, 76–78
    medications and, 75, 79,
        100–101, 103, 106, 110–12,
        114, 116, 118, 120–22
    mental health care professionals
        and, 37–38, 40, 42–44,
        49–52, 60, 67–68, 73, 78, 80,
        91, 93
    observing and recording, 49–50,
        60, 73–78, 100, 102
    parental relationships and, 241,
        249–50, 254
    parental self-care and, 87,
        229–30, 234
    period after, 99–100
    schools and, 71, 75, 79–80, 83,
        86, 89, 91–92, 94, 101, 186,
        188
    secret codes for, 80–82
    siblings and, 81, 84–87, 89, 97,
        256, 258, 260, 262
    triggers of, 72–74, 78–81, 85–86,

        100–101, 117, 126, 135, 147,
        272
mood stabilizers, 51, 111–13, 120
mornings, 133
muscles, muscle relaxation, 16, 96
musical instruments, 77, 88, 137

National Alliance for the Mentally Ill
    (NAMI), 18, 34, 44–45, 61,
    161, 166, 183, 202, 213, 221,
    223, 237–38, 245, 252–53
National Institute of Mental Health
    (NIMH), 20, 65–66
negotiable limits, 246–47
neuroimaging techniques, 17,
    22–25, 34
nighttime, 137–38
no, daily life and, 130–31
noisemakers, 77
Noll, Kathy, 208

obsessive-compulsive disorder
    (OCD), 14, 26, 42, 137–38
omega 3 fatty acids, 119–20, 282
open-label studies, 63
oppositional behavior, 41, 52, 56,
    240
oppositional defiant disorder
    (ODD), 35, 103–4, 186–87
organizational skills, 20, 52, 178, 270
other health impaired (OHI), 178

panic attacks, panic disorder, 21,
    94–95, 216
paranoia, 152, 249
    helping with, 81, 89–91
    schools and, 186–87
parent bullies, 207–9
parents, parenting:
    abundance focus for, 233–34
    attitude-adjusting ideas for,
        232–33

bipolar disorder in, 240–41, 251
as challenged vs. trapped, 231–33
isolation of, 235–37
martyr role of, 234–35
relationships between, 239–54
self-care for, 87, 229–38
spousal issues of, 230, 234–35, 237
tag team, 249–50
united front presented by, 247–49
partial hospitalization programs, 156
partnering, 279
pediatricians, 124, 140, 155
selection of, 37–38, 57–58
Pender Greene, Mary, 230, 233–36, 246–47
photo albums, 232
physical illness, 58
pictures, 77
play therapy, 42
positron emission tomography (PET) scans, 23, 181
pregnancy, 110
privacy, 85, 274
parental relationships and, 248–49
private school placement, 188–89
productive expression, 83
psychiatrists, 5–9, 62, 157–59, 216, 242
daily life and, 138, 140, 146
diagnoses and, 14–15, 17–22, 26–29, 34–35
family finances and, 282–83, 286
frequency of visits with, 40, 46
hospitalization and, 151–53, 155, 158–59, 166–67
medications and, 106–7, 113, 115, 120, 124
moods and, 73, 78, 80, 91, 93
parental relationships and, 245, 252
questions for, 48–49

schooling and, 180–82
selection of, 36, 39–40, 45–46, 48–51, 53, 57–58, 282
psychologists, 3, 9, 64, 80, 152, 242, 245
schooling and, 180, 182
selection of, 38–41, 43, 45–46, 282
punching bags, 77
punishments and rewards, 102
daily life and, 125, 128–29, 131–32, 134, 138
hospitalization and, 155, 160, 168–69, 259
schools and, 187–88
siblings and, 258–60, 263

quiet zones, 144

rages, 4–9, 54, 112, 161, 190, 276
diagnoses and, 13, 15, 21, 28
helping with, 71–72, 85–89, 95, 97, 99–101, 104
parental relationships and, 249, 252
parental self-care and, 229, 231, 234
Rakestraw, Jennie, 194
reality, 90–91, 112
rechanneling, moods and, 88
record keeping, 192
mental health care professionals and, 60–61, 64
moods and, 49–50, 60, 73–78, 100, 102
regeneration, 99–101
relaxation techniques, 95–96
research studies, 61–66
hospitalization and, 152, 165
types of, 62–63
residential treatment centers, 156–57, 189–91, 276

residential treatment centers *(cont.)*
    family finances and, 284, 287–88
    laws and, 217, 221
retrospective studies, 62
rewards, *see* punishments and re-
    wards
Risperdal, 113, 122, 163
Ritalin, 6–7, 26, 117
routines, 186
    daily life and, 125, 132, 138–39

sadness, 1, 4, 105
    diagnoses and, 14, 20, 31
    helping with, 72, 80–81, 92–94
safety, 119
    hospitalization and, 160–64
    moods and, 86–88, 104
    siblings and, 263–65
schedules, scheduling, 156, 231,
        251, 276
    adhering to, 139, 141, 148
    daily life and, 128–29, 138–39,
        141–42, 144, 146, 148
school, schools, schooling, 3–5,
        8–10, 157, 177–95, 199–200
    advocacy and, 180–83, 199, 243
    daily life and, 125–26, 128,
        130–35, 137, 140–41, 145, 148
    diagnoses and, 13, 15, 18–19, 21,
        32–34, 178, 181–83, 189, 199
    evaluations and, 178–80, 183
    explaining your child's condition
        and, 204, 207, 209
    family finances and, 193–94, 281
    at home, 193–95
    hospitalization and, 161, 169–72,
        181, 185, 193
    IEPs and, 184, 191–92, 195, 213
    laws and, 179, 181–83, 188,
        191–94, 212–14, 220
    medications and, 123, 177–78,
        191, 193

mental health care professionals
    and, 36–37, 41, 54, 59, 68,
    180–82
moods and, 71, 75, 79–80, 83, 86,
    89, 91–92, 94, 101, 186, 188
options available in, 184–91
out-of-district, 188
parental relationships and,
    243–44, 248, 251–52
parental self-care and, 229, 231,
    233, 235–36
SECs and, 180–84, 188, 236
siblings and, 260, 262–63
work and, 269, 271, 275–78
seasonal affective disorder (SAD), 80,
    93, 126
sensory integration therapy, 68–69
separation, separations, 21, 94, 175,
    272
Seroquel, 6, 113
serotonergic agents, 110, 114
serotonin, 16, 98–99, 177
severely emotionally disturbed
    (SED), 178
sexual inappropriateness, 84–85
shame, 165, 261
shelter, 135
siblings, 1–5, 157–58, 176, 220,
    255–65, 271
    abuse of, 263–65
    accommodations for, 262–63
    as caregivers, 260–61
    copycat behavior in, 4, 9, 255,
        257–58
    daily life and, 132, 135
    explaining your child's condition
        and, 205, 207, 256–57
    fairness to, 258–60, 263, 265
    family finances and, 285, 288–89
    friends and, 255, 257, 261–63
    hospitalization and, 160, 164–65,
        168, 259, 265

mental health care professionals
and, 49, 53, 60, 257–58
moods and, 81, 84–87, 89, 97,
256, 258, 260, 262
parental relationships and, 241, 252
understanding from, 256–57
sick days, 139–40
single parents, 252–54, 271
single photon emission tomography
(SPECT) scans, 22–24
sleep, 3–5, 16, 161
daily life and, 125–26, 129–30,
132–33, 138, 141
diagnoses and, 21, 24–25, 28
medications and, 114–18
moods and, 75, 92, 94
social security payments, 284–85
social skills, 52, 237
camps and, 196, 198–99
diagnoses and, 21–22
schools and, 178, 183–84,
186–87, 189–90
social workers, 158, 180, 245
family finances and, 282, 284
selection of, 39–41, 43, 45, 282
Special Education Committees
(SECs), 180–84, 188, 236
stimulants, 116–17, 120, 122
Stoltz, Mike, 273–74, 278
suicidal thoughts and acts, 1, 3–4, 8,
37, 143, 161
diagnoses and, 13–14, 21, 30
helping with, 92–93
laws and, 212, 217
supplemental needs trusts, 288
supportive therapy, 42
Swanson, Mona, 190

taxes, 283
television, 85, 177
daily life and, 135, 140–41
theme parks, 147

therapeutic support programs
(TSPs), 187–88
therapists, therapy, 106, 155–59,
207, 220, 233, 242, 257
alternative, 41, 66–69, 118
camps and, 198–99
changing of, 54–56
daily life and, 134, 137
family finances and, 281, 286
goals of, 52, 67
hospitalization and, 151–53,
155–56, 158–59, 165, 170
moods and, 73, 75, 78, 80, 82,
88, 91, 98, 100
parental relationships and, 245, 252
questions for, 49–50
schooling and, 180–81, 183,
187–88, 193
selection of, 40–43, 46, 49–54,
57, 59–60
types of, 41–42
work and, 275, 278
Thorazine, 113, 163
thought problems, 22
tranquilizers, 117–18, 159, 163
Transition Form for Bipolar Kids,
126–27
transitions, 196, 278
daily life and, 125–32, 135, 139, 141
easing, 127–28, 132
hospitalization and, 165, 167–68,
170
parental relationships and, 252–53
schooling and, 181, 184, 188
Treatment Goal Worksheets, 52–53
tricyclic antidepressants, 115
Trudeau, Tracey Lynn, 134, 170–71,
181, 186
trustees, 290
trusts, 288–90

videos, video games, 85, 140, 144

visualization, 95–96, 138

waiting, 90
Welch, Bryant, 217–18
Wellbutrin (buproprion), 114–15
Wellstone, Paul, 44
work, workplace, 2–3, 9, 175, 230, 251, 269–81
  accommodations at, 273–75
  creative solutions for, 278–80
  daily life and, 126, 134
  demands of, 272–73

exiting, 275
  explaining absence from, 277–78
  explaining your child's condition and, 273–74, 278
  family finances and, 269, 275–76, 280–81
  at home, 269, 280
  laws and, 214–16, 220, 273–75
  reentering, 276–77
  staying home vs., 271–73

Zyprexa, 112, 122–23, 113